THE PHILOSOPHY OF
THOMAS AQUINAS
Introductory Readings

Edited by Christopher Martin

ROUTLEDGE
London & New York

First published in 1988 by
Routledge
11 New Fetter Lane, London EC4P 4EE

Published in the USA by
Routledge
a division of Routledge, Chapman & Hall, Inc.
29 West 35th Street, New York NY 10001

Reprinted 1989

British Library Cataloguing in Publication Data

Thomas *Aquinas*.
    The philosophy of Thomas Aquinas.
    1. Philosophy
    I. Title   II. Martin, Christopher
    100   B765.T5

    ISBN 0-415-00295-8
    ISBN 0-415-00296-6 Pbk

Library of Congress Cataloging-in-Publication Data

    ISBN 0-415-00295-8
    ISBN 0-415-00296-6 Pbk

Photocomposition by Pat and Anne Murphy,
Highcliffe-on-Sea, Christchurch, Dorset
Printed and bound in Great Britain
by Billing & Sons Limited, Worcester

Contents

Preface

I had considered not giving any preface to this work. There is an explanation and justification of it included in the first chapter, 'An introduction to reading the philosophy of Aquinas'. To write a preface, too, means mentioning the people one is indebted to: I have had no time to ask their permission, and I feared that they might think that this work did me and them no credit. On reading over it again, though, I find that my debt to Professor P. T. Geach is so apparent on every page that it would be criminal not to acknowledge it explicitly. It is from Geach that I have learnt everything that I know about Aquinas: if this book turns out to be of value to the student, it is to him they owe it. If it is of no value, it is my own fault entirely.

My thanks are also due to Mr David Mitchell, of Worcester College, who first taught me how to be a philosopher; to Professor Alejandro Llano, of the University of Navarre, who taught me how to do metaphysics; and to my colleague in Glasgow, Dr Alexander Broadie, whose idea this book was. None of them, alas, has been able to have any part in writing it: so, let me stress again, all the shortcomings are entirely my own work. If the book does no credit to those I have cited, I am sorry for it: but they have at least the profound gratitude and affection of an incompetent.

This is the first book of mine to see the light of day. I dedicate it, as is customary, to my parents.

Christopher Martin

Abbreviations and Manner of Giving References

Passages collected here are referred to by their numbers in this collection. The works of St Thomas cited are usually referred to here by their full names. In other works which the reader may have occasion to consult, self-explanatory abbreviations are usually used, e.g. *S. T.* or *S. Th.* for the *Summa theologiae*, *S.C.G.* for the *Summa contra gentiles*, *De Ver.* for the *De veritate*, *In Perih.* for the *In Perihermeneias*, etc.

Some titles occasionally give difficulty. The *Summa theologiae* is also known as the *Summa theologica*, or just as the *Summa*, without qualification. The *Summa contra gentiles* is sometimes called *De veritate catholicae fidei*, or *On the truth of the catholic faith* in English. The *In Perihermeneias* is the commentary on the work of Aristotle that we call the *De interpretatione*. *In Perihermeneias* is the usual title given to this work: in the case of other commentaries I have preferred to refer to, for example, the *Commentary on the Ethics* rather than to *In decem libros Ethicorum ad Nicomachum expositio*.

The manner of referring to parts of the text varies in detail from work to work, but is basically the same. The *Summa theologiae* is divided into three parts, of which the second is again divided into two. Thus there are in effect, four parts: the first part, the first part of the second part, the second part of the second part, and the third part. These are often referred to in Latin: *Prima*, *Prima Secundae*, *Secunda Secundae*, and *Tertia*. These are abbreviated as 1a, 1a2ae, 2a2ae, and 3a, or as I, I–II, II–II, and III. Within each part there are questions (abbreviated as 'q.') and articles (abbreviated as 'a.'). Each article consists of objections, a body of the article (abbreviated as 'c.' for *corpus*), and replies to the objections (abbreviated as 'ad', 'to'). Hence I q.12 a.4 ad 3: first part, question 12, article four, reply to the third objection. The division into questions and articles is the same in the *Quaestiones disputatae*.

The *Summa contra gentiles* is divided into books and chapters, and the commentaries on Aristotle into books and *lectiones*. In the *Summa contra gentiles* and the commentaries the Marietti texts, which have been used here, divide into paragraphs or sections. The section divisions have been kept here, but the numbering of sections has been made to run from the beginning of the passage selected, not from the beginning of the work. (On the Marietti texts, see Notes on Reading.)

1

An Introduction to Reading the Philosophy of Aquinas

The purpose of this book

There already exists at least one collection of philosophical texts selected from the writings of St Thomas Aquinas: there is already more than one excellent introduction to his philosophy. This book contains elements of both kinds of work. But it is not intended to rival either. Rather its aim is to be an introduction to the reading of St Thomas's philosophy. Many people starting the study of Aquinas must have found difficulties when they turned from one of the books that introduce his philosophy to the texts themselves. The introductions are often lucidly written by people who have studied Aquinas for a long time, to whom his writing presents no problem. This is indeed a feature of his writing: once one has the knack of it, it is nearly always remarkably clear. But one needs to have the knack, and the introductory books do not teach it.

It is, indeed, a knack: a skill that cannot be taught but only acquired through practice. The beginner has the problem, however, of knowing where to start. Much of St. Thomas's philosophical is hidden away in impenetrable theological contexts to which the philosophy student may have no clue. But it is not always helpful to turn instead to a selection of philosophical texts. These texts are often very short indeed: shorn of their theological context, the texts appear shorn of all context whatsoever. This would pose an obstacle to the understanding of any philosopher.

This obstacle is particularly important in the case of St Thomas. To sum it up in a few words: St Thomas, like his master Aristotle, needs to be read in bulk, but understood in detail. One needs to read in bulk, to grasp the breadth and the connected nature of the

1

thought of both of them: but one needs to understand in detail, by a careful examination of individual applications of the wide-ranging doctrines, in order to appreciate their subtlety. When people are taught to read Aristotle well, they are taught to read him in this way: and this, indeed, is the way that St Thomas himself read Aristotle. There is a need for an aid to learning to read St Thomas in this way.

Criteria of selection of passages

To this end, then, the texts which have been chosen here are texts from a non-theological context. This has sometimes meant taking an early expression of St Thomas's views, which he may refine on in the *Summa theologiae*. It is felt that this is a price that has to be paid. St Thomas's thought does develop, though perhaps not very much with regard to the basic philosophical concepts he uses. Still, on the one hand even his less mature views are of philosophical interest; and on the other the *Summa theologiae* is fairly easily available to most university students. For most of the passages collected here there is a reference given to a parallel passage, or parallel passages, in the *Summa theologiae*. Those who wish to compare what he says in the texts collected here with what he says in the *Summa* will not find it hard: and after looking at the notions in a non-theological context here, they should find it easier to follow them in the theological context there.

The texts have been chosen, then, according to the criteria of choosing texts from non-theological contexts, as far as possible, and of choosing them from contexts which are not easily available in English, if at all. It is fortunate, given the comparison made above between the reading of Aristotle and the reading of Aquinas, that it has been possible to choose a good number of them from Aquinas's commentaries on Aristotle. It is hoped that the application of these admittedly rather trivial criteria will increase the book's usefulness. But its main pretension to usefulness comes from other criteria of selection, that have to do with the content, rather than the context, of the passages chosen.

In general, the texts have been chosen with one of two aims in mind: either to allow Aquinas to explain some of his key philosophical concepts, or to show Aquinas contributing to some perennial philosophical debate which is still alive today. Thus, under the first head, there are texts on substance and accident,

matter and form: under the other, texts on the truth of future contingent statements, on the existence of God, on the immortality of
the soul, and on free will. A number of the texts would warrant
inclusion under either head: for example, the passages on the
theory of predication, on existence, on truth and knowledge, and
on human well-being.

If this book differs from the usual kind of selection from
Aquinas's writings, it also differs from the usual kind of introduction to his philosophy. It is not intended to rival the unmatched
essay by Geach in *Three philosophers*, for example: an introduction
that should be read by anyone beginning to study Aquinas's
philosophy (see Notes on Reading). The aim has been rather to
give people practice in reading Aquinas's philosophy, letting the
texts speak for themselves as far as possible.

But in order that the texts should speak for themselves as far as
possible, it has proved necessary to give a thematic introduction to
each group of texts: an introduction to logic, to metaphysics, to
God in Aquinas's philosophy, to truth, knowledge and the soul,
and to human action and ethics. Frequent attention has had to be
drawn to three features of Aquinas's philosophy that the reader
nowadays has difficulty in appreciating: his Aristotelianism, his
essentialism, and the systematic nature of his thought. By a
strange coincidence they are also the features that we most need to
understand to make progress with the contemporary problems of
philosophy.

St Thomas and Aristotle

If St Thomas is neglected, and considered difficult to understand,
among English-speaking philosophers, perhaps that is only the
penalty that must be paid for living abroad and dying more than
seven hundred years ago. But Aristotle has become the object of a
tremendous amount of attention within the same circles during
this century; and he lived even farther abroad, and died over three
times as long ago. St Thomas is no more difficult than Aristotle:
indeed, his language is usually easier. This is perhaps not the place
to investigate the reasons for the neglect, but we should at least be
aware of it. This neglect makes it hard for us to approach him: at
first sight his ideas are alien to us, there is no tradition of
discussing them.

But the difficulties are not as great as this might suggest. In the first place, St Thomas is an Aristotelian. His basic concepts and categories are those of Aristotle, and when they are developed beyond the point at which Aristotle left them they are developed in an Aristotelian manner. No one who is familiar with Aristotle should have much difficulty with Aquinas.

Empiricism and essentialism

But perhaps we are not as familiar with Aristotle as we ought to be: or perhaps Aquinas's Aristotle is different from ours. It is hard not to draw this latter conclusion when one reads a great deal of modern Aristotle scholarship. Modern scholarship in English-speaking countries is deeply affected by the legacy of the empiricist philosophers: and this tends to warp our appreciation of Aristotle. Aristotle, and Aquinas after him, insist on the importance of observation by the senses as being the origin of all our knowledge. But they do not hold, as the empiricists held, that this is the end of the knowledge that we can have. They both held that there is a more profound knowledge of the world which our intellect can come to. This intellectual knowledge has, indeed, its origins in the senses: but it is not limited to the manipulation and combination of concepts which are available to the senses. The lesson has been slowly re-learned by some this century that our ordinary language and indeed all our ordinary thought presuppose the Aristotelian – Thomistic view of knowledge, and the metaphysics which lies behind it. No matter how much we may profess empiricist or positivist ideas, we cannot express them in the language that we normally use, and cannot, either, do more than sketch — with very broad strokes, sometimes — the language that would be appropriate to them. It is also clear that such an empiricist language would not be capable of expressing what we actually do know, but should on empiricist grounds be incapable of knowing. This includes, of course, the truths of modern science.

This century, philosophers have been coming to see the bankruptcy of empiricism. But old habits die hard. The brilliant puzzles of Hume are still set for the study of undergraduates, and no alternative system is given which will explain and organise the unconscious metaphysics that we all use, the metaphysics that Hume seeks to expose as unfounded. So philosophers continue to be influenced by empiricism. This is where the value, and the difficulty, of the study of Aquinas become evident. He is not an empiricist, and indeed largely ignores the epistemological questions to which empiricism seeks to give an answer. He is a metaphysician: and he uses the concepts of Aristotle to systematise the unconscious metaphysics that we all share. He represents a step forward, as it were, on the road at whose beginning we are standing. Frege and Kripke, among others, have brought us to the start of this road: the one by relegating problems of epistemology to their rightful place, the other by drawing attention to our unconscious metaphysics. What we need to do is to develop and systematise that metaphysics, and defend it against attack. It is much to be regretted that very few are attempting to make progress along that road. Our unconscious metaphysics has a presumptive correctness, but that presumption can be defeated. But it can also be defended, and should be: it is not enough merely to draw attention to it.

Aquinas's development and systematisation of Aristotle, though not his only philosophical achievement, may be his most important contribution to our present needs. It is also the feature of his work which is most unfamiliar to us, and thus merits this lengthy preamble. Unless we get it fixed in our heads that St Thomas is an essentialist, and a non-empiricist, that he holds that our grasp of the real essences of things is no less firm, and far more important, than our perceptions, we will learn nothing from him.

St Thomas's philosophy as a system

Furthermore, St Thomas is a systematic philosopher. Systems are temporarily out of vogue in the world of English-speaking academic philosophy, though as influential as ever in the intellectual world at large. But it is with systems as it is with ideologies: the more one tries to avoid them, the more one falls into one that is all the more dangerously rigid through being unconscious. Some of the remarks above about the legacy of empiricism are relevant here. It will come as a relief to philosophical readers, though, to discover that while there is a great deal of system in the philosophy of St Thomas — it is enough to read the few passages collected here and notice the frequent interconnections of thought they contain to realise that — the system is complicated and subtle. It is not a question of applying one category or system of categories upon the whole of reality, and lopping off unwelcome bits of evidence. Rather it is a matter of seeing connections between

5

concepts in different philosophical fields. One can apply to Aquinas the words of C. Day Lewis on Virgil:

> But chiefly dear for his gift to understand
> Earth's intricate, ordered heart.

Intricate but ordered: that is surely the way the world is, and it is something of a relief to find a philosophy that reflects this.

Features of the translation

This long parenthesis on these features of St Thomas's philosophy which are alien to us today began as an attempt to explain why there are quite lengthy thematic introductions to each group of passages in this book. It was claimed that the intention was to let the texts speak for themselves, and that therefore they needed introducing, if they were not to be broken up by detailed notes.

This intention of letting the texts speak for themselves has had its influence on the manner of translation. Every translation is a compromise: all one can hope for is that one's own compromise may be less unhappy than it might be. Here a compromise has been made between comprehensibility and putting the reader in as close a contact as possible with St Thomas's own way of doing philosophy. Liberties that have been taken are to split up the lengthy sentences St Thomas sometimes indulges in, and to change the order of clauses within sentences, for the sake of the sense. Strictness has come in the attempt — not always successful — to translate one technical term or group of cognate technical terms in Latin by one technical term or group of cognate technical terms in English. The technical term used in English has not always been the one that might be expected: for example, 'description' has been used throughout for one clearly identifiable sense of *ratio*, and 'awareness' and 'being aware', so far as possible, for *cognitio* and *cognoscere*. Another liberty that has been taken is to put in supplementary words or examples in square brackets. Nothing in square brackets is Aquinas's: it is merely a gloss or interjection of the translator. Since it proved necessary to use this device to make the texts run anything like smoothly, the liberty has been taken to interject the occasional remark in square brackets which would normally go into a footnote. It was felt that to have the text interrupted by both brackets and footnotes would be intolerable, so since brackets there had to be, footnotes have been abandoned. There have also been unflagged omissions from the text, but they are in all but one case omissions of Aquinas's references to the text of Aristotle that he is commenting on: 'Then, when he says "The existent, however" ', and the like. The only omission which is not of this kind has been in one place to drop the repetition of one qualifying phrase that made no difference to the sense but made the sentence impossible for the reader to parse, even with the cleverest of punctuation.

If Aquinas's own references to phrases in Aristotle's text have been dropped, it is hoped that the insertion of modern references to Aristotle where he makes a specific reference that is important in the context will be taken as a fair exchange, and not as a further outrage. When Aquinas refers to other authors, for example Hilary of Poitiers or Augustine, full references have not been given. It is felt that to do so would clutter up the text yet more, and that in any case Aquinas's use of *auctoritates* is not to be wrongly assimilated to a modern author's use of authorities.

2
Aquinas on Logic

An introduction to Aquinas on logic

Aquinas's logic

Perhaps the best place to start reading the philosophy of St Thomas is with his logic. This is not because it is easier: it is certainly the most difficult part of his philosophy to translate, and probably the most difficult to read as well. It is rather because most of those interested in philosophy nowadays in English-speaking countries are probably more familiar with logical problems than they are with the problems of metaphysics. However, as we shall see, St Thomas does not seem to wish to keep logic and metaphysics rigidly apart.

The two texts which are collected here are both from the commentary on Aristotle's *De interpretatione*, or *In Perihermeneias* as Aquinas calls it. They deal with his theory of predication — on which St Thomas held views that were far from standard in his own day, though they are similar to current views — and on the problem of the truth of propositions about future contingents. It should be noticed that the *De interpretatione* was divided into two books in Aquinas's time, at 19b5: hence his occasional references to the 'second book'. Most of them, being statements about a future contingent state of affairs, turn out false: for some reason he never completed his commentary on this work, leaving off at 19b31.

Unlike many other great mediaeval thinkers, St Thomas was not a professional logician. He wrote no textbook, and there is little of outstanding interest in his commentaries on the logical works of Aristotle, beyond the two texts chosen here. But in these two texts and in other writings we get an interesting and unusual view on certain major logical problems.

The reference of predicable expressions

One problem of enormous importance in logic — in the contemporary reflowering of logic no less than in that of the Middle Ages — is that of the reference and manner of referring of predicable expressions. (It is to be hoped, by the way, that no one beginning the study of Aquinas will be under the false impression, which is still occasionally found, that the Middle Ages was a logical desert. The Middle Ages was a period of immense logical fertility, during which a remarkable amount of remarkably good work was done. It has been surpassed in the last hundred years only, and then only in one particular field.) The problem with predicable expressions is the following. When I say 'Socrates is a human being' it is clear that the name 'Socrates' refers to Socrates. No problem there: but what about the expression 'human being'? Does it refer to a Form, as Plato thought, or to something more down-to-earth? Does it not, perhaps, refer to Socrates again?

Nowadays, we unanimously reject this last simple answer, that the expression 'human being' refers in this sentence to Socrates. We hold that the semantic role of names, such as 'Socrates', is quite different from that of predicable expressions, such as '— is a human being'. Frege, who initiated this way of thinking, did indeed hold that predicable expressions referred to something: but what they referred to was a 'concept', something incomplete and entirely different from an individual and self-contained object such as Socrates or the number four. A serious problem in modern discussions is how to uphold this great Fregean insight — which is embodied in the form of all modern logical notations that stem from his work — without falling into Platonic realism about concepts.

Most of the great logicians of the Middle Ages gave the simple answer, that in 'Socrates is a human being', 'human being' stands for Socrates again. Ockham, Paul of Venice and Buridan had no hesitation in giving this answer, and they were followed by all except a very few. They found evidence for it in Aristotle. Though in the *De interpretatione* Aristotle makes a distinction between 'nouns' and 'verbs' — more literally, 'names' and 'words' —

9

which seems to answer to our modern distinction between names and predicable expressions, he went on later to a theory in which an e⁻pression which was a name in one proposition could become a predicate in another without change of sense. As a result, most logicians by Aquinas's time paid little heed to the distinction between nouns and verbs, tending to say that the verb was just another kind of noun in which the copula had somehow got included. There is support enough for this in Aristotle, too. (See passage 1, *lectio* 5, section 15; and passage 3, section 9.) It should be noticed, however, that at no time was the distinction between nouns and verbs merely a grammatical one: all these authors, like Aquinas, would include e.g. 'wise', or 'pale' — which are grammatically adjectives — among 'nouns' in this sense.

There were always a few logicians and philosophers, however, who did not consider the verb to be simply another kind of noun, and they include such great names as Peter of Spain, Walter Burleigh, and Aquinas.

Aquinas, faithful to Aristotle, repeats the view that nouns and verbs are akin. He also repeats Aristotle's surely mistaken view in the *De interpretatione* that verbs, no less than nouns, should be syntactically simple: that, as he says, no part of them should signify on its own (passage 1, *lectio* 5, sections 2 and 3).

Aquinas on nouns and verbs

Despite the view that verbs and nouns are akin, Aquinas holds that there are important differences between them. One, on which Aristotle laid great stress, is that nouns signify without time, while verbs signify with time, or 'consignify time' as the mediaeval technical term has it (passage 1, *lectio* 4, section 7 below). Obviously, it makes no difference to the truth of a sentence at what time a name is applied: but it does make a difference at what time the predicate applies. This clearly indicates the predicative nature of verbs — and also how mistaken Aquinas and Aristotle were to insist that they should not have 'parts that signify when separated'.

This difference between the noun and the verb is brought out yet more clearly by considering their different roles. Together they make up a proposition; but a proposition is a unity in a stronger sense than is a list, or a proposition formed by connecting two other propositions by 'and'. Aquinas accordingly holds that the two parts of the proposition have different natures, which enables them to come together in a fully united whole. He compares them to 'matter' and 'form': to the bronze a statue is made of and the shape in virtue of which the bronze is the statue. Thus, naturally, they do not need a copula to join them, any more than the shape of the statue needs to be glued on to the bronze.

The name is analogous to the matter, the bronze: that about which the proposition is made, that out of which the statue is made. The verb is analogous to the form or shape: it makes this a proposition about this subject matter, just as the shape makes a statue of this bronze. Aquinas even uses the word *compositio*, composition or making up, of the way in which noun and verb fit together: the same word as he uses to describe the way a body or a statue is made up or composed of its matter and its form (passage 1, *lectio* 5, sections 3–4 below).

The verb, in Aquinas's terms, is always predicative: 'always the sign of those things that are predicated of another'. He is aware, however, that there are sentences which have a noun in predicate-position, or, as we would say, have a noun as part of their predicate: for example 'Socrates is a human being' (passage 1, *lectio* 5, section 4 below). Here he has to work hard to overcome the tendency to consider nouns as names, but in the end he succeeds. In the first place, he distinguishes nouns that refer to an individual from those that refer to a nature. Common nouns refer to a nature: he has a discussion in the *Summa theologiae*, I q.13 a.9, in which he draws attention to the fact that the word 'sun' can be taken as a proper name, referring to a certain individual only, or as a noun that refers to a nature. The fact that as a matter of fact this potentially common nature is possessed only by one individual is not relevant to the logic (compare also *In Perihermeneias I*, *lectio* 10, sections 4–5).

Suppositio

He elsewhere applies a concept of mediaeval logic which is not to be found in Aristotle: that of *suppositio*. This notion is not easy to define, but it can perhaps be best explained as the way in which a word has a signification. Thus the word 'runs', as Aquinas explains, sometimes has formal *suppositio*, as in the sentence 'Socrates runs'. A word used with formal *suppositio* is taken to signify that which it is imposed to signify: in this case, a certain activity. But the same word can also be taken with material *suppositio*, in which case it is taken to signify not what the word stands for but the word itself: as in ' "Runs" is a verb' (passage 1, *lectio* 5, section 6). (There were no inverted commas in mediaeval times, just as there are none in speech: hence the little gesture that lecturers often make to indicate, not always successfully, that the word they are uttering is being mentioned, not used.)

A distinction of kinds of *suppositio* which is more relevant to our present concerns is made by Aquinas when he tells us that a common noun in subject-position is taken to stand for some individual of the nature that it signifies, while in predicate-position it is taken to stand for the nature itself (*S. Th.* III q.16 a.7 ad 4). We have in English the definite and indefinite articles to help us make this clear: we say 'The cat was sick' but 'Ludo is a cat'. In Latin, where there are no articles — though Aquinas mentions at passage 1, *lectio* 5, section 5 the use of the definite article in 'vulgar Latin', presumably Italian or French — we have to maintain the distinction of *suppositio* to make it clear that the role of *felis*, cat, is quite different in *Felis erat aeger* and *Ludo est felis*.

Composition and the copula

In such a sentence, which has a noun in the predicate position, we also have the copula to convey the composition of the subject, Ludo, the material part, and the predicate, the formal part, cat. St Thomas wants to draw attention to the difference between an *oratio*, translated as 'expression' below, and a proposition or indicative sentence, *enunciatio*. An *oratio* is always a complex expression: it *may* be a propositional one such as 'A human being is pale' — one that 'signifies something true or false', as Aquinas would say — or it may be a non-propositional one such as 'A pale human being'. It is the copula here which 'conveys the composition' and turns the expression into a proposition (passage 1, *lectio* 5, sections 8 and 22).

It is worthwhile noticing here, by the way, that even before we have finished stating Aquinas's theory of predication, elements from his metaphysics are already creeping in: not only the analogy of the composition of a sentence to the composition of matter and form, but even the notion of nature or essence. This is already an example of the connectedness of Aquinas's thought. He shows up well in this respect in contrast with his contemporaries, who shared his metaphysics, to a great extent, but did not trouble to bring their logic into line with it: and also in contrast with ourselves, who share a great part of his views on logic, but fight shy of discussing the metaphysics which it implies.

Manners of predication

Linked with this connectedness is Aquinas's view that there are different manners of predication. The field of logic is not self-contained, for Aquinas: it has continually to take into account what we are talking about. Hence he holds, e.g., that in 'Socrates is a human being' and 'Socrates is pale' the two different predicates are actually said of the subject in two different manners: 'human being' is said of Socrates *per se*, in its own right, 'pale' is said of him *per accidens*, coincidentally (see passage 3, sections 1–4 below). The reason for this is clearly that Socrates is a human being in his own right: he could not be Socrates without being a human being, while he merely happens, as it were, to be pale. Even if, as a matter of fact, he is always pale — even if he is an albino — Aquinas would hold that this is something that is merely coincidentally true of him. This thesis is vulnerable to evidence: for example, if we were to discover that Socrates's paleness is caused by some property of his genetic make-up such that he could not have been Socrates without being pale, then 'Socrates is pale' may turn out to have been said in its own right. In any case, 'The human being is pale' — a kind of unquantified sentence that the Aristotelians were very fond of — is certainly a *per accidens*, coincidental predication.

We shall see when we move on to the metaphysics that there are also connected notions of 'being one and the same thing in one's own right' and 'being one and the same thing coincidentally' (passage 3). This also has a logical aspect, of 'being said to be one and the same thing in one's own right' and 'being said to be one and the same thing coincidentally'. Also of importance is the distinction between 'being a cause in one's own right' and 'being a cause coincidentally'. An example of the former would be the action of parents in generating children, an example of the latter the actions of parents generating prosperity for manufacturers of prams. It is not in so far as they are parents that they generate prosperity for pram-manufacturers: and there are many other concomitant causes which go to bring about the same effect.

Another distinction of kinds of predication is that between 'being predicated in its own right' or 'predicated essentially', as in 'Socrates is a human being' or 'Red is a colour', as opposed to 'denominative' or 'concretive' predication, in which an accident is predicated of a substance.

The signification of names

Another important distinction which St Thomas makes is between that in virtue of which a name is imposed, and that which a name is imposed to signify (passage 1, *lectio* 4, section 9). This distinction is often used to make points made by Frege by means of the sense–reference distinction, and made by Kripke by means of the distinction between the reference of a name and the fixing of a reference. The noun 'God', for example, is imposed in virtue of God's governance of the world — that is what is used to fix the reference: but the reference of the noun, what it is imposed to signify and does signify, is the unknown nature of that which does govern the world. Equally, 'the wisdom of God' and 'the goodness of God' have the same reference — they signify one thing, God himself — but they have different senses, which arise from being imposed in virtue of different perfections in creatures.

In this context, as in many others, St Thomas makes use of the notion of *ratio*. This is perhaps the most difficult word to translate in his logical vocabulary. This word takes over most of the duties and difficulties of *logos* in Greek. It can mean 'reason' and also 'argument', but its most frequent use is the one that is translated here throughout by some use of the English word 'description'. This description is to be understood as a mental description of a thing, which may or may not be equivalent to its definition. A thing has only one definition, but several descriptions, and can be referred to or thought of under any one of them. Thus the words that are used to refer to it may be different in virtue of different descriptions. The reader will find many places in which the context would demand in English a word such as 'sense', as was used in the paragraph above (cp. especially passage 8, article 1).

Analogy

Linked with this notion of *ratio* is also the notion of analogy. Aquinas holds that when we consider the meanings of a word we do not have to choose between claiming that the word is univocal, and signifies just one thing — like 'aardvark', so far as one can see — and claiming that it is equivocal, and signifies two or more entirely different things, like 'bank'. He thinks that there is a third category, that of analogical expressions: expressions or words which have different related senses, which are said 'according to a principal sense and secondary related senses'. He thinks that most of the major metaphysical terms are analogical in one way or another: 'existence', 'truth', 'unity', 'identity', 'action', 'actuality', 'potentiality' would all be analogical expressions.

Indeed, in all their analogical related senses they are also related one to another.

Expressions of existence

For example, there is a strong connection between truth and existence in the mind of St Thomas. We shall see something of this when looking at his metaphysics, but even within his logic it has its importance. Certainly it makes translation difficult. One and the same verb *esse*, to be, has to be translated sometimes as 'to exist' and sometimes as 'to be the case'. In passage 1 it has proved impossible to disentangle the notions, and all parts of the verb *esse* have been translated with parts of the English verb 'to be' throughout. Passage 2 presents a related difficulty: St Thomas shuttles between talking about the truth or falsity of future indicative statements and the existence or non-existence of some future thing, or occurrence or non-occurrence of some future event. This complication, though, does not seriously affect the points that are made: he manages to make it clear which he is talking about. The reader should be warned, though, that he talks much more about occurrence and existence, and much less about truth, than a present-day logician would.

Future contingents

St Thomas's views on the theory of predication and related topics, valuable and original though they are, have to be gleaned piecemeal from his writings. His other most valuable contribution to logic, however, his view on future contingents, can be gathered direct from his treatment in passage 2, from the *Commentary on the De interpretatione*, Book I, *lectiones* 13 – 15. There are also interesting related views in the *Summa theologiae*.

St Thomas holds that all statements about the past and present, even singular ones, are 'determinately' true or false. From this he holds that it follows that they are in some sense necessarily true or false. This sense of 'necessarily' is one that was important to both Aristotle and Aquinas, but is unfamiliar to us. The nearest approach there has been to it in recent discussions is Prior's notion of being now-unpreventable (in e.g. 'The formalities of omniscience' — see Notes on Reading). The question is then put, what about singular statements about the future? (*lectio* 13, sections 4–6).

The problem

Aquinas draws out at length the consequences of saying that singular statements about the future are determinately true: it rules out all contingency in the world (*lectio* 13). He regards this conclusion as 'unsatisfactory' (*inconveniens*), and goes on to prove, in *lectio* 14, that it is in fact impossible. But first he closes off one important possible escape route: it cannot be that singular statements about the future are not true or false at all. If 'There will be a sea-battle tomorrow' is neither true nor false, he maintains, this can only be because tomorrow there will neither be nor not be a sea-battle: a clearly absurd conclusion (*lectio* 13, section 12).

He also gives us, in *lectio* 14 (sections 8–24), long discussions of different notions of necessity and possibility, of fate, and of God's foreknowledge and will. On this last point he adopts Boethius's comparison of God to a watcher on a high tower who can see the ordering of a long procession of people all at once, while the people in the procession can only experience a few bits of it. This passage seems to imply that the human experience of temporal ordering is in fact a misperception of another kind of ordering which can be seen by God all at once: a view which entails difficulties for Christian doctrine. Accordingly, Aquinas elsewhere gives a different, but less conclusive view, which safeguards his belief that even God cannot change the past. What is of particular interest here, however, is the notion that though God necessarily brings about whatever he wills — there is no possibility of thwarting God — some of the things he wills to bring about are contingent results of contingent causes. Contingency and free-will in the world are not in spite of God's foreknowledge and will, but because of it.

The solution

In *lectio* 15 Aquinas gives an answer to his problem. He grants that there is a sense of 'necessarily' — the sense he illuminates by his use of 'determinately' — in which it is necessary that Socrates is sitting down when he is sitting down. But this necessity is conditional or hypothetical: there is no absolute or unqualified necessity involved. Hence, it was not necessary before Socrates sat down that he should sit down: the necessity of Socrates' sitting down is only conditional on his in fact sitting down, not absolute.

So it was not 'determinately' or necessarily the case that Socrates was going to sit down before he did sit down, since the condition is not fulfilled. What is necessary is that Socrates should sit down if he sits down: that Socrates should sit down is contingent (section 2).

In the same way, it is necessary that at 10 a.m. tomorrow either Socrates should be sitting down or that Socrates should not be sitting down: clearly he cannot be neither sitting down nor not sitting down at 10 a.m. tomorrow. But Aquinas holds that from this it does not follow either that Socrates will necessarily be sitting down or that Socrates will necessarily not be sitting down. Hence, though necessarily either 'Socrates will be sitting down at 10 a.m. tomorrow' is true, or 'Socrates will not be sitting down at 10 a.m. tomorrow' is true, neither of them is necessarily true: the one which is true is contingently true, the one which is false is contingently false. Aquinas calls this 'necessity under a disjunction', and considers it to be analogous to the conditional or hypothetical necessity mentioned above (passage 2, *lectio* 15, section 3).

Passage 1: Predication

Aquinas's commentaries on Aristotle seem to have had their origin in a fear that young students would be misled by studying Aristotle with Averrhoes's commentary, which was then the only one available. Despite their form, manner, and frequent verbal references to the text, it does not seem that Aquinas ever gave them as lectures. Where possible, Aquinas worked with a new translation of Aristotle, or at least a revision of the older one. His ability to penetrate the obscurities of the Latin translations and get to what we are now confident is Aristotle's meaning is remarkable. The commentary on the *De interpretatione*, or *In Perihermeneias* as he calls it, seems to date from 1270–71, in Paris. Why it was left unfinished is not known. Those who wish to know more about Aquinas's logical theories should read the whole of question 13 of the first part of the *Summa theologiae*.

In Perihermeneias, Book I, lectiones 4 – 5
(Aristotle's text: 16a19 – 16b25; commentary: Marietti, sections 36 – 73)

Lectio 4

1. After settling the question of the order in which utterances [*voces*] have signification, the Philosopher [i.e. Aristotle] now turns to discuss the utterances themselves that signify. He is principally interested in the indicative sentence [*enunciatio*], which is the subject of this book. Now, in any study, one ought first to know the originating principles of the subject; so here he first settles the question of the originating principles of the indicative sentence [i.e. its parts, the noun and the verb]. Then he turns to discuss the indicative sentence itself [in *lectio* 7].

On the first [the principles of the indicative sentence] he does two things. First he settles the question of what we might call the material originating principles of the indicative sentence, i.e. the parts that make it up. Then [in *lectio* 6] he raises the question of the formal originating principle of the indicative sentence, i.e. the expression [*oratio*], which is the category to which the indicative sentence belongs.

On the first of these [the material principles] he does two things. First [here in *lectio* 4] he settles the question of the noun, which signifies the substance of a thing. Then [in *lectio* 5] he settles the question of the verb, which signifies an acting or being acted on. Acting and being acted on have their origin in a thing.

On the first [the material principles] he does three things. First he defines 'noun' [sections 2 – 8 below]. Then he expounds its definition [section 9]. Thirdly he rejects some terms which do not completely meet the description of 'noun' [section 13].

2. On the first [the definition of the noun], we should realise that the definition is said to be a limit, because it encloses the whole thing. That is, the definition encloses the thing in such a way that nothing that belongs to the thing remains outside the definition, i.e. that the definition does not apply to. Nor is there anything different that falls under the definition, i.e. that the definition does apply to.

3. So he puts five elements into his definition of 'noun' [as 'utterance that signifies at will, without time, of which no separate part signifies']. First, he gives us 'utterance' as its category, thus distinguishing it from all other noises which are not utterances. An utterance, as it says in Book Two of the *De anima* [420b12], is a noise produced by an animal's mouth, accompanied by some imagination. Then he gives the first specific difference of the noun, namely 'that signifies'. This distinguishes it from utterances that do not signify anything, whether they be utterances which can be written down and are articulated (like 'tra-la-la'), or utterances which cannot be written

down and are not articulated, like idle whistling. He has already spoken about the signification of utterances, and so concludes from that here that a noun is an utterance that signifies.

4. But an utterance [in this sense] is something that exists naturally. A noun, on the other hand, is not something natural: it comes from human convention. Hence it might seem that he should not give 'utterance' — which is something natural — as the category to which the noun belongs. He should rather give 'sign', which is something conventional. So he should say: 'a noun is an uttered sign'. This is just as [if to say] it would be a more satisfactory definition of a bucket to say that it is a wooden vessel, rather than that it is wood formed into a vessel.

5. But we should answer to this that artificial things belong to the category of substance as far as their matter is concerned, but to the category of the accidents as far as their form is concerned. This is because the forms of artificial things are accidents. A noun which stands for an artificial thing, then, signifies an accidental form as it is made individual in its subject.

Now, in the definition of any accident one should include its subject. So if nouns signify an accident in the abstract [e.g. paleness or snubness], in their definition the accident should be in the nominative, since it is the category to which it belongs. The subject in which the accident exists should be in the genitive, as the specific difference. For example, we say 'snubness is curvedness of the nose'. But if the nouns signify an accident which is made individual [e.g. snub, pale], we should include in their definition their matter or subject as the category that they belong to, and the accident as their specific difference. For example, we say 'snub is a curved nose'.

So if the nouns which stand for artificial things signify accidental forms, as they are made individual in their natural subjects, it is more satisfactory that we should include the natural thing in their definition as the category they belong to. Hence, for example, we should say a bucket is wood of a certain shape; and, likewise, a noun is a significant utterance. It would be different if the nouns which stand for artificial things were taken to signify the artificial forms in the abstract.

6. Then he gives the second specific difference, saying: 'at will'. This means 'by human convention, which has its origin in human will'. This is the way in which the noun is different from utterances which have their significance by nature, like the groans of the sick or the utterances of brute animals.

7. Then he gives the third specific difference, i.e. 'without time'. This is the way in which nouns are different from verbs. But this would appear to be wrong: after all, the noun 'day' or 'year' signifies a time.

We should answer that there are three things we can consider in thinking about time. First, time itself, in so far as it is a sort of thing. Considered in this way time can be signified by a noun, as can any other sort of thing. Secondly, we can consider that which time measures as such: this is principally and chiefly change. Change is what acting and being acted on are; and so the verb, which signifies acting or being acted on, signifies with time. But a substance considered in itself, in so far as it is signified by a noun or a pronoun, has no reason to be measured by time as such: it is only in so far as it is subject to change, and is signified by a participle, that it is so measured. Thirdly, we can consider the character of time itself, the measure: and this is signified by the adverbs of time, such as 'tomorrow', 'yesterday', and the like.

8. Lastly, he gives the fourth specific difference when he adds 'of which no separate part signifies'. That is, no part signifies when separated from the noun as a whole. The part is related to the signification of the noun [only] in so far as it is a part of the whole. This is so because the signification is the form of the noun, as it were. No separated part has the form of the whole: a hand separated from a human being [is not something human,] does not have the human form. This is the way in which nouns are distinguished from expressions. The parts of an expression, e.g. 'a just man', do signify when they are separated.

9. Then he proves the definition he has given. He proves the last element of it first, then the fourth [section 11]. This is because the first two elements are obviously true from what has already been said; while the third, 'without time', is proved in the next discussion, on the verb. On the first point above [proving the last element] he does two things. First, he proves what he has said by means of composite nouns [in this section]. Then he shows the difference there is in this respect between composite nouns and simple ones [section 10].

He proves first, then, that separated parts of a noun do not signify anything, by drawing our attention to composite nouns, in which it looks as if they do. In the noun 'wildcat' the 'wild' part does not signify in its own right [or on its own] what it signifies in the expression 'wild cat'. [Literally, *equiferus*, a species of wild horse, as opposed to *equus ferus*, a wild horse.] The reason for this is that a noun is imposed in order to signify one simple concept. We should distinguish between that in virtue of which a noun is imposed from that which the noun signifies. The noun 'hydrogen' is imposed in virtue of its producing water. The noun 'hydrogen' does not signify producing water; it is imposed in order to signify the concept of some sort of thing. [Literally, *lapis*, a stone, from *laedens pedem*, hurting the foot — a false etymology]. This is why a part of a composite noun which is imposed in order to signify a simple concept [such as 'wild' in 'wildcat'] does not signify a part of the composite conception in virtue of which the noun is imposed. An expression, however, [such as 'wild cat'] does signify that composite conception; hence its parts do signify the parts of the composite conception.

10. Then he shows what the difference is in this respect between simple and composite nouns. He says that things are not the same with respect to simple nouns as they are with respect to composite nouns. In simple nouns the parts not only do not signify at all in fact, they do not even appear to [e.g. no one would suppose that 'ice' in 'justice' signifies ice.]. In composite nouns, however, it looks as if they do signify, though in fact they do not, as we have said about the noun 'wildcat'. The reason for the difference is this: that simple nouns are imposed in order to signify some simple concept, and also are imposed in virtue of some simple concept. Composite nouns, on the other hand, are imposed in virtue of some composite conception; hence it looks as if their parts signify.

11. Then he makes clear the third part of the above definition, ['at will']. He says that it is said that 'a noun signifies at will' because nothing is a noun by nature. A noun is a noun because it has a signification. It does not have a signification by nature, but by convention. Hence he adds, 'when it is known', i.e. when it is imposed, in order that it may have a signification. This is because that which has a signification by nature does not come to be a sign [and so is not imposed], but just is a sign by nature. This is what he means when he speaks of 'unlettered noises, as those of the beasts': he means that they cannot be signified by letters. He speaks of 'noises' rather than utterances, because some animals cannot utter, since they have no lungs. They do, however, naturally signify what is happening to them by certain noises: but none of these noises is a noun. Hence we are clearly given to understand that a noun does not signify by nature.

12. But you should know that there was a difference of opinion in some quarters on this subject. Some said that nouns do not have significance by nature in any way at all. They even said that different things' being signified by different nouns is not natural either. Others said that nouns have signification entirely by nature: as if nouns were natural likenesses of things. Others again said that nouns have no natural signification in so far as their signification is not by nature — which is what Aristotle means here — but they do have signification by nature in so far as their signification fits the natures of things. Plato said this [in the *Cratylus*]. The fact that one thing is signified by more than one noun is no objection to this view, since one thing can have many likenesses. In the same way more than one different noun can be imposed on one thing in virtue of its different properties.

We should not understand his remark 'There is no noun here' to mean that the noises made by animals have no nouns applied to them. There are some nouns that name them, such as the *roar* of a lion or the *lowing* of an ox. What he means is that none of these noises is a noun, as has been said.

13. Then he excludes some things from falling under the description

of being a noun: firstly, the 'indefinite' noun; then, grammatical cases or inflections of nouns.

He says first, then, that 'not-man' is not a noun. This is because every noun signifies some determinate nature, as 'human being' does, or some determinate person, as pronouns do, or some determinate nature and determinate person, as 'Socrates' does. The example given, however, 'not-man', does not signify either a determinate nature or a determinate person. It is imposed in virtue of the negation of 'man', and this is predicated equally well of what exists and of what does not exist. Hence 'not-man' can be said just as well of that which does not exist in the real world as it is of that which does: we can say 'The chimaera is a not-man' and 'The horse is a not-man'. If the noun were imposed in virtue of a privation [as 'invalid' is], it would require a subject, at least, that really exists; but since it is imposed in virtue of a negation, it can be said equally of that which exists and that which does not, as Boethius and Ammonius comment. But because it has a signification in the way that a noun has, i.e. in such a way that it can be either a subject or a predicate, there needs to be an individual [to which it refers] in the mind at least.

In Aristotle's time there was no name given to classify this sort of locution [*dictio*]. They are not expressions, since no part of them has signification on its own — just like composite nouns. Nor are they negations, i.e. negative sentences, since such a sentence adds negation to an affirmation. There is no question of this here. So he imposes a new name on this kind of locution, and calls it an 'indefinite' noun on account of the indeterminacy of its signification, which we explained.

14. Then he excludes the grammatical inflections of nouns, and says that *Catonis* [Cato's] and *Catoni* [for Cato] and suchlike are not nouns. Only the nominative inflection is said to be a noun in the central sense, as it is with this inflection that a noun is imposed to signify something. The other kinds are called the 'oblique' inflections of the noun. This is because they fall off obliquely from the nominative as their starting point: the nominative is called 'the upright' because there is no falling-off. The Stoics, however, also called the nominative an inflection [literally 'a case', i.e. 'a falling']. The grammarians follow this terminology, as they hold all of them fall — i.e. have their origin — from the interior conception of the mind. The name 'upright inflection' applies because there is no difficulty about something falling in such a way that it remains upright, like a pen which falls and sticks in a plank.

15. Then he shows how, as a consequence, the oblique inflections are related to the noun. He says the description which a noun signifies is the same for all the inflections of the noun. The difference consists in that a noun [in the nominative] joined to the verb 'is' or 'will be' or 'was' always signifies something true or something false, while this is not so with the oblique inflections. It is to be noticed that

he gives an example using a 'substantive' verb, 'to be' [i.e. a verb which requires a personal subject]. This is because there are other verbs, called 'impersonal', which do signify something true or false when joined to an oblique inflection. For example, 'It's upsetting for Socrates': here the actuality expressed by the verb is understood to affect [what is referred to by] the noun in the oblique inflection. It is as if we said, 'Socrates is upset.'

16. But there is an objection to this. If indefinite nouns and inflections of nouns are not nouns, then the definition we gave of 'noun' is unsatisfactory, since it fits them. We have to reply, following Ammonius, that the above definition of a noun is a rather general one, but afterwards Aristotle restricts the signification of 'noun' by making these exceptions. Or we could say that the definition given does not fit them without qualification: for the indefinite noun does not signify anything determinate [and so does not 'signify' without qualification], while grammatical inflections of nouns do not have their signification by the sheer will of the person who sets up the convention, which is what was said in the definition.

Lectio 5

1. After settling the question of the noun, here the Philosopher discusses the verb. On this he does three things: first, he defines the verb [section 2], then he excludes some things from falling under the description 'verb' [section 10]. Thirdly he shows how the verb and the noun are akin [section 15].

On the first point, [the definition of the verb], he does two things: first, he states the definition of the verb and then he explains it [section 7].

2. We should notice that for the sake of brevity Aristotle does not include in the definition of the verb those elements which are common to both the verb and the noun. He leaves this to be understood by the reader from what he has said in the definition of the noun.

He puts three elements into his definition of the verb [as 'that which consignifies time, of which no part signifies on its own, and is always the mark or sign of those things that are predicated of another']. Of these the first, that it consignifies time, distinguishes it from the noun. (It was said in the definition of the noun that the noun signifies without time.) The second element, that its parts do not signify anything on their own, as he says, distinguishes the verb from the expression.

3. But this was also included in the definition of the noun; so it might seem that it should have been omitted here, as is the point about being an utterance which signifies at will.

Ammonius's answer to this was that this element was put into the

23

definition of a noun to distinguish the noun from expressions which are composed of nouns, like for example 'the human being is an animal'. Since there are some expressions which are composed of verbs, e.g. 'to walk is to move', this element has to be repeated in the definition of the verb as well.

Another answer would be that verbs convey composition, which brings to completion an expression which signifies something true or false: so verbs are more akin to expressions than are nouns. Verbs are the formal part of an expression, while nouns are the material or subject part. Hence it has to be repeated. [But if this is so 'verbs' are here being assimilated to predicates, so the demand that no part of them should signify on its own is surely an error: C.M.]

4. The third element distinguishes the verb not only from the noun, but also from the participle, which signifies with time. He says that it is always the mark or sign of those things that are predicated of another. He says this because nouns and participles can be used as either subjects or predicates, while the verb is always a predicate.

5. A counter-example to this claim would seem to be that of verbs in the infinitive mood, which are sometimes used as subjects: as, for example, in 'To walk is to move'.

The answer is that verbs in the infinitive, which are used as subjects, have the force of nouns. Hence both in Greek and in the idiom of vulgar Latin [i.e. Italian and French] they can have the article tacked on to them, as nouns can. The reason for this is that the distinguishing mark of nouns is that they signify something as if it were something that exists in its own right, while the distinguishing mark of verbs is that they signify some kind of acting or being acted on.

Now, an acting can be signified in three ways. The first way of signifying an acting is to signify it in the abstract, in its own right, as if it were a kind of thing. In this case it is signified by a noun, as when we say 'an acting', 'a being acted on', 'a walk', 'a run' and the like. Another way of signifying an acting, is to signify it in the way which is proper to an acting, i.e. as something which proceeds from a substance and inheres in a substance as [an accident inheres] in its subject. In this way it is signified by verbs in some mood other than the infinitive, which are applied in predicates. But [there is a third way:] an acting's very proceeding from a subject or inhering in it can be grasped by the intellect, and signified by it, as if it were some sort of thing. Hence verbs in the infinitive, which signify the inherence of the acting in the subject, can be taken either as verbs, under the description of something individual [perhaps as in such a sentence as 'to be pale is occurring to Socrates'], or as nouns, in so far as they signify the action as if it were a sort of thing [as in 'to walk is to move'].

6. Someone might object to this that apparently even verbs in

moods other than the infinitive are sometimes used as subjects, e.g. in ' "Runs" is a verb'.

The answer to this is that in s᾿   . a sentence the verb 'runs' is not understood formally, i.e. in such a way that its signification bears on reality. Instead it signifies materially, i.e. it signifies the utterance itself, which is taken to be some kind of thing. When verbs, or any kind of part of an expression, are used materially, they are taken with the force of nouns.

7.   Then he explains the definition he has given. Firstly, he explains the point about 'consignifying time'; then he goes on to what he said about it being 'the mark of those things that are predicated of another' [section 8]. He does not explain the element of 'no part signifying on its own', as he has already explained it while dealing with the noun.

He explains first, then, that the verb consignifies time by means of an example. The word [a] 'run' signifies an acting: but not in the way which is proper to an acting, but in the way which is proper to a thing which exists in its own right. So it does not consignify time, since it is a noun. 'Runs', however, is a verb that signifies an acting, and so it does consignify time. It is proper for change to be measured by time. An acting comes to our notice over a period of time. We have said above [*lectio* 4, section 7 above] that to consignify time is to signify a thing that is measured in time. Hence there is a difference between signifying time in a primary way, as if it were a kind of thing, which can be done satisfactorily by a noun, and signifying *with* time. This cannot be done satisfactorily by a noun, but only by a verb.

8.   Then he explains another element. We should notice here that the subject of an indicative sentence is signified [by a noun] in the way that is proper to a thing in which something inheres, while the verb signifies an acting in the way which is proper to an acting. It belongs to the things that fall under that description to inhere in something else. Hence the verb is always used as a predicate, never as a subject, unless it is taken to have the force of a noun, as we have said [*lectio* 5, sections 4 – 5 above].

It is said, then, that 'the verb is always the mark of those things that are said of another'. This is because a verb always signifies that which is being predicated, and because there must always be some verb in any predication. This is because the verb conveys composition, by which a predicate is composed [put together] with a subject.

9.   But what follows seems doubtful: he says '[the mark of those things which are said of another,] either as of a subject or as in a subject'. Now it seems that a thing is said *of* a subject when it is predicated in the way which is proper to essences, e.g. 'the human being is an animal'. But '*in* a subject' would mean as when an accident is predicated of a subject, as for example 'the human being is pale'. If, then, verbs signify an acting or a being acted on, i.e. an

25

accident, they must always signify those things which are said as *in* a subject. It is superfluous, then, to say 'in a subject or of a subject'.

Hence Boethius says that both are about the same thing. This is because an accident is predicated of a subject, and is in a subject.

But Aristotle says 'either', so it would seem that he means something different by either expression. So we could say that when Aristotle says, 'A verb is always the mark of those things which are predicated of another' we should understand him to be saying this: it is not what is signified by the verbs which is predicated; rather it is the verbs themselves which are predicated. It is not that they signify things which are predicated. This is because predication seems to have to do more specially with composition. [That is, Aristotle is changing his usage: he uses the word 'predication' here to describe the relation between the verb and the subject, not that between what the verb stands for and the subject.]

We should understand, then, that a verb is always the sign that something is being predicated. This is because every predication is carried out by means of a verb, [considered] under the description of being that which conveys composition. This will be so whether that thing is predicated in the way proper to essences or in the way proper to accidents.

10.   Then he rules out some things from falling under the description 'verb': firstly, the 'indefinite' verb: then, the verb in the past or future tense [section 12].

He says first, then, that 'is not-running' or 'is not-working' are not properly called verbs. This is because it is proper to the verb to signify something in the way appropriate to an acting or a being acted on. These locutions do not do this: rather than signifying some determinate acting or being acted on, they remove some acting or being acted on. But though they cannot be said to be verbs in the proper sense, what has been put in the above definition of the verb does fit them. The first of these was that the verb signifies time, since it signifies acting and being acted on. These occur in time, and so does the privation of them. This is why 'being at rest' is measured by time, as the sixth book of the *Physics* says [238b26 ff]. The second is that they are always used as a predicate, as the verb is. This is because a negation is put in the same category as its affirmation. Hence, just as the verbs that signify an acting or a being acted on signify something as existing in something else, in the same way the above-mentioned locutions signify the removal of some acting or being acted on.

11.   But someone might object: if the definition of the verb fits the locutions just mentioned, then they are verbs. The answer to this is that the definition of the verb given above is a definition of the verb in a general sense. We are saying that these locutions are not verbs, because they fall short of the *complete* description of the verb.

Here, too, there was no name for this kind of locution before Aristotle's time. Since they are akin to verbs in some things, but fall short of the definite description of the verb, he calls them 'indefinite' verbs. He gives the reason for this name by saying that each of them can be said indifferently of that which is and of that which is not. This is because the negation which is attached to them is taken to have the force of sheer negation, not privation. Privation supposes a determinate subject [cp. *lectio* 4, section 13 above]. This kind of verb differs from negative verbs, since these indefinite verbs are taken to have the force of one locution, while negative verbs have the force of two locutions. [We might suggest 'is motionless' or 'is idle' as verbs that express a privation rather than a negation.]

12. Then he rules out verbs in the past and future tenses from being verbs. He says that just as indefinite verbs are not verbs without qualification, so neither 'will run', which is in the future tense, nor 'ran', which is in the past tense, are verbs. Rather they are 'inflections' of the verb. The difference between these and verbs is that the verb consignifies the present time, while these signify time on one side or other of the present.

It is important that he says 'present time', and not just 'present', so that the reader does not understand the indivisible present, i.e. the present instant. In the present instant there is no change, and hence no acting or being acted on. We should take 'present time' to be the time that measures an acting which has begun and has not yet been determined [had a limit set to it] by the achievement of what is being done.

It is quite correct to say that the things that consignify past or future time are not verbs in the strict sense. This is because a verb, strictly speaking, is that which signifies acting or being acted on. Hence, strictly speaking, a verb is that which signifies actually acting or actually being acted on: that which signifies acting or being acted on without qualification. Acting or being acted on in the past or future is acting or being acted on in a relative sense.

13. It is also reasonable to call verbs in the past or future tense 'inflections of the verb'. The verb consignifies present time, and 'past' and 'future' are said with relation to the present. The past is what was present, the future is what will be present.

14. The way the verb inflects varies according to mood, tense, number and person. But variation according to number or person does not constitute an inflection of the verb, as such variation arises in relation to the subject, not in relation to the acting. Variation according to mood or tense, however, has reference to the acting itself, and so both constitute inflections of the verb. Verbs in the imperative and the optative moods are said to be inflections of the verb, as are verbs in the past and future tenses. But verbs in the present tense and the indicative mood are not said to be inflections, whatever their person or number.

15. Then he shows the way that verbs are akin to nouns. He does

two things on this: first, he sets out what he means, then he proves what he has set out [section 16].

He says first, then, that verbs themselves, said in their own right, are nouns. Some have explained this as being a reference to verbs taken with the force of nouns. We have spoken of this: they may be either in the infinitive mood, as when I say 'To run is to move', or in some other mood, as when I say ' "runs" is a verb'. But it seems that Aristotle does not mean to say this, as what follows does not fit this intention. We have to say something else, then: that 'noun' here is taken in the sense it generally has of 'some locution imposed to signify something'. Acting and being acted on are sorts of things, and hence verbs themselves, in so far as they name, i.e. signify, some acting or being acted on, fall under 'nouns' taken in this general sense. But a noun, in so far as it is distinguished from a verb, signifies a thing in a determinate way, namely, in so far as it can be thought of as existing in its own right. Hence nouns can be both subjects and predicates.

16.   Then he goes on to prove what he has said. He does this first, from the fact that verbs signify something, as nouns do: secondly, from the fact that they do not signify anything true or false, as is also the case with nouns.

He says first, then, that by saying that verbs are nouns, he is saying that they signify something. He proves this: he has said above that significant utterances signify something thought of. Hence it is the special mark of a significant utterance that it should produce some thought in the mind of the hearer. So to show that a verb is a significant utterance, he assumes that the person who pronounces a verb produces some thought in the mind of the hearer. To show this he alleges that the person who hears the verb is at rest.

But this appears to be false: for only a complete expression makes the intellect be at rest, not a noun or a verb, if it just be said on its own. For if I say 'human being', the mind of my hearer is in suspense, waiting to hear what I have to say about it; and if I say 'is running', his mind is in suspense, waiting to hear of what I am saying this.

The answer to this is that there are two kinds of performance of the mind, as we maintained above. A person who pronounces a noun or a verb on its own does produce a thought which is the first kind of performance, the simple conceiving of something. To this extent the hearer's mind, which was in suspense before the noun or verb was uttered, and its utterance completed, is at rest. But the speaker does not produce a performance of the second kind, i.e. the operation of thought of one who composes and divides. So to this extent the speaker does not put the mind of the hearer at rest.

18.   So he immediately goes on to say that the verb does not yet signify anything in the way of composing and dividing, i.e. does not yet signify anything either true or false. This is the second point which he tries to prove.

He proves it, in fact, by considering those verbs which appear to signify truth or falsity more than any other, i.e. 'to be' and the 'indefinite' verb 'to not-be'. Neither of these, said on its own, signifies truth or falsity in reality: so still less does any other verb. Or, indeed, one can understand that this point is being made quite generally about all verbs. This is because when it has been said that this verb does not signify that a thing is or is not, he shows as a consequence that no verb signifies the being or not-being of a thing, i.e. that it is or is not. Although every definite verb implies being — since to run is to be running — and every indefinite verb implies not-being — since to not-run is to not-be running — nevertheless no verb signifies the following whole: that *a thing is* or *is not* [or 'exists or does not exist', or 'is or is not the case'].

19.   He proves this as a result of what he says: 'Even if you say a plain "is" it itself is nothing'. One should notice that the Greek says, 'Even if you say a bare "being", it itself is nothing.'

To prove, then, that verbs do not signify that a thing is or is not, he takes up the source and origin of what it is to be, i.e. being itself. Alexander comments that he says that 'being is nothing' since 'being' is said equivocally of the ten categories. No equivocal term means anything when said on its own; it needs something added to determine its signification. Hence not even 'is', said on its own, means that something is or is not.

But this explanation seems unsatisfactory, for three reasons. 'Being' is not equivocal, but said in a principal sense and secondary related senses: so when said on its own it is understood to mean that of which it is said in the principal sense. Also, equivocal locutions signify many things, rather than nothing: the same locution signifies sometimes one thing, sometimes another. Also, this explanation does not help forward the present discussion.

Hence Porphyry gives a different explanation. This word 'being' does not signify the nature of anything, as the nouns 'human being' or 'wise' do. Rather it merely designates a joining together. Hence Aristotle adds that it 'consignifies some composition, which cannot be understood without the things composed'. But this appears unsatisfactory as well, since if it does not signify any thing, but only a joining together, it would be neither a noun nor a verb, but like prepositions and conjunctions.

So we must give another explanation, as Ammonius does. His claim is that 'being itself is nothing' means that it does not signify truth or falsehood. Aristotle gives the reason for this when he adds: 'It consignifies a certain composition'. As Ammonius points out, we have to take 'consignify' not in the same sense in which it was used when we said that the verb consignifies time, but rather as 'signifying together with something else'. This means that when joined to something else it signifies a composition. A composition cannot be understood without its terms. But this point is common to all nouns and all verbs: so it looks as though this explanation is not what Aristotle meant. Aristotle takes *being* itself to be something special.

To stick closer to the words of Aristotle we have to remember that he did not say that the *verb* does not signify that a thing is or is not, but rather that not even *being* itself signified that a thing is or is not. Hence he says 'it is nothing', i.e. it does not signify that anything is. This is most obvious by the use of the word 'being', since a being just is that which is. Hence it seems to signify a *thing* in virtue of the 'that which', and *being* in virtue of the 'is'. If, then, this locution 'being' were to signify the act of being in its principal sense (as in fact it signifies a *thing* which has an act of being), it would doubtless signify that something is. But it does not in a principal sense signify the composition, which is what is conveyed by this word 'is'; rather it con-signifies it in so far as it signifies a thing that has an act of being. Hence this consignifying of composition does not suffice for truth and falsehood, because a composition, in which truth and falsehood are found, cannot be grasped except in so far as it connects the terms of the composition. [That is, it is the proposition as a whole that signifies something true or false, not any part of it.]

21.   But if we read 'a plain "is"', as our text has it, the sense is clearer. He proves that no verb signifies that a thing is or is not by using this verb 'is'. This verb, said on its own, does not signify that something is, although it does signify being. *To be* seems to be some kind of composition: hence this verb 'is', which signifies 'to be', could seem to signify a composition, in which the true and the false are to be found. But to rule this out he adds that the composition which the verb 'is' signifies cannot be grasped without the things which are being composed. A grasp of the composition depends on the terms. If they are not there, there is no complete grasp of the composition, such that there could be true or false in it.

22.   So he says that this verb 'is' consignifies a composition. This is because it does not signify it in a principal sense, but in a secondary way, since it signifies first of all that which comes into the mind in the way of something actual, without qualification. 'Is', said without qualification, signifies 'to be actually'. Hence it signifies in the way that a verb signifies. The actuality which this verb 'is' principally signifies is, generically, the actuality of every form, or of every substantial or accidental actuality. Hence whenever we want to signify that some form or actuality actually inheres in some subject, we signify this by means of this verb 'is'. This may be done without qualification or relatively. It is done without qualification in the present tense, and relatively in the other tenses. Hence as a result this verb 'is' signifies a composition.

Passage 2: Future contingents

Aquinas had a great deal of interest in the question of future contingents, and returned to it again and again. Parallel passages are to be found at *Summa theologiae* I q.14 a.13, and *De veritae* q.2 a.12. A. N. Prior discusses the latter in his paper 'The formalities of omniscience' in his *Papers on time and tense* (see Notes on Reading).

In Perihermeneias, Book 1, *lectiones* 13 – 15 (Aristotle's text: 18a27 – 19b4; commentary: Marietti, sections 164 – 204)

Lectio 13

1.   The Philosopher has just settled the question of the opposition of indicative sentences, and shown how opposed indicative sentences divide up the true and the false between them. Here he looks into a matter which might be doubtful, namely whether that which has been said [that of two contradictory sentences one must be true and the other false] is true in the same way for all indicative sentences or not.

On this he does two things: first, he puts forward the argument for there being indicative sentences which are not like this, then he proves it [section 7].

2.   On the first point, we should remember that the Philosopher has earlier made three different divisions of indicative sentences. Firstly, he distinguished between indicative sentences according to their unity, i.e. according to whether an indicative sentence is one without qualification, or one by conjunction [17a7 ff]. Then he distinguished between indicative sentences according to their quality, i.e. according to whether they are affirmative or negative. Thirdly he divided them according to their quantity, that is according to whether an indicative sentence is universal [e.g. 'Every human being is rational'] or particular [e.g. 'Some human beings are rational'], indefinite [e.g. 'The human being is rational'] or singular [e.g. 'Socrates is rational'] [17a37 – b16].

3.   Here he touches on a fourth division of indicative sentences: a division according to their time. Some are about the present, some about the past, and some about the future. This division can be accepted on the basis of what has gone before: for it was said above that every indicative sentence must necessarily be made with a verb or with an inflection of a verb [17a10]. The 'verb' is that which consignifies present time, while 'inflections of the verb' are those words that consignify past or future time.

We could admit a fifth division of indicative sentences, according to their matter. This division arises from the relation of a predicate to its subject. If a predicate is in its subject in its own right, it will be called an indicative sentence in a necessary matter or in a natural matter, e.g. 'the human being is an animal' or 'the human being is able to laugh'. But if the predicate in itself is repugnant to the subject and, as it were, rules out the description of the subject, it will be called an indicative sentence in an impossible or removed [or remote] matter, e.g. 'the human being is a donkey'. But if the relation between predicate and subject is in between, i.e. if it is neither in its own right repugnant to the subject, nor in the subject in its own right, it will be called an indicative sentence in a possible or contingent matter.

4. Now we have looked at these differences between indicative sentences: the judgement on truth and falsity in each of these kinds is not the same. Hence the Philosopher says, drawing a conclusion from what has gone before, that 'in those things that are the case' — i.e. in propositions about the present — and 'in those things which have become the case' — i.e. in indicative sentences about the past — it is necessary that an affirmation or a negation be determinately true or false. But there is a difference here, according to the quantity of the indicative sentence. In indicative sentences in which something is universally predicated of a universal subject, it is necessary that it is always the case that one of the two, i.e. either the affirmation or the negation, is true, and the other, which is opposed to it, false. [For example, 'Every human being is a donkey' and 'Not every human being is a donkey'.]

This is because, as it was said above, the negation of a universal indicative sentence in which something is universally predicated is not a universal negative indicative sentence but a particular one. It works vice-versa, too: the universal negative indicative sentence is not directly the negation of a universal affirmative indicative sentence, but of a particular affirmative indicative sentence. Hence, according to what has been said, it has always to be the case that one of them is true and the other false, in any matter whatever. The same argument applies in singular indicative sentences, which are also contradictorily opposed one to another, as has been maintained above. But in indicative sentences in which something is predicated non-universally of a universal subject, it is not necessary that always one should be true and the other false, as they can both be true at the same time, as was shown above. [For example, 'The human being is pale' and 'The human being is not pale' can both be true.]

5. This is how things are with propositions about the past or the present. But if we take indicative sentences about the future, they behave the same with regard to oppositions which are about universals, whether taken in a universal way or in a non-universal way. For all affirmative indicative sentences in a necessary matter are determinately true, whether they be about the future or about the past or about the present, and the negative indicative sentences are false. [For example, 'All human beings will be rational' is true and 'It is not the case that all human beings will be rational' is false]. And in an impossible matter, vice-versa. But in a contingent matter the

universal indicative sentences are false and the particular indicative sentences true, whether they be future or past or present. [For example, 'Every human being is pale' is false and 'Some human being is pale' is true.] Indefinite indicative sentences are both true at the same time, about the future as well as about the present or the past.

6.   But there is a difference with regard to singular future indicative sentences. In indicative sentences about the past or present necessarily one of the opposed indicative sentences is determinately true and the other determinately false, in any matter. But in singular indicative sentences about the future it is not necessary that one should be determinately true and the other determinately false. This is being said in the case of a contingent matter: for with regard to necessary and impossible matters the same argument applies to future singular propositions as to present and past ones. Aristotle does not mention 'contingent matters'. This is because things which properly belong to singular individuals are those things that turn out contingently; things that are in singular individuals in their own right, or are repugnant to them in their own right, are attributed to them in virtue of their falling under some universal description.

So this is the purpose of the whole present discussion: is it necessary that one of an opposed pair of singular indicative sentences about the future, in a contingent matter, should be determinately true, and the other determinately false?

7.   Then he proves the differences he has just alleged. He does two things on this: first, he proves it by drawing unsatisfactory consequences [from denying it]. Secondly, he shows that these consequences are [not just unsatisfactory, but] impossible [*lectio* 14, section 2].

On the first of these he does two things: first, he shows that in singular future indicative sentences truth cannot always be determinately attributed to one of the two opposites; then he shows that it cannot be the case that neither of them is true [section 12].

On the first of these he gives two arguments. The first draws a consequence, namely that if every affirmation or negation is determinately true or false, in singular future indicative sentences as in others, it follows that everything must either determinately be the case or not the case.

Then when he says 'Because if someone says' — or, as in the Greek, 'If, therefore, someone says', he proves the consequence he has alleged. Let us suppose that there are two people, one of whom says that something will happen, e.g. that Socrates will run, while the other says that this will not happen. If we take up the position mentioned, i.e. that it is contingent that one of a pair of singular future indicative sentences — either the affirmative or the negative — is true, it would follow that it is necessary that one of the two is saying the truth, and not the other. This is because it cannot be that both of a pair of singular future propositions be true, i.e. both the negative and the affirmative. This is possible only in indefinite pro-positions. But from the fact that necessarily one of them is saying the truth, it follows that it is necessary that it is determinately the case or not the case. He proves this as follows: these two propositions are interchangeable, that what is said is true, and what is said is really the case.

He makes this clear afterwards by saying that if it is true to say that it is white it follows of necessity that such is really the case; and if it is true to deny this, it necessarily follows that such is not the case. And vice-versa, too: if such is really the case, or is not the case, it necessarily follows that it is true to affirm it or to deny it. The same interchangeableness appears in what is false, too: if someone lies, saying something false, it necessarily follows that such as he affirms or denies is not really so: and vice-versa, if such as he affirms or denies is not so, it follows that by affirming or denying he is lying.

8. The way this argument proceeds is as follows. If it is necessary that every singular future affirmation or negation is true or false, then it is necessary that everyone who makes an affirmation or a negation determinately utters a truth or a falsehood. But from this it follows that as regards anything it is necessary that it is or is not the case. So if every affirmation or negation is determinately true [or false], it is necessary that everything is determinately the case or not the case. And from this he concludes, further, that everything is the case of necessity. By this conclusion three kinds of contingent things are ruled out.

9. Some things are contingent and occur in a minority of cases, e.g. the things that occur through chance or luck. Others are two-way: i.e. they are not more inclined to occur one way more than another; these are the things that come from choice. And some occur in the majority of cases, e.g. a person's growing grey in old age, which has a cause in nature. But if everything turns out as it does by necessity, none of these contingent things will be the case. So he says ['nothing is the case, and nothing comes to be the case, either by chance or two-way; or will be or will not be':] 'nothing is the case', referring to the continuance of those things that continue contingently 'and nothing comes to be the case', referring to the production of those things that are caused contingently; 'either by chance', referring to those things that occur in a minority or small number of cases, 'or two-way', referring to those things that are inclined to occur either way indifferently, i.e. can occur or not, and are not determined to either. This is what he means when he says 'or will be, or will not be'.

Of a thing which is more determined to go one way we can deter-minately say truly that this will be the case or will not be the case, e.g. the doctor truly says of the patient who is recovering, 'This person is going to get better', even though perhaps his getting better may be obstructed by some accident. This is why the Philosopher says in the second book of the *De generatione* [337b7], 'The one who is

going to jump will not jump.' For one can truly say of one who has a
determined purpose of jumping 'This person is going to jump', even
though his jumping may be obstructed by some accident.

The two-way, however, is not determined more one way than
another, and so it is a mark of such a thing that one can determinately say of it neither that it will be the case, nor that it will not be
the case. But he goes on to show that it would follow that nothing is
two-way, on the foregoing hypothesis. He does this by adding that if
every affirmation is determinately true, it must be that either the
person affirming or the person denying is saying the truth. This rules
out the two-way; for if there were anything two-way it would tend
equally to its occurrence or its non-occurrence, and not more one
way than the other.

But we should notice that the Philosopher does not explicitly rule
out the contingent which occurs in the majority of cases. This is for
two reasons. The first is, that such a contingent thing does not rule
out that one of a pair of opposed indicative sentences is determinately
true, and the other false, as we have mentioned. The second is that
once the contingent which occurs in a minority of cases — that which
occurs by chance — is ruled out, as a result the contingent which
occurs in a majority of cases is also ruled out. There is no difference
between that which occurs in a majority of cases and that which
occurs in a minority of cases, other than that it is its failure to occur
that is less often the case.

10.   Then he gives a second argument to show the difference he has
spoken of, by drawing an impossible conclusion. If truth and falsehood were to be found alike in present-tense indicative sentences and
future-tense indicative sentences, it would follow that whatever is
true about the present has also been true about the future, in the
same way as it is true about the present. But it is now determinately
true to say of some individual thing that it is white: so 'first', i.e.
before it turned white, it was true to say of it 'it will be white'. But
the same reasoning applies to what is near and what is distant: so if
the day before it was true to say 'this will be white', it follows that it
was always true to say of anything that occurs 'it will be the case'.
But if it is always true to say about the present that it is the case, or of
the future that it will be the case, it cannot be that it is not the case, or
that it will not be the case.

The reason for this conclusion is obvious: these two sentences are
inconsistent: 'so-and-so is truly said to be the case', and 'so-and-so is
not the case'. It is, after all, part of the signification of 'true' that
what is said is the case. So if we suppose that what is said about the
present or about the future is true, it cannot but be the case at present
or in the future. But that which cannot but be the case is the same as
that which it is impossible not to be the case: and that which is impossible not to be the case signifies the same as that which it is necessary
that it be the case. This will be explained more fully in the next book.

It follows from what has gone before, then, that it is necessary that
everything which will occur will occur. It further follows, that there is

nothing two-way, or by chance, since what is by chance is not by necessity, but occurs in a minority of cases. Aristotle abandons this conclusion as unsatisfactory: so the first premiss is false, i.e. that as regards everything such that it is true that it will be the case, it has been determinately true to say that it will be the case.

11.   To show this we must notice that since 'true' signifies that what is the case is said to be the case, a thing is true in the way in which it is or exists. Now, when something is or exists in the present, it possesses its act of being or existence in itself, and for this reason we can truly say of it that it is or exists. But when something is yet to come, it does not yet exist in itself: it does exist, however, in its cause, in some way. This can happen in three different ways.

First, it may be that it exists in its cause in such a way that it should come from it by necessity. In this way it has existence determinately in its cause, and so one can determinately say of it that it will exist.

Secondly, it exists in its cause in such a way that the cause has a tendency to its effect, but can be obstructed. This too is determined in its cause, but in a changeable way. Of this one can truly say that it will be, but not with complete certainty.

Thirdly, it exists in its cause merely potentially. This potentiality is not more determined one way than the other. Hence it is clear that it is in no way possible to say determinately of it that it will be: [we must say] rather, that it will be or not be.

12.   Then he shows that truth is not completely lacking to a pair of opposed future singular indicative sentences. First of all, he sets out what he means to do by saying that it is not true to say that in such a pair one of them is determinately true; but similarly it is not true to say that neither is true. This would be as if we said 'It will neither be nor not be'.

Then he proves this contention with two arguments. Of these the first is as follows: an affirmation and a negation divide up the true and the false between them, as is clear from the definition of 'true' and 'false'. After all, the true is just to say that what is the case is the case, or what is not the case is not, and the false is just to say that what is the case is not the case, or what is not the case is. Hence if an affirmation is false, it must be that its negation is true, and vice-versa. But according to the position taken above the affirmation 'This will be the case' is false: but the negation is not true either. In the same way, the negation will be false, without there being any true affirmation. Hence the position taken above is impossible, since it means that neither of a pair of opposites is true.

The second argument he gives is as follows: if it is true to say something, it follows that what is said is the case. For example, if it is true to say that something is large and white, then it follows that it is both. This is the same for the future as for the present. It follows that tomorrow something is the case, if it is true [today] to say that it will be tomorrow. If, then, the above position is true, which maintains that neither it will be the case tomorrow, nor it will not be the case, it must then [tomorrow] neither be the case nor not the case. This goes against the description given of the two-way: the two-way can go either way [but not neither]. For example, a sea-battle will occur tomorrow or not occur. And so from this there follows the same unsatisfactory conclusion as there did above.

Lectio 14

1. The Philosopher has shown above, by drawing unsatisfactory conclusions, that truth and falsehood are not to be found determinately in one or other of a pair of opposed singular future indicative sentences, in the same way as he had said they were in other indicative sentences. Now he shows that the unsatisfactory conclusions to which he has arrived are impossible.

On this he does two things. First, he shows that what follows is impossible: then he concludes what the truth really is on this point [*lectio* 15].

2. On the first of these he does three things: first, he puts forward the unsatisfactory conclusions that follow; then he shows that these unsatisfactory conclusions do follow from the position taken up above [section 3]; then he shows that the unsatisfactory conclusions that have been mentioned are in fact impossible [section 5].

He says first, then, as a conclusion of the foregoing arguments, that if we suppose that it is necessary that one of a pair of opposed indicative sentences must be determinately true, and the other false, in singular indicative sentences just as in universal ones, the following unsatisfactory conclusions follow: namely, that nothing which occurs is two-way, but everything is and comes to be of necessity.

And from this he draws two further unsatisfactory conclusions. The first is that one must not deliberate on anything, since it has been proved in the third book of the *Ethics* that there is no deliberation about things that are of necessity, but only about contingent things, that can be the case or not [1112a21 ff].

The second unsatisfactory conclusion is that all human actions which are done for the sake of some end — e.g. business, which is done for the sake of getting rich — will be vain. This is because if everything happens of necessity, what we are trying to bring about will occur whether we do anything or not. But this goes against human intention: for people seem to deliberate and do business with the intention that if they do so-and-so, such-and-such a result will follow, while if they do some other thing, such-and-such other result will follow.

3. Then he proves that these unsatisfactory conclusions do in fact follow from the position taken up.

On this he does two things: first, he shows that the above-mentioned unsatisfactory conclusions follow [if we grant] a certain possible hypothesis: then he shows that they follow even without this hypothesis.

He says first, then, that it is not impossible that a thousand years ago, when none of the things which are being done at present among human beings had been thought of or pre-ordained, someone should have said 'So-and-so will happen' — e.g. that such-and-such a state will be overthrown — and that someone else should have said that this will not happen. But if every affirmation or [its] negation is determinately true, necessarily one or other of them will determinately have said the truth. Hence it was necessary for one of the things said to have happened of necessity. The same argument goes for any other case; so everything happens of necessity.

4.   Then he shows that the same follows even if we do not suppose this possible hypothesis. It makes no difference to the reality or occurrence of a thing whether when one person has affirmed that it will happen, another should have denied it, or not. Things will be the same whether this has been done or not. The course of reality, or something's existing or not existing, does not change just because of our affirming or denying. This is because it is not the truth of our indicative sentence that causes reality, but rather vice-versa. In the same way, it makes no difference to what is happening now whether somebody affirmed or denied it a thousand years ago, or indeed ever. So if at some time past the truth of indicative sentences was such that it was necessary that one of a pair of opposite indicative sentences should be said truly, and if from that it follows that something that was said is necessarily true, it follows that everything that happens is such as to happen by necessity.

He gives a reason for this conclusion: if we suppose that someone said truly that this will be the case, it is impossible that it will not be the case. In the same way, suppose that a human being exists: it is impossible that it not be a mortal rational animal. This is what is signified, when we say that something is truly said, namely that things are as it is said. But the relation between what is said now and the things that are to come is the same as the relation there was between what was said earlier and the things that are present or past. Thus everything has happened, is happening, and will happen of necessity; because it was always true to say that what is now the case, was going to happen, whether it be something that is happening now or something that happened in the past.

5.   Then he shows that what has gone before is impossible; first, by argument, and then from examples of things we can see [section 7].

On the first point he does two things: first, he shows what he plans to show in human affairs, then also in other things [section 6].

As far as human affairs are concerned, then, he shows that what has been said is impossible. It is obvious that human beings are the originating principle of those things in the future that they do as the controllers of their own acts, and that they have in their power to do or not to do. If you deny this originating principle, you remove the whole structure of human intercourse, and all the principles of moral philosophy. If you deny this, there is no point in persuasion, or threats, or punishment or reward, by which people are encouraged to do good and discouraged from doing evil, and so the whole science of society becomes vain.

The Philosopher takes it as an obvious premiss that human beings are originating principles of things in the future. But they are not originating principles of things in the future except by deliberating and acting in some way. Things which act without deliberation have no control over their actions, in the way of judging about what is to be done. They are rather moved to act by some natural instinct, as is clear in the case of the brute animals. Hence the above conclusion, that we must not do business or deliberate, is impossible. Hence the premiss from which it follows, namely that everything happens of necessity, is also impossible.

6.   Then he shows that this is so in other matters, too. It is obvious even in natural matters that there are things which are not always actually existing. These things, then, can exist and not exist, contingently. If it were not so, they would either always exist or never exist. But that which does not exist begins to exist through becoming what it is: as something that is not white begins to be white through becoming white. If it did not become white it would continue to be not-white. So things which can exist or not contingently can come to exist or not, contingently. Such things, then, do not exist, and do not come to exist, of necessity, but they have in them a nature which is possible, through which they are able to come to exist and not come to exist, to exist and not exist.

7.   Then he shows what he has alleged by examples which are available to the senses. Suppose, for example, that there is a new coat; it is obvious that it can be cut up, as there is nothing to prevent its being cut up, either on the part of the person who does the cutting or on the part of what gets cut up. But he proves that at the same time as it is possible that it should be cut up, it is possible that it should not be cut up. He does this in the same way as he proved in an earlier chapter that two indefinite indicative sentences which are opposed to each other can both be true, i.e. by assuming the contrary. For just as it is possible for this coat to be cut up, it is also possible for it to wear out, i.e. to be destroyed by age. But if it wears out it is not cut up. Therefore either is possible, namely, that it should be cut up and that it should not be cut up.

From this he draws a universal conclusion, that in other future things that do not always actually exist but can exist, it is clear that not everything exists or comes to exist of necessity. Some of them are two-way: they do not tend more to the affirmation than to the denial. Some of them are such that one is the case for the most part, while in the minority of cases the other is true, and not that which occurs in the majority of cases.

8.   We should notice that there have been different views on the possible and the necessary, as Boethius points out in his *Commentary*.

There were some who distinguished them according to the outcome, like Diodorus. He said: that which will never be the case is impossible; that which will always be the case is necessary; that which will sometimes be the case, and sometimes not, is possible.

The Stoics, on the other hand, distinguished between them according to external prevention. They said: that which cannot be prevented from being true is necessary; that which is always prevented from being true is impossible; while that which can be prevented or not is possible.

Both these two ways of distinguishing [the necessary from the possible] seem faulty. The former, Diodorus's view, has the cart before the horse: it is not that something is necessary because it will always be the case; rather, it will always be the case because it is necessary, and (obviously) so on. The latter, the Stoic view, is external and, as it were, coincidental. It is not that something is necessary because it is not prevented, but rather that it cannot be prevented because it is necessary.

Hence others made this distinction in a better way, which depends on reality. They said that that which is determined in its nature solely to exist is necessary; that which is determined solely not to exist is impossible; and that which is not wholly determined to either is possible, whether it tends more one way than the other or tends either way indifferently, i.e. the two-way contingent. This is the view attributed by Boethius to Philo.

But it is clearly Aristotle's view here. He attributes the description of being possible and being contingent, in the things which are in our power, to the fact that we can deliberate, and in other things to the fact that the matter is in potentiality to either of two opposites.

9.   But this argument does not seem sufficient. We see that there is in perishable bodies a matter which is in potentiality to existence and non-existence; in the same way we see that heavenly bodies have a potentiality to be in different places. Nevertheless in heavenly bodies there are no contingent events, only necessary ones. Hence we have to say that the two-way possibility of matter, generally speaking, is not a sufficient condition for contingency. We have to add, on the side of the potentiality of the agent, that it should not be completely determined one way. If it were so determined one way that it could not be prevented, then as a result it would bring the passive potentiality into actuality of necessity, in the same way.

10.   Some noticed this, and suggested that the potentiality which is in natural things acquired a necessity from some cause, determined one way, which they called *fate*. Among such authors, the Stoics put fate into their series or web of causes. They supposed that everything that happens in this world has a cause, and that once one supposes the cause, the effect follows of necessity. If one cause on its own were not enough, then many causes coinciding in one effect were put

under the description of one sufficient cause. Hence they concluded that everything happened of necessity.

11.   But this argument was resolved by Aristotle in the sixth book of the *Metaphysics* [1027a30–b16], by refuting both the assumptions they made. He says that not everything that comes into existence has a cause: only that which exists in its own right has a cause. That which is coincidental does not have a cause, since properly speaking it is not an existent. It should rather be ranked with the non-existent. Plato said the same. So 'being a musician' has a cause, and so does 'being pale': but 'Someone pale being a musician' has no cause. It is the same for all such things. It is also false that when a cause — even a sufficient cause — is supposed, one must necessarily suppose the effect to follow. This is because not every cause, not even every sufficient cause, is such that its effect cannot be prevented. Fire is a sufficient cause of the burning of wood, but you can prevent the burning by pouring on water.

12.   If these two suggestions were true, then it would undoubtedly follow that everything happens of necessity. If every effect has a cause, this would be to bring back the effect — which is to happen in five days' time, or after any period — to some earlier cause. In this way one would get back to a cause which exists now in the present, or existed already at some past time. So if, once the cause is supposed, one must necessarily suppose the effect, the necessity would reach along the causal ordering right to the last effect. For example, if he eats salt, he will be thirsty; if he is thirsty, he will leave home to have a drink; if he leaves home, he will be killed by robbers. But he has already eaten the salt: so he will necessarily be killed. Aristotle rules this out by showing that both suggestions are false, as we have said.

13.   Some people objected to this that every coincidental existent can be brought back to something that exists in its own right: hence an effect which is coincidental should be brought back to something that is a cause in its own right. They did not notice that that which is coincidental is brought back to something that exists in its own right because it is something that coincides in something that exists in its own right. For example, being a musician is something that coincides in Socrates, and every accident is something that coincides in some subject that exists in its own right. In the same way, everything that is coincidental in some effect is thought of as connected with some thing that is an effect in its own right. This effect, in so far as it is an effect in its own right, has a cause in its own right: but it has no cause in its own right with regard to that which is coincidental in it, only a coincidental cause. An effect should be proportionately related to its cause, as is said in the second book of the *Physics* [195b26] and the fifth book of the *Metaphysics* [?1013b29–1014a16].

14.   But there were some who paid no attention to the difference between effects which are coincidental and effects which are effects

in their own right, and tried to bring every effect which occurs here below back to some thing that is a cause in its own right. They said that there was a power in the heavenly bodies — which is where they localised fate — and that fate just was the influence of the positions of the stars. But from such a cause we cannot derive necessity in everything that is done down here.

Many things are done here as a result of thought and will, which are not, in themselves and directly, under the power of the heavenly bodies. Thought — or reason — and the will which is in the reason, are not the activities of any bodily organ. This is proved in the *De anima* [429a26]. So it is impossible that thought or reason, and the will, should be directly under the power of the heavenly bodies. This is because no bodily power can act in its own right on anything but a body. Now, the sensitive powers, in so far as they are the activities of bodily organs, are coincidentally subject to the action of the heavenly bodies. Hence the Philosopher, in the *De anima*, ascribes the view that the human will is subject to the movements of the heavens to those who did not make the intellect any different from the senses [427a22]. But the power of the heavenly bodies does indirectly affect the intellect and the will, i.e. in so far as the intellect and the will make use of the sensitive powers. But it is clear that what happens to the sensitive powers does not bring any necessity to bear on the reason and the will. For the self-controlled person has base desires, but is not led astray by them, as the Philosopher makes clear in the seventh book of the *Ethics* [1145b12]. Hence there is no necessity that comes from the power of heavenly bodies in what is done by reason and will.

There are also other bodily effects in perishable things in which there is no necessity. In bodily effects in perishable things there are many things that happen coincidentally. But that which is coincidental cannot be brought back to any natural power as to something that causes it in its own right. This is because natural powers tend to one outcome, while that which happens coincidentally is not one outcome. This is why Aristotle has said in a previous chapter that the indicative sentence 'Socrates is a pale musician' is not one thing, since it does not signify one thing. Hence he says in his book on sleeping and waking that many things of which there previously occur signs in the heavens, e.g. rain and storms, do not occur, because they are prevented, coincidentally [*De divinatione per somnium* 463b23 – 31]. Now, that preventing agent, considered in itself, can be brought back to some heavenly cause. But the meeting of these two heavenly causes is something coincidental, so it cannot be brought back to any cause that acts by nature.

15.　But we should notice that the coincidental, e.g. someone pale's being a musician, can be grasped by the intellect as one thing. Even though in itself it is not one thing, it is taken by the intellect as one thing, when it forms one indicative sentence by composition. Hence it can happen that something that in itself happens coincidentally and by chance can be brought back to some intellect that preordains it.

For example, the meeting of two servants in a certain place is coincidental and by chance as far as they are concerned, since the one knew nothing of the other. But it can be intended by their master, who has sent both precisely in order that they should meet in a certain place.

16.   Hence some claimed that everything that is done in this world, even the things that appear fortuitous or by chance, can be brought back to the ordering of divine providence, on which, they said, fate depended. Some foolish people denied this because they judged the divine intellect according to the measure of our intellect, which does not know individual things. But this is wrong: the divine thought and the divine will are both God's own act of existence. Hence, since his act of existence, by its power, extends to everything that exists in any way — i.e. in so far as everything exists by sharing in his existence — in the same way what he thinks of and can think of extend to everything that is known or can be known, and his will and his willing extend to everything good that is or can be desired. So in so far as anything can be known, it falls under his knowledge, and in so far as anything is good it falls under his will; just as in so far as anything exists, it falls under his active power, which he grasps perfectly, as it depends on his active intellect.

17.   But if divine providence is, in its own right, the cause of everything that happens in this world, or at least of everything good, it seems that everything happens of necessity.
     Firstly, because of his knowledge. His knowledge cannot err, so it seems that what he knows must necessarily happen. Secondly, because of his will. God's will cannot be thwarted: so it seems that whatever he wants happens of necessity.

18.   But these objections come from weighing up the divine intellect and activity according to the measure of our own intellect and activity. They are very different, however.

19.   Firstly, as far as awareness or knowledge are concerned. A power of knowing which is in some way contained within the order of time is related to the things that happen in the order of time quite differently from a power of knowing which is completely outside the order of time. A satisfactory example can be drawn from spatial order: as the Philosopher says in the fourth book of the *Physics*, what comes first and second in change, and hence in time, follows on from what comes first and what comes second in size [219a15–20]. So if there are a lot of people going along a road, then each of them, contained within the order of the travellers, is aware of those before and those behind, just in so far as they are before and behind. This is part of spatial ordering. So any of them can see those who are beside him and some of those in front of him: he cannot see those who are behind him. But if there were someone out of the whole ordering of travellers, e.g. someone standing on a high tower from which he

could see the whole road, he would see all those on the road at the same time. He would not, however, see them under the description of before and behind, relative to his view. He would see them all at the same time, and how each one goes before another.

Our knowledge falls under the ordering of time, either in itself or coincidentally. (This is why the mind, in composing and dividing, needs to include time, as it says in the third book of the *De anima* [430b12 ff].) Hence things fall under its knowledge under the description of present, past and future. Thus it knows present things as actually existing and in some way perceptible by the senses. It knows past things, as recalled. And future things it does not know in themselves, because they do not yet exist, but it can know them in their causes. It can know them with certainty, if they are totally determined in their causes, in such a way that they come from them of necessity. It can know them conjecturally, if they are not so determined that they cannot be prevented. (This is the case with the things which occur for the most part.) It cannot know them at all, if, in their causes, they are wholly in a state of potentiality which is not more determined one way than the other. This is the case with the two-way. This is because a thing cannot be known, in so far as it exists potentially, but only in so far as it exists actually, as the Philosopher makes clear in the ninth book of the *Metaphysics* [?1051a29–34].

20. But God is wholly outside the order of time, standing, as it were, in the high citadel of eternity, which is all at one time. The whole course of time is subject to eternity in one simple glance. So at one glance he sees everything that is done in the course of time; he sees everything as it is in itself, not as if it were future relative to his view. It is only future in the ordering of its causes. (Though God does see that ordering of causes.) In a wholly eternal way he sees everything that is the case at any time, just as the human eye sees the sitting down of Socrates as it is in itself, not in its causes.

21. The fact that some human being sees the sitting down of Socrates does not take away the contingency of this event: contingency has to do with the ordering of cause and effect. Nevertheless the human eye does see the sitting down of Socrates most certainly and without any possibility of error, while he is sitting down. This is because everything is already determined in so far as it is the case, in its own right. We are left, then, with the conclusion that God knows everything which happens in time most certainly and without possibility of error; but in spite of this the things that happen in time are not necessarily but contingently the case, and do not necessarily come to be the case, but contingently.

22. We have to notice a difference, too, as regards the divine will. The divine will should be thought of as being outside the ordering of existent things. It is the cause which grounds every existent, and all the differences there are between them. One of the differences

between existents is between those that are possible and those that are necessary. Hence necessity and contingency in things have their origin in the divine will, as does the distinction between them, which follows from the description of their proximate causes. God lays down necessary causes for the effects that he wants to be necessary, and he lays down causes that act contingently — i.e. that can fail of their effect — for the effects that he wants to be contingent. It is according to this characteristic of their causes that effects are said to be necessary or contingent, even though they all depend on the divine will, which transcends the ordering of necessity and contingency, as their first cause.

The same cannot be said of the human will, or of any other cause. Every other cause falls under the ordering of necessity and contingency. Hence either the cause can fail of its effect, or its effect is not contingent but necessary. The will of God cannot fail: but in spite of that, not all its effects are necessary; some are contingent.

23.   There is another notion at the root of contingency, which the Philosopher mentions here to conclude what we have been discussing, which some people attacked. They wanted to show that the will, in choosing, is moved of necessity by the desired object. Since good is the object of the will, it seems that the will cannot be turned from desiring what seems good to it; just as the reason cannot be turned from assenting to what seems true to it. Hence it seems that choice which follows on deliberation always comes of necessity; and so everything which we orginate as a result of deliberation and choice come of necessity.

24.   We should answer that we have to notice a similar distinction with regard to both the good and the true. There are some truths which are known in their own right, e.g. the first unprovable premisses, to which the intellect assents of necessity. But there are other truths which are not known in their own right, but by means of something else.

These are of two kinds. Some follow by necessity from the premisses, so that they cannot be false, if the premisses are true. This is the case with the conclusions of logical demonstrations. The intellect assents to such truths of necessity, once it has grasped the way they are ordered to the premisses, though not before.

But there are others which do not follow from their premisses of necessity. They can be false, though their premisses are true. These are matters of opinion, and the intellect does not assent to such of necessity, though there may be something else that inclines it one way rather than the other.

In the same way there is such a thing as a good that is desired for its own sake: e.g. well-being, which falls under the description of being the last end. The will is necessarily fixed on this of necessity, since everyone desires to live well, by some kind of natural necessity. But there are other goods which are desired for the sake of some end. These are related to the end as are conclusions to their premisses, as the Philosopher makes clear in the second book of the *Physics* [200a21 ff].

So if there are certain goods without which no one can live well, they will be necessarily desired, especially by someone who grasps their ordering to their end. Perhaps existence, life, thought, and any others like them there may be are such goods. But individual goods, which is what human actions are about, are not of this kind: nor are they included under that description 'things without which there can be no well-being'. For instance, eating this food or that, or not eating at all. But they do have in themselves something in virtue of which they move the will, according to some good which we consider in them. Hence the will is not led to choose them of necessity.

Hence it is significant that the Philosopher points to deliberation as the root of contingency in the things that come to be through us. Deliberation is about those things that go towards an end, but are not determined. In those matters in which the means are determined, there is no need for deliberation, as he says in the third book of the *Ethics* [1112b5 ff].

All these things have been said to preserve the roots of contingency which Aristotle mentions here, though they seem to go beyond the limits of the task of the logician.

Lectio 15

1.   The Philosopher has now shown that what follows from the positions set out above is impossible. Here he rules out those impossible conclusions and gives the truth as his own conclusion.

On this he does two things. The argument to the impossible conclusion went from indicative sentences to things. He has already excluded the unsatisfactory conclusion about things which followed. Now he reverses the order, and first shows how the truth about things is, then how the truth about indicative sentences is.

On the first of these he does two things. First, he shows how truth and necessity are related in reality, when they are considered without any relation to anything else: then, how they are related in reality in relation to their opposites.

2.   He says first, then, in a sort of conclusion from what has gone before, that if the above is unsatisfactory — i.e. that everything happens of necessity — we have to say the following: necessity and truth are related in reality in such a way that everything that is the case necessarily is the case when it is the case, and everything that is not the case necessarily is not the case when it is not the case. This necessity is based on the following principle: it is impossible for something to be and not be the case at the same time. So if something is the case, it is impossible that it should not be the case at the same time. So it is necessary that it should be the case at that time.

This is because 'It is impossible that it should not be the case' signifies the same as 'It is necessary that it should be the case', as will be said in the second book. In the same way, if something is not the case, it is impossible that it should at the same time be the case. Hence it is necessary that it should not be the case, since these two ['impossible' and 'necessary that not'] also signify the same thing. So it is an obvious truth that whatever is the case necessarily is the case when it is the case, and everything that is not the case necessarily is not the case, at the time at which it is not the case. This is not necessity in an absolute sense, but in a hypothetical sense. One cannot, then, just barely say that everything that is the case, necessarily is the case, and that everything that is not the case necessarily is not the case. These two: 'Everything that is the case, when it is the case, of necessity is the case' and 'Everything that is the case of necessity is the case', without qualification, do not signify the same: the first signifies hypothetical necessity, the second absolute necessity.

And what has been said of being the case should be understood in the same way of not being the case. It is one thing for something not to be the case of necessity, without qualification, and another for it not to be the case, of necessity, while it is not the case. By this argument Aristotle is seen to be denying what was said above, that if at present one of a pair of opposites is determinately true, then even before it came to be the case it was determinately going to be the case.

3. Then he shows how truth and necessity are related to reality in relation to their opposites. He says that the same argument applies in the case of contradiction, as it did in the hypothetical cases.

Something that is not absolutely necessary becomes necessary on the hypothesis that it is the case: it necessarily is when it is. In the same way that which is not in itself absolutely necessary becomes so by being put in a disjunction with its opposite. This is because it is necessary that anything is or is not the case, and that it will be or will not be the case, under a disjunction. This necessity is based on the principle that it is impossible for contradictories to be true or false at the same time. Hence it is impossible for something to neither be the case nor not be the case; and therefore it is necessary that it should be the case or not. But if either of the pair is taken on its own, it is not necessary, in the absolute sense, for it to be the case.

He makes this clear by an example. It is necessary that a sea-battle will take place or not take place tomorrow. But it is not necessary that a sea-battle will take place tomorrow, and likewise it is not necessary that it will not take place. These belong to absolute necessity. But it is necessary that it will either take place tomorrow or not take place: this belongs to necessity under a disjunction.

4. Then, as a result of what he has shown about reality, he shows how things are with regard to expressions.

First, he shows how truth in expressions is uniformly related to the way things are or are not in reality. Then he finally determines the truth of the whole question.

First, then: expressions of the indicative sentence kind are related

47

to truth as things are to their existence or non-existence. This is because an expression is true or false according to whether a thing exists or not. So with regard to everything that is two-way — and with regard to everything that is such that its contradictory can contingently occur, whether equally either way, or one way in a majority of cases — it necessarily follows that the contradiction of indicative sentences will be the same way, [i.e. two-way etc.].

And he shows, as a consequence, that there are things whose contradictory can contingently occur. There are things, he says, that neither are always the case, as necessary things are, nor are always not the case, as impossible things are, but rather sometimes are the case and sometimes are not. And he shows, further, that it is the same way with regard to contradictory indicative sentences. He says that, of a pair of contradictory indicative sentences about contingent things it is necessary that one side of the contradiction be true or false under a disjunction. But it is not necessary that one or the other should be true or false determinately: it is two-way. And even if it should happen that one side of a contradiction is more true — as happens with contingent things that occur in a majority of cases — even so it is not the case that therefore it is necessary that one of the two sides be of necessity determinately true or false.

5.   Then he draws his main purpose to a conclusion and says that it is clear from what has gone before that it is not necessary that in every kind of opposed affirmation and negation, one should be determinately true and the other false. This is because truth and falsity are not related in the same way to things which are already now the case, and to things that are not the case, but can be or not. They are related, as we have said, in the following way. In those things that are the case it is necessary that one should determinately be true and the other false. This does not happen in future things which can be or not be the case.

And this is the end of the first book.

3

Aquinas on Metaphysics

An introduction to Aquinas on metaphysics

Existence

It was mentioned in 'An introduction to Aquinas on logic' that it was Frege who re-established in recent times the absolute category-distinction between names and predicable expressions. We also owe to Frege our modern doctrine on existence, according to which 'existence is a second-level predicate', as the slogan runs: to say that something exists, that there is a so-and-so, is not to predicate anything of any individual. It is rather to say something about what the predicable expression 'so-and-so' — which can itself be true of individuals — stands for.

Here, too, Aquinas anticipated him. In a number of passages of great subtlety he observes that the Latin verb *esse* (to be) which is used to express existence 'is said in many ways'. Often — in passage 3, for example — there is a blurring of the distinction as to whether we are talking about manners in which things can exist or senses in which the verb 'to exist' can be used. This does not lead to any serious confusion in the writer's mind.

The sense which is relevant to logic, and which is most familiar to us, is the sense he calls *esse ut verum*, existence in the sense of the true (passage 3, sections 11–12). We would say that when we say that there is a God, or there is such a person as Socrates — incidentally, using a part of the verb 'to be' to express existence, as Aquinas did — what we are saying is that something belongs to the kind we are talking about. Aquinas says that by such a statement we mean that there is a proposition such as 'The Lord is God' or

'That man over there is the person called Socrates' which is true. Hence the label of 'existence in the sense of the true'.

Aquinas also says, interestingly, that in sentences which express 'existence in the sense of the true', such as 'There is blindness', the verb 'to be' is used as the copula. Recent linguistic research suggests this is true in both Greek and English, and thus presumably in Latin too: the point at stake here is that it is the sentence as a whole that conveys existential import, presumably in so far as this elliptical sentence with its dangling copula depends for its truth on the truth of some other sentence such as 'Some animal is blind'.

Actual existence

This sense needs to be carefully distinguished from another sense with which we are less familiar. Aquinas holds that there is another sense of *esse* in which it can genuinely be predicated of individuals. This, he often says, is equivalent to '— is alive' when it is a living thing that we are talking about: 'actually exists' would be the closest rendering into English. Things that can be said to be existents in the *esse ut verum* sense need not be existents in the 'actual existence' sense. In the *esse ut verum* sense even blindness exists, since it is true to say, for example, that Homer is blind. Indeed, in this sense even the dead exist, since it is true to say that Homer is dead. Blindness, though, is by no means an actual existent: rather it is the lack of a certain power in the blind subject, a power that ought to exist and normally does exist in other animals. Equally, a dead man — not to be confused with a corpse — is clearly not an actual existent.

It is to be hoped that readers will not be reluctant to admit the notion of actual existence. One difficulty may be the general acceptance of the slogan 'existence is not a predicate', and the fear that to admit a notion of existence that can be expressed as a predicate which can be true of individuals is to lay oneself open to the clearly fallacious 'ontological argument' for the existence of God. This fear is unfounded. The existence that 'is not a predicate' is the notion of existence that Aquinas calls 'existence in the sense of the true': he is capable of using it to achieve all the insights on this notion which we have had since Frege, and also to avoid the ontological argument.

But if readers do find it hard to accept this notion, then there is little that they can do, except, perhaps, to close the book and devote themselves to other philosophers. The notion of the actual existent is of crucial importance to Aquinas, and, arguably, to metaphysics in general. There can surely be no genuine study of the existent as such, including the non-actual existent: no such thing as an object-theory, as Meinong asked for, or a quite general ontology, a study of all the entities. Such a study would have to include not only sub-atomic particles, stocks and stones, plants and animals, human beings and angels, the world and God — already a dizzying list — but also numbers, functions, senses and propositions: perhaps even the mysterious and chimerical *facts* which were so beloved by early twentieth-century philosophers. They would all have to be studied 'as such': what is the suchness that provides the description, the *ratio*, under which they would all admit study?

It is true that there is a more or less respectable part of logic called 'ontology' which does consider everything that can be said to exist in any way. But here the 'can be said' is crucial: the *ratio* in virtue of which they form a unified field of study is that of the contribution that the expressions which stand for them make to sentences. This is properly a part of logic: it is a study of what is or can be named. Aquinas would have no difficulty with such a field of study: it is already included within his conception of logic, and within his conception of 'existence in the sense of the true' that goes with it. We need not find any difficulty with this either. But a theory of objects as such, or the existent as such, is doomed to failure: they have no 'such'.

Real and Cambridge changes

Still, it is not enough to abuse the opposition: some positive defence of the notion of the actually existent must be put forward. This is not easy: the concept is such a basic one that those who uphold it find it hard to understand why anyone else should not do so, while those who oppose it find it hard to understand what the devil the others are going on about. An example which Geach gives (in 'What actually exists' in *God and the soul* — see Notes on Reading) is usually crucial. He distinguishes between what he calls 'real' changes and 'merely Cambridge' changes. A Cambridge change occurs whenever we have a sentence 'a is F' true at one time and false at another. It will be immediately apparent that a vast number of Cambridge changes are in some sense not real: they do not imply any 'real' change in their subject. When Socrates was fifty-five and Theaetetus was thirteen 'Socrates is taller than Theaetetus' was true: when Socrates was sixty and Theaetetus was eighteen 'Socrates is taller than Theaetetus' was false. It is clear that while there has been a Cambridge change in Socrates, this is a *merely* Cambridge change: the real change is in Theaetetus. If one had watched Theaetetus closely enough during the five years one would have noticed his height changing: not so by watching Socrates.

Equally well, when I come to think about Jerusalem, there has been a real change in me, but not in Jerusalem: though, of course, there has been a merely Cambridge change in Jerusalem, as 'Jerusalem is not being thought about by me' has come to be false. A suitable investigation of my mind, could one be performed, would discover something that has changed in me: but there is just no kind of scrutiny of Jerusalem that could have revealed the merely Cambridge change taking place.

It looks fairly obvious that merely Cambridge changes depend on real changes: there will be no merely Cambridge change unless there is a real change somewhere. Since the difference between the two kinds of change consists in the fact that a real change involves some new actual existent coming to be in its subject — a greater height, a thought — this would back up Aquinas's belief that the notion of actual existence is in fact more basic than the notion of existence in the sense of the true.

It was said above that Geach's use of the distinction between real and merely Cambridge changes to illustrate the distinction between actual existence and existence in the sense of the true is crucial. The word 'crucial' was meant literally: the distinction is far from being universally convincing. Students of philosophy appear to be divided between those who are immediately convinced that here is a genuine and potentially important notion, and those who can see nothing in it. Gilson, a great exponent of Aquinas, used to claim that this notion was 'ineffable', and had to be grasped by a kind of 'intuition'. He has occasionally been mildly abused for this claim, particularly by those younger Thomists who have been trained in English-speaking universities, who have seen in it a bad case of what is sometimes wittily called 'Thomysticism'. Certainly the claim seems to be false, if taken as a theoretical point: or at least, there seems to be no good reason why this should be so. But when one considers the sheer inability of someone, like C. J. F. Williams, who lacks neither brilliance nor good-will towards Aquinas, to appreciate that there is any genuine notion involved here at all, one is inclined to think that on a practical level Gilson may have had a point. (Cp. his *What is existence?*, pp. 230–6.)

The existent in its own right and the coincidentally existent

The actually existent (*ens*) can be divided into two: the actually existent in its own right (*ens per se*) and the actually existent co-incidentally (*ens per accidens*) (passage 3, sections 1–10). The actually existent in its own right is that which is a genuine existent individual: it is one and the same thing in its own right (*unum per se*) as well. A human being would be an existent in its own right, as would any other individual substance. But the individual proper-ties of an individual — its accidents, as Aquinas would say — such as Socrates's paleness, the snubness of his nose, etc., are also in this sense existent in their own right. It is clear that they cannot exist without Socrates, of course: they are not subsistent or self-existent. But they are nevertheless genuine existent individuals: Aquinas in fact insists at some length on this fact, even, in a couple of passages collected below, going through the list of different kinds of accident to remind us of it (e.g. passage 3, section 8).

We can see what this means by attending to the clear difference between individual accidents, such as the paleness of Socrates, and coincidentally actual existents such as Socrates's house or Socrates's lunch. The individuality and existence of the latter are only the individuality and existence of the combination of actually existent things in their own right which make them up. Equally well, the events or states of affairs expressed by the sentences 'Socrates is having lunch', or 'Socrates is pale' are not genuine individual existents in their own right: their existence is only co-incidental.

That which exists coincidentally, then, is a complex existent which results from the comparison or relating of two (or more) things that exist in their own right. This is why St Thomas always picks out a coincidental existent by means of a complex expression, *oratio*, such as 'pale human being' or 'A human being is pale'. It is important, in this context of the discussion of existence, to notice that while St Thomas, like Aristotle, is often glad to use the presence of the copula 'is' in a sentence as a pedagogic device to draw attention to the existential import of the proposition (e.g. at passage 3, section 9), he does not seem to rest his claim for existen-tial import on this presence. He is happy to say, for example, that in sentences that express a coincidental existent the verb 'is' just means 'coincides in' (passage 3, section 3).

We should return for a moment to compare these actual existents, whether they are so coincidentallly or in their own right, with what can be said to exist in the sense of 'existence in the sense of the true'. Is the blindness of Homer an actual existent? We have claimed that it is not. Clearly it is not an actual existent in its own right, as Homer himself, or his musical talent was. Could it not be an actual existent coincidentally? Not even this is the case. 'Homer was blind' describes a real state of affairs, it is true: but the only actual existent about which this sentence tells us is Homer, an actual existent in his own right. It is true that it implies something about certain other actual existents, such as that there were such-and-such dispositions of Homer's eyes and brain: and the dispositions of Homer's eyes and brain were themselves existents in their own right, as was the snubness of Socrates's nose. But implying is not saying: and the only actual existent that we are told about in 'Homer was blind' is Homer himself.

It is important, then, to realise that not every true sentence is true in virtue of the existence of some actual existent. St Thomas would indeed claim that the sentence 'Homer is blind' can be brought back to — reduced, he would say — Homer, as he is the only actual existent it tells us about. If the sentence is true then there will be something about Homer — some actual existent in its own right in him, or some coincidentally actual existent in which he is a part — on whose actual existence the truth of this sentence is based. It is on this actual existence that the 'existence in the sense of the true' of Homer's blindness is based. But this bringing back or reduction is a long road: and though St Thomas claims that there always is a road, he perhaps would not claim that we can always go over it. In the example we are using, we cannot, as we have no information about the cause of Homer's blindness.

We would perhaps nowadays be less sanguine than St Thomas about the possibilities of this bringing back or reduction. What about numbers, for example? Numbers are clearly not actual existents, either in their own right or coincidentally: St Thomas, with Aristotle, rather brusquely dismisses as implausible the idea that they are (passage 4, sections 2–3). They do not, as actual existents do, initiate or undergo any acting or being acted upon. St Thomas, as a matter of fact, clearly thought that all true sentences could be brought back or reduced to some actual existents. But he does not make it clear what actual existents these are in the case of sentences about numbers. Perhaps he might think that a sentence about the number four could be brought back to the legs of a table, or perhaps to the human mind in which operations with numbers are performed; or even perhaps to the divine mind. Perhaps this last is the most likely — it would clearly be absurd to think of God creating the numbers, so they must be something prior to the existence of the world. But no plausible attempt at this bringing back was made by St Thomas: and all other *prima-facie* plausible reductions were shown to be ridiculous by Frege in the *Grundlagen*.

Potentiality and actuality

The last distinction Aquinas makes within the notion of existence is between that which exists potentially and that which exists actually: between potentiality and actuality, as he says (passage 3, section 13). We should perhaps rather say: between that which can exist and that which does exist. It is to be noticed that when he speaks of potentiality here he means something that does actually exist in one way, but can come to exist in another way. The stone which will make up the statue actually does exist at present as part of an unformed block: it is actually stone, but only potentially a statue. Equally, the finished statue is actually a statue, but potentially a heap of chippings. Potentiality always rests upon actuality, in two senses: a potentiality is always a potentiality for something, and it is always some other actuality. If the lump of stone can be a statue, then a statue is what it can be: there is no *mere* potentiality. It can never be the case that a thing just 'can be': it can be *something*. Also, if it can be something, then it already is something different now. Hence, following Aristotle, Aquinas points out that we often say that there is something even when it exists only potentially (passage 3, section 13). We say the statue is in the stone, that people know even when they are asleep and not exercising their knowledge, or that they are resting when they have no work to do, even if they are in fact pacing up and down their room smoking and fretting.

It is clear, then, that St Thomas has made a number of very subtle distinctions within the notion of existence. He is able to account for the logical notion which we have been familiar with since Frege's time, the notion of existence in the sense of the true, and also to go beyond this — and behind it — to his own metaphysical notion of the actually existent. It is with the actually existent that his philosophy is concerned. Admittedly, he thinks that there is a lot more that is actually existent than the empiricists would think: not only individuals, but also real essences and potentialities. But in spite of this his metaphysics is pleasingly down-to-earth.

Form and individual

A metaphysical distinction of great importance to Aquinas is that between the individual thing that is F and the form of F, that in virtue of which it is F. This can be approached in a number of ways: one way is by logic. We have seen, in the section on logic, a reference to this distinction in Aquinas's doctrine that predicates are taken formally: they do not refer to an individual but to a form, essence or nature. This doctrine is less obscure than it appears. Geach is justly famous for a paper 'Form and existence' (collected in *God and the soul* — see Notes on Reading) in which he drew a parallel between this doctrine and Frege's doctrine on the reference of predicable expressions or concept-words. Frege made an absolute category-distinction between names, which stood for individual objects, and concept-words, which stood for concepts. Concepts are not individuals: they are in some sense incomplete. Frege compared them, rightly, to functional expressions in mathematics: these stand for a function, but a function is not a number. Only a function *of* a number can be a number. Aquinas, as we have seen, made much the same point, though he did not have Frege's valuable parallel available to him. (See 'Function and concept' and 'On concept and object' in *Translations from the philosophical writings of Gottlob Frege*, edited by P. T. Geach and M. Black, Oxford: Basil Blackwell, 1952, pp. 21–55.)

But there is an important difference here. Frege starts with expressions and moves on to postulate what the realities they stand for must be if the expressions are to stand for them. He expresses no other views about the realities that the expressions are supposed to stand for. The claim is only: this is the way that language works. If someone has metaphysical problems with the idea of concepts, that is no concern of Frege's. As a result of this way of approach, he concludes that every predicate stands for a concept: '— is the square root of two' stands for a concept, and so does '— is red or round'.

Aquinas starts the other way in: from realities. He thinks that it is a fact that there is something in virtue of which Socrates is a human being: and there is something in virtue of which Socrates is pale. These are forms: but not Platonic Forms. They are in themselves — if such a phrase may even be permitted — as incomplete as Frege's concepts. Human nature does not exist anywhere in the world or out of it except in Socrates and his fellows: paleness does not exist anywhere except in certain surfaces. All the human nature there is is the human nature of this or that individual of the species. 'Human nature' does not exist, and neither does paleness: only the human nature of Socrates and Plato, the paleness of Callias and of the apple-blossom.

But forms or natures are nevertheless in some sense actual. They are fully actual when they exist in an individual: and even when considered in themselves they are such as to be actual when made individual, or 'concrete', as Aquinas often says. This is not the case with Frege's concepts: the very brilliance of Geach's parallel has sometimes confused other writers here. We saw that in Fregean terms there is a concept of being red-or-round. For Aquinas, on the other hand, while there is a form of being red, which is made individual in such things as Socrates's nose during a symposium, and a form of being round, which is made individual in such things as the drachma piece in Socrates's pocket, there is no such form as that of being red-or-round which can be made individual by anything: not even a tomato. Forms, when made individual, are themselves individual existents in their own right, though they may be of an accidental kind. The human nature of Socrates, at any given time, just is Socrates: and the redness of Socrates's nose is also a genuine existent in its own right, though of an accidental kind, with even a spatial location and a history. The predicable expression '— is red or round' does not stand for any such form: there could be no such form, as were it made individual — when the predicate is instantiated — it would not be an individual existent in its own right. Even '— is red and round' does not stand for a form: even though when it is instantiated it certainly stands for an existent, it is an existent that is only one and the same existent coincidentally, not in its own right.

Substance

Within actually existent individuals we can distinguish substances and accidents: thus we will have also to distinguish substantial forms from accidental forms. St Thomas draws attention to these differences in more than one way. One way he calls the 'logical' way: it can be found in the *Commentary on the Metaphysics* V, 10, and VII, 2 (passages 4 and 5 below). The other way is developed in, for example, the commentary on the *Physics*, and is called 'the way of change'.

It is important to notice that while manuals of Aristotelian and

Thomistic philosophy nearly always introduce the notion of substance by opposing it to that of accident, and using what Aquinas calls 'the way of change', neither he nor Aristotle seems to think that this is the only way, or even the best way. Both of them make just as much use of what Aquinas calls the 'logical way', introducing the metaphysical notion of substance by way of the logical notion of subject. Aquinas says, for example, that what needs to have a subject included in its definition is not a subject in a principal sense, and so cannot be a substance (passage 5, section 14). Another related way which Aquinas uses to reach the same notion is to ask what counts as a proper answer to the question 'What is it?'

It is relevant to consider here the fact that Aristotle, and Aquinas, think it necessary to notice the Pythagorean–Platonic view that such geometrical entities as points and lines are substances (passage 4). This view strikes us as plain silly: but this is because we have had 2,100 years more Aristotelianism than Aristotle himself, and 700 years more of it even than St Thomas. The notion may not seem so silly when we consider that the notion of substance is supposed to provide the ultimate answer to the question 'What exists?'

There is clearly a connection between being individual and identifiable; being comprehensible; and existing. This connection impressed the ancients and the mediaevals more than it does us, but one can find evidence of its importance even today by reading almost any modern book of philosophical logic on the notion of existence.

Mathematical beings are supremely individual, identifiable, and comprehensible: much more so than the rather confused and blurred concepts that we have of the things around us. We know very well when we are dealing with one number and when we are dealing with two: it is only when we get to notions such as 'plant', 'animal', 'human being' and 'personality' that we get confused. What is easier, then, than to say that the basic structure of the world is a mathematical or geometrical one? That is all we are sure of, after all: we know that numbers exist, they cannot do otherwise. Everything else is quite a lot vaguer.

Aristotle and Aquinas rejected this view so strongly that they have made it sound odd for us to say that numbers or points are substances: 'substance' has for us Aristotelian overtones. We should notice, however, that it is only the concept of actual existence, however tacit it may be in our minds, that gives us any right to avail ourselves of their straightforward rejection of the Pythagorean – Platonic view. It is noticeable that Quine began in *From a logical point of view* by denying the possibility of any notion of existence other than that which St Thomas calls 'existence in the sense of the true' — thus denying the notion of actual existence — and ended up unable to see why the world should not be a structure of numbers.

Since Aquinas seems to be willing to look at substances from a number of points of view, we perhaps should not make too close a connection between the notions of accident and substance, and the conception of change. Quite often too close a connection has been made, ending in an erroneous view of substance as being something unchangeable, and indeed unknowable. It is but a step from there to the conclusion that it does not exist at all: a step that separates Locke from Hume, for example. Nevertheless, change does need examining in its own right, and its proper analysis does help with the concepts of substance and accident. So with these warnings in mind, we can begin with 'the way of change'.

The analysis of change

The Aristotelian analysis of change, which St Thomas takes over, is of course an analysis of real change, not merely Cambridge change. It arises from the typical puzzles of the pre-Socratic philosophers. When can we say that something has changed, rather than that something has ceased to exist and another thing come to exist? Why do we say that Socrates's nose has changed from pale to red during the symposium, rather than saying that the pale nose of Socrates has ceased to exist and a red nose come into existence in the same place? When the princess kisses the frog and he turns into a handsome prince, what would warrant us in saying that the frog has indeed changed into a handsome prince, rather than that he has ceased to exist and a handsome prince appeared in his stead?

Aristotle's answer is that for there to be a change there must be a subject of change and two termini of change. We know that Socrates's nose has changed as regards its colour, rather than that one pale nose has ceased to exist and another red one come in its place, because we know that it is one and the same nose. Socrates's nose is the subject of this change, its paleness and redness the two termini. We should demand evidence, which might not be forthcoming, that the frog was the same person as the prince in order to determine whether there really was a change rather than a sudden death of a frog and the sudden birth of a handsome prince.

We say, then, that Socrates's nose is the subject of the change: before the change it actually was pale and was capable of being red — was pale in actuality, and red in potentiality, as Aquinas's terminology has it — and after the change it actually is red, or is red in actuality. Every change is a change of a subject from being F in potentiality to being F in actuality.

Change and initiators of change

It is an important Aristotelian doctrine, which St Thomas makes great use of, that a change can only come about in virtue of the influence of something that actually exists (cp. especially passage 7, and 'An introduction to Aquinas on God'). There are a number of different aspects to this doctrine. One is the modest claim that nothing that comes into existence as the result of a change can be the cause of that change: that nothing causes its own existence. When Socrates's nose changes from pale to red, it is not the redness of Socrates's nose that causes this change. This is surely unexceptionable.

If the redness of Socrates's nose cannot cause the change by which the nose becomes red, then, what can? A possible answer, which Aquinas need not reject out of hand at this stage, would be that it is the paleness of Socrates's nose which causes it to turn red. It would not be possible, though for the blueness of Socrates's nose, while his nose is pale, to cause its redness: if the nose is pale, then there is no blueness there to be causing anything. Hence we have the doctrine that nothing can change from potentiality to actuality except by the influence of something which is in actuality.

This doctrine has been misunderstood. Some have thought that it means that that which is potentially F can become F actually only through the influence of something that is actually F — as if Socrates's nose could be turned red by Burgundy but not champagne — but Aquinas did not hold this obviously false doctrine.

Omne quod movetur ab alio movetur

Nevertheless, the apparently true and unexceptionable doctrine is closely associated in Aquinas's mind with a more far-reaching claim — so far-reaching, in fact, that he uses it in a number of his arguments for the existence of God. This claim is that which is quoted in the heading above: that everything that is in process of change has that change initiated in it by something else. This claim looks like a straight denial that there are self-movers or initiators of

their own change: a denial that, for example, animals initiate
changes in themselves. It is not so simple — or so obviously false
— as that. The claim is based on the doctrine outlined above.
When a dog starts barking it is clearly not the barking of the dog
that causes the barking. It might be some outside initiator of
change: some experimenter might have found out how to connect
up electrodes to the dog's brain in such a way as to start it barking.
More likely, though, it is, as we would say, the dog itself that just
starts barking.

Aquinas would claim, as we have seen, that a dog can only start
barking in virture of some non-barking aspect that it has. But this
non-barking aspect cannot be just 'its aspect of non-barking': if
the barking cannot cause itself, then neither can the non-barking,
as such. It has to be some other actually existing aspect of the dog
that causes the barking. So though the dog does initiate its own
change in a sense, strictly speaking it is one aspect or part of the
dog which initiates a change in another aspect or part. Thus the
dog does not initiate its own change in what Aquinas would call the
chief or principal sense of this expression: and he claims that this
holds good for all material things. Things which initiate their own
change in the chief or principal sense are things in which the whole
initiates the change of the whole: in material things it is always one
part that initiates a change in another part. There are, then, no
initiators of their own change in the chief or principal sense in the
material world: and so everything that is in process of change has
its change initiated by something else (cp. especially passage 7,
and 'An introduction to Aquinas on God').

Subject and substance

But let us return to our example of the change in Socrates's nose:
we have not yet clearly applied the analysis of change. What
exactly is the subject of the change? We have spoken as if the
subject were Socrates's nose. Clearly this is one way of describing
the change, while to try to speak as if the subject of the change
were the redness or the paleness themselves is not to describe a
change at all. But is Socrates's nose the ultimate subject of the
change? If we ask, 'What is it that has changed?' is 'Socrates's
nose' the only or the best answer?

Clearly not. If Socrates's nose has changed then Socrates has
changed as regards his nose. If we ask 'What is it that has
changed?' then the answer 'Socrates's nose' already includes
another subject, Socrates. Socrates's nose is an individual, is

existent, is a 'this something', only in so far as it is Socrates's: if it were to cease to be Socrates's, through an unfortunate accident with a bacon-slicer, then it would cease to be a nose at all. If, on the other hand, we follow Aristotle and St Thomas and say that Socrates has changed as regards the colour of his nose, then we have got back to an answer that does not include another more basic subject. Hence, they would say, the answer to the question 'What is it?' in its most basic sense is a substance, a substantial individual like Socrates, or the cat, or the tree outside the window, or this lump of gold: not an accident or accidental individual like Socrates's paleness, or even a part of a substantial individual like Socrates's nose.

Of course we often do refer to accidental individuals as subjects, and do say that they have changed: this wave of the sea, for example, is moving towards the shore, or that humming noise from the word-processor is getting louder. We also refer to coincidental individuals, made up of the coincidence of many substances and their accidents: the battle gets fiercer, the depression is moving in a south-easterly direction from Iceland, the house is getting dilapidated, or the lecture gets boring. But the claim is that in each of these cases we could bring back our reference to the substances in which these accidents exist or inhere, or the substances that make up the coincidental existent. It is not the wave which is moving, but the sea which is taking up a wave-shape over successive parts of its surface: it is not the humming which is getting louder, or even the word-processor which is humming more loudly, but the individual substances which go to make up the word-processor which are co-operating in such-and-such a way and thus humming more loudly. It is not the battle that gets fiercer, but the soldiers: not the depression which is approaching, but the air which is decreasing in pressure nearer to us: not the house which gets dilapidated, but lumps of slate that fall off: not the lecture that gets boring but the lecturer.

Substance and accident

In this way, or in these ways, the distinction between substance and accident is established. It will be noticed that while we began with a discussion based on change, we continued it with the consideration of what is the ultimate subject: a consideration that belongs to 'the way of logic'. People often talk as if the accidents were that which can change, and the substance that which does not change: this is very alien to the manner of speaking of Aristotle and Aquinas. For them, it is precisely the substance that changes, that is the subject of change: the accidents do not change at all, strictly speaking. They merely (in some sense) cease to exist and come into existence. The other way of talking has its dangers — apart from the fact that it is in any case nonsense. That other way of speaking has often led people in the past to speak as if it were, e.g. the colour of Socrates's nose that is really red, and could change to being pale: thus Socrates, whose nose can adopt or take on such a variety of colours, would have no colour in himself. Obviously there is, as a matter of fact, no colour that Socrates's nose has to be, and this obvious truth, which could be expressed loosely by saying 'Socrates's nose has no colour in itself', perhaps tends to incline people towards the erroneous way of talking. But it is certainly not the case that Socrates's nose does not have to have some colour, and still less that in itself it does not have any colour. No: in itself it has the colour it has while it has it. It is true that it does not, indeed, have that colour in so far as it is a human nose, or even in so far as it is Socrates's nose. But what about the colour of Socrates's eyes? Is Socrates not coloured as regards his eyes at least in so far as he is this human individual, the son of these parents? As soon as Socrates came to exist he had eyes of that colour, and they could not have been other. This fact does not make the colour of his eyes any less of an accident.

The erroneous way of talking leads people in the end to suppose that the substance is a 'bare particular', that has no accidents, that has no colour or shape, that is a 'something I know not what' that is completely unknowable. This degenerate scholastic doctrine — associated chiefly with the name of Locke because he was the first one brave enough to put it into English — has, sad to say, sometimes been attributed to Aquinas and Aristotle: but it is definitely not their doctrine.

It is true that Aquinas sometimes talks in a way that suggests the false doctrine. For example, in passage 5, section 13, he suggests that we can have a substance without accidents. This must be taken either as elliptical for: 'this substance can exist without these accidents, but these accidents cannot exist without this substance', or simply as a mistake. It is not clear, anyway, how this remark supports the contention which it is meant to support: that a substance is temporarily prior to its accidents. The meaning of this contention is in any case obscure: if it means that a substance can come into existence without any accidents, it is false, while if it means that any accidents that a substance may have at any moment of its existence were probably preceded by some other accidents it appears to be true but of no interest.

Aquinas's serious doctrine, odd and inconsistent passages aside, is that it is the substance that changes, the substance that has the accidents: the accidents only exist in so far as they are accidents of this substance. This substance cannot exist without some accidents: but these accidents cannot exist without this subject. It is important to notice — as one can see in passage 5, section 9 — that accidents in the abstract are not existents at all, let alone existents in their own right. This is a blunt rejection of Platonism. An equally blunt rejection of the later scholastic notion of accidents as separate individuals that are somehow attached to a substance is the remark that what is signified by a name of an individual accident — e.g. 'the paleness of–' — would not be an existent at all if it did not inhere in another thing or exist in a substance (passage 5, section 10).

The erroneous way of talking is related to a mistake about the nature of forms, which Aquinas here rejects. Those who talk in this way talk as if the paleness of Socrates's nose were an individual in its own right, which could be stripped off him, leaving him essentially the same as before. This is not the case. The paleness of Socrates's nose is simply that in virtue of which Socrates is pale as regards his nose: how could it be stripped off him? Admittedly, it can cease to exist in some sense, in that Socrates's nose can turn red: but does this imply the erroneous way of looking at things? Socrates cannot lose the accident of pale-nosedness without acquiring some other accident in its place: Socrates cannot cease to be pale as regards his nose without becoming coloured in some other way as regards his nose. Noses, unlike angels, cannot exist without being coloured in some way. And if they are coloured in some way, they will be coloured in that way in virtue of some accidental form.

Linked with the Lockean view of substance is the idea that accidents — qualities, Locke would say — are in some way prior to substances in the order of knowledge. Again, Aquinas rejects this idea. Clearly, since some accidents can be sensed, and all our knowledge comes originally from the senses, there is a sense in which Locke's idea is true. But Aquinas holds that when it is a question of an intellectual apprehension, accidents are secondary to substances. We can have sensations of colour without a grasp of the substance, if any, in which the colours may inhere. But this, for Aquinas, would not be a grasp of the accidents as accidents.

What makes the colour of a cat different from the colour of the night sky is that the colour of the cat is an accident of the cat, and can be grasped intellectually as an accident of that substance. It cannot be grasped as a genuine accident, a genuine existent in its own right outside of ourselves, rather than as something in our eyes and brain, except in so far as it is grasped as the accident of a substance.

Matter and substantial form

The same problems and misunderstandings appear when we consider substantial changes. All the changes we referred to above were accidental changes: changes in which a substance is the subject, in which a substance changes as regards some accident it has. What happens when it is not an accidental determination of a subject that ceases to exist, but the substance itself that ceases to exist? All the substances we mentioned above can cease to exist: people, cats and trees all die, and even lumps of gold can be destroyed. This is clearly a change, but a change of a different kind: the substance is no longer the subject, but one of the termini of the change.

What then is the subject here? Clearly when a human being dies, something has changed: there has not been an instantaneous annihilation of a human being and creation of a corpse, any more than when Socrates's nose flushed a ruddier hue there was an instantaneous annihilation of one nose and the creation of another. What is the subject?

The answer of Aristotle and Aquinas is that this lump of stuff has changed: before, it was one substance, a human being: now it is a heterogeneous and rapidly decomposing heap of different substances. Or take the other end of life: these two small lumps of stuff have joined and ceased to be two gametes, but have become one individual substance of the human species.

This 'stuff' is what Aquinas calls 'matter' or 'first matter', and it is again a very basic and very simple notion (passage 6). Nevertheless there have been people who have failed to understand it. Obviously, this lump of stuff — 'this stuff', Aquinas would say — is not anything apart from a human being at one time, and a whole heap of other substances at another: there is not anything — flesh, for example — which it is all the time. In the same way, there is no colour that Socrates's nose is all the time: at one time it is pale, at another red. This does not mean, as we saw, that Socrates's nose is a permanently colourless bare particular: nor is this lump of stuff, this amount of first matter, a permanently bare particular stuff that is never any stuff in particular. On the contrary, any lump of matter you care to point to at any time will at that time be some kind of substance: but there is no kind of substance that it has to be all the time. If the corpse is eaten by vultures, then the same stuff — or part of it — will be later on part of a vulture.

What makes this lump of matter to be a human being rather than a heap of other substances is the human form, the form of a human being: that in virtue of which this lump of stuff is a human being rather than a whole heap of other substances. If it were a whole heap of other substances, of course, then it would be so in virtue of a number of other substantial forms. The matter, then, which at some time makes up a substance, just is that substance in so far as it can become another substance: while the form is that substance in so far as it is a substance of that kind rather than another.

This is what is meant by saying that first matter is 'pure potentiality'. At any time it will be some substance, in virtue of some substantial form or forms. The substantial form is that in virtue of which this lump of matter is a substance of this kind, rather than a substance of some other kind, in virtue of some other substantial form.

In the case of human beings and animals there is in Greek and Latin a word for the substantial form, for that in virtue of which this lump of matter is a cat, say, and not a bundle of different kinds of stuff held together by fur. The word is *psukhe* or *anima*, soul: that which makes the difference between a hedgehog racing across the road and a flat parcel of different kinds of spiky stuff under the wheels of an articulated lorry. This is all that the word translated as 'soul' means in Aristotle and Aquinas. It is important to insist on this point, as for most people nowadays the word brings with it connotations of surviving after death. Hence people nowadays who do not believe in any survival after death tend to say that they do not believe in the existence of the soul. Aquinas certainly believed in some kind of survival after death — he argues for it in passage 10. Aristotle, however, did not: and they would both have had difficulty in understanding a claim not to believe in the existence of the soul. They would have understood it to mean that there was no difference between being alive and being dead: a claim so incredible as to be incomprehensible. The claim which our contemporaries wish to make would have been expressed by Aristotle and Aquinas rather by saying that the soul does not survive, that it is not a 'this something', or even that the soul is no more than the good relation of the parts of the body. They would find such claims perfectly comprehensible, even if they would disagree about what parts of them were true.

Every substance, of course, has a substantial form, even if we do not use the word 'soul' of it. There is something in virtue of which this lump of stuff is a lump of gold: that is its substantial form. 'Soul', we should insist, means no more than this: that in virtue of which this lump of stuff beside a word-processor is a human being.

Aquinas uses another way to explain these notions in one of the passages collected here. He claims that the notions of matter and form are best understood by means of the analogy of artificial things: the artificial thing itself bears an analogy to the substance which is made up of matter and form, the specific kind of stuff that it is made out of bears an analogy to the first matter, and the shape or arrangement of the parts which make this stuff into this artefact bears an analogy to the form (passage 6, section 8).

Once the distinction is made, he claims that in some sense form is more substance — or perhaps one should say 'is more what the substance is' than is the matter (passage 6, sections 9–10). This is important to maintain. There were those, like the pre-Socratics, who thought that matter was some previously existing and otherwise specifiable kind of stuff (passage 6, sections 12–16). Such people naturally tended to think that this specific matter was what things really were: hence, 'more substance' than the form, which was more of an accidental determination of this basic substance. The Aristotelian conception of matter, according to which matter is not anything specific that is different from the made-up substance which it is made to be by a form at any given time, cannot admit this notion. Matter is not a kind of thing: it is merely that in any thing which can become another thing. The matter which makes up a human being, so long as it is a human being, just is a human being and nothing else. It can become all kinds of other substances, but it is not them at present, nor is it anything except a human being.

We should, incidentally, conclude from this that if molecules of iron on their own are substances — as Aquinas would probably claim — then the molecules of iron which chemical analysis can reveal in our red blood cells are not in fact molecules of iron at all: they are just bits of us that have all the properties of molecules of iron. Aquinas, following Aristotle, points out that the error of the ancients here was caused by their not having the notion of substantial form. We might say, equally, since form and matter are correlatives, that it was caused by their not having the notion of first matter, as opposed to a specific matter of a particular kind. They thus made all changes out to be accidental changes. This kind of view is too common nowadays for us to take kindly to the rival view of Aristotle and Aquinas: but we should notice that only the Aristotelian view can avoid the opinion that human beings, say, are just a collection of sub-atomic particles in a certain arrangement.

St Thomas also brings in a logical consideration to help make these points, based on a discussion of different manners of predication. Being a substance is predicated of a lump of matter in the same way that, e.g. 'being pale' is predicated of Socrates. Aquinas calls this 'denominative' predication, as opposed to 'essential' predication. An example of 'denominative' predication is 'Socrates is pale' and of 'essential' predication, 'The human being is rational' or 'White is a colour'. Just as you can say 'Socrates is pale' but not 'Socrates is paleness' or 'Humanity is paleness', you can say 'This lump of matter is a human being' but not 'This lump of matter is humanity' or 'Matter is humanity'. This is taken to be evidence in favour of the genuineness of the distinction between form and matter (passage 6, sections 18–21).

Another difficult part of Aquinas's teaching on matter and form is the claim that while the notion of the individual substance made up of form and matter is in a way obvious to us, as is that of matter itself, the notion of form is obscure (passage 6, section 27). Aquinas himself finds this difficult in that it is in virtue of its form that a material substance is what it is and can thus be thought of. We shall see a discussion of this in 'An introduction to Aquinas on truth, knowledge and the mind'. How then is the notion of form an obscure one, one which the pre-Socratics were unable to grasp?

Aquinas explains this at length at the end of passage 6 by pointing out that what is most easily grasped by the mind in itself may be most remote from our normal order of acquiring knowledge. Material substances made up of form and matter are obvious to our senses: we can see them. Matter can be grasped very simply by means of the analogy with the stuff from which artefacts are made. But form, though it is that in virtue of which the material substance is in fact thought of, and in virtue of which we understand the analogy with artefacts, is something that is remote from

our senses or from any analogy with things sensed. It would perhaps make things clearer if Aquinas had said that though forms are
eminently intelligible, the *notion* of form is a rather obscure and
recondite one.

The principle of individuation

Each of us, then, is a human being in virtue of the human form or
soul. But what makes us different human beings? The answer of
Aristotle and Aquinas is again so straightforward as to appear
almost simple-minded: we are different individuals of the same
kind or species in virtue of the fact that we are different lumps of
stuff with the same human form. Of course, once we are different
individuals in virtue of being different lumps of stuff, then the
form in virtue of which we are human is an individual, too. That
in virtue of which Socrates is a human being is as distinct from that
in virtue of which Plato is a human being as Socrates is from Plato.
But the individualised form in Socrates is a distinct individual in
virtue of being the form of this distinct lump of matter, not in
virtue of being a form of this kind. In so far as it is a form of this
kind, it is formally identical with all other forms of that kind: in so
far as we are human, we are no different one from the other. It is
in so far as we are different lumps of matter that we are different.
In a similar way, the redness of Socrates's nose may be formally,
qualitatively identical with the redness of Agathon's nose: but it is
a different individual redness through its existence in Socrates
rather than Agathon. A frequent parallel drawn by Aquinas is that
of two different statues from the same mould: the shape is the
same, but the statues are different. In the same way, the human
form in Socrates is the same form as the human form in Callias,
but they are different human beings.

Essence

The form should not be confused with the essence. The essence is
what the definition defines: so since the definition of a human
being includes his or her being a material thing, the essence will
include matter. The substantial form, which is introduced precisely in terms of that which makes a lump of matter to be a thing
of a certain kind, does not. We should notice, though, that the

essence of a human being includes matter, not *this* matter. For a start, the essence can be universal as well as individual: we can speak of the essence of the human race, as well as of the same essence as made individual in Socrates. So the universal essence has to include matter in such a way that the definition does not fit Socrates alone, as it would do if it included *this* matter, which at present is Socrates. But there is more to it than that: the matter of Socrates is constantly changing, as Aquinas was well aware. So even the individual essence of Socrates could not be defined in such a way as to include this matter, as otherwise in seven years' time Socrates would not have the same essence, and would thus be a different human being. At any moment Socrates is made up of *this* matter in virtue of this form: but his essence is to be made up of *matter*, without qualification, in virtue of this form (passage 9, article 5).

Another word for essence is nature: this has a slightly different nuance, and signifies an essence in so far as it is the originating principle of actions. Had this word not existed, perhaps no one would have felt any need to invent it: but there it is, and this is how it is used by Aquinas.

The topic of essence has received a new lease of life in recent years in some sectors of English-speaking philosophy. This is to be welcomed: but there are different shades of meaning to be found in the contemporary uses, which might mislead us with regard to Aquinas's use. Nowadays the term 'essence' tends to be used solely in the sense of 'individual essence': a certain determination belongs to Socrates's essence if Socrates has it in all possible worlds in which he exists, or some such phrase. The notion of individual essence is certainly used by Aquinas, but it is less important to him than the notion of the essence of a species. This affects his idea of individual essence, too: what belongs to Socrates's individual essence is only that which belongs to Socrates in so far as he is human. It certainly belongs to Socrates in all possible worlds to be the son of such-and-such parents, and Aquinas would uphold this truth: but he would not say, on account of that, that Socrates is essentially the son of such-and-such parents. Moreover, essence for Aquinas is something metaphysical, something real, something actually existent that brings about real changes in the world. He would never say, as contemporary authors would, that it belongs to the essence of Socrates not to be a square root. It is true that Socrates is essentially a human, and being human entails not being a square root. Nevertheless, there is no actual not-being-a-square-rootedness about Socrates, while what really does belong to his essence — his rationality, say — is an actuality in him: in this case, a certain essential power.

Powers, properties and tendencies

This brings us to another important point about St Thomas's notion of essence. For St Thomas, things have real powers, properties and tendencies in virtue of what they are. This goes directly against the empiricist tradition. St Thomas would not object to the empirical claim that we can only know about a thing's real powers and tendencies — what it can do, what it tends to do — by observing what it does do: he does not believe in the existence of a sort of metaphysical eye by which we perceive occult powers. But he would object to the empiricist claim that when we observe what a thing does do, that is all we are doing: that we are not also observing what it can do, and what it has a tendency to do. Hume's view on causality, as being merely a tendency in our mind which is habituated to expect a certain succession of events from the experience of constant conjunction, would strike him as a false ingenuousness.

St Thomas does not believe, as Hume appears to have believed, that our notion of causality is associated with a belief in a certain kind of necessity. In fact, we have seen him explicitly denying that all causes necessitate their effects, in passage 2. Thus he would not be worried by Hume's arguments that there is no basis in our experience for this belief. St Thomas does believe that certain causes do necessitate their effects, but, as we have seen, he thinks that the effects of nearly all causes can be obstructed. This view has the merit of matching our experience. Hume would tell us, for example, that our repeated experience of a heavy body being free from all support is always in constant conjunction with our experience of it falling to the ground. One's limited experience of watching conjurers should be enough to disprove this claim. To be sure, we know there is a trick when the lady remains suspended in mid-air: but we cannot know there is a trick on the basis of our experience of the constant conjunction of ladies in spangles having the chairs that supported them on stage being removed, and their falling to the ground. Our experience in this line, limited as it is, goes quite the other way — unless we have been very unlucky in our choice of conjurers to watch. We know there is a trick because we know that ladies, whether in spangles or not, have a tendency to fall to the ground when chairs supporting them are drawn away. We know that this tendency will be fulfilled unless obstructed, so we know that there is a carefully concealed obstructing agent, or trick, as we say.

It is important to notice that the whole of science rests on a Thomistic kind of assumption. It is one of the most surprisingly successful bluffs in the history of philosophy that has caused empiricism to be taken to be specially apt for the explanation of science. Scientists do not bring things into conjunction and watch the outcome which always follows from it. If they did, not only would science be rather less developed than it is; but science as we know it would not exist. What scientists do is bring bodies *of certain kinds* into conjunction, and watch the result for confirmation of their hypotheses about the natural properties and tendencies of bodies of those kinds. The first rule of experimental science, it is said, is that if the experiment doesn't give the expected outcome, there is something wrong with the experiment. This is often said jokingly, but it enshrines a great truth. We know the properties and tendencies of the things being experimented on, and if the experiment does not bear out our beliefs the probability is that there is an unnoticed obstructing agent.

Aquinas, then, would not laugh outright at the seventeenth-century doctors of medicine who said that opium put people to sleep because it had a dormitative power. He would instead say — as we should say — that what is wrong here is that the sketch of an answer is being given as a complete answer. The doctor should be able to find out what that dormitative power consists in, what properties of opium it depends on. If modern doctors are rather more knowledgeable than seventeenth-century ones it is because they have found out how to fill out the sketch-answer. What would be truly laughable would be someone who should say that opium puts people to sleep because in our experience an administration of opium is always followed by a falling asleep. This is not only less informative than the 'dormitative power' answer, it is almost certainly false as well. The administration of a dose of opium, when immediately preceded by the administration of a dose of a powerful emetic, is probably never followed by a falling asleep.

Properties and natures

A thing of a certain kind or essence has the properties, powers and tendencies which belong to that essence. From those properties, powers and tendencies follow its specific or essential activities, operations or performances. Aquinas would again insist in his down-to-earth manner that the only way in which we can get to know the essential powers, properties and tendencies of a thing is by observing its specific performances. Indeed, he would say that the only way in which we can describe or think of these powers, properties and tendencies is as powers or tendencies to perform a certain kind of operation, or as properties from which certain activities spring. This does not mean we are limited to sketch-descriptions of the 'dormitative power' kind: we can discover that opium contains such-and-such a chemical compound, which causes people to fall asleep by acting in such-and-such a way on such-and-such zones of the brain, and so on. We can specify the description we give of opium, in terms of its chemical constitution: and so we can specify the description of the dormitative power by describing it in terms of a more specific power in a more specific component of opium. But even if we specify down to the level of the mechanics of chemical bonding, we will still be describing more and more specific tendencies in terms of more and more specific activities to which they are the tendencies.

Tendency and teleology

The way of describing tendencies, then, is teleological: in terms of what they are tendencies to. It cannot be stressed enough that this is the only way of describing tendencies, and that the only possible alternative is to give up talk of tendencies — and hence science — altogether. People nowadays are suspicious of teleological explanations. This is probably rather similar to the fear of the notion 'soul' which so many share. It would seem to have a purely accidental, historical origin. In the late eighteenth and early nineteenth centuries there was a vogue for natural theology and apologetics which were based on the existence of teleology in the world. As a result, people are afraid that if they admit teleology they will have to admit the existence of God as well, something which many contemporaries are unwilling to do. It seems that this is merely a psychological prejudice. St Thomas thinks that you need to have an argument to pass from the existence of finality in the world to the existence of God: in the fifth of his five ways in question two, article three, of the first part of the *Summa theologiae* he sketches that argument for us. But it is only a sketch, and contains a rather questionable premiss which he does not there defend or explain. (In passage 7, the passage on the existence of God collected here, he does not even sketch the argument, but rather waves towards it, at section 35.) He has other arguments in the same places to prove the existence of God from the existence of a series of efficient causes: so if we have a prejudice against believing in God it should logically extend to disbelieving in efficient causality as well. (Perhaps that was at the back of Hume's mind.)

Be that as it may, we should fight against the prejudice. Admitting final causality may psychologically cause some people to make a leap at once to admitting the existence of God, but Aquinas would hold, surely correctly, that there is no rational immediate connection. We ought rather to investigate the notion of finality more carefully: we need it for our science, and it is genuinely to be found in the world. If an acceptance of these facts made people embrace the existence of God without rational argument, then that would perhaps be far from ideal. But closing one's eyes to the truth is still farther from being ideal.

Specific or essential tendencies arise from the essences — or natures, as Aquinas would say in this context — of different kinds of things. So since different kinds of things are of different kinds in virtue of their form rather than their matter, things act in virtue of their form. Aquinas would go further, and say that things exist in virtue of their form, and thus also act in virtue of their act of existence. Existence is shown by operation or performance, as are essence and form. This point is of importance to him in arguing for the imperishability of the soul, in passage 10.

Kinds of potentiality

We must thus recognise various kinds of potentiality in things. There are passive potentialities — the potentiality of Socrates to be hit on the head by a brick, or to be killed by poisoning — which are, as we would say, merely potential. They are based on actual properties in the subject, of course, but they are not themselves anything actual in the subject. Active potentialities, on the other hand, do have actual existence in the subject: Aquinas even goes as far as to call them 'first actuality', as opposed to 'second actuality', which would be the operation, performance or activity of those potentialities (cp. passage 12, *lectio* 10, section 2). There are many different degrees of potentialities, according to the manner of existing of the things that have them. Socrates has an active potentiality to run away from his execution, but one could not say that it amounts to a tendency. He has, on the other hand, an active potentiality that amounts to a real tendency to await his execution: and an active potentiality that can scarcely be frustrated to carry on doing philosophy right up to the moment of his death. Lastly, he has an active tendency to being a rational animal that cannot be frustrated at all short of killing him, a tendency that amounts to a genuine natural necessity. Meanwhile, the potentiality of the stone bench Socrates is sitting on to remain put is presumably a passive potentiality, which is being actualised by the force of gravity. But it has this passive potentiality in virtue of the active potentialities of its mass.

Kinds of necessity

These different kinds of potentiality are unfamiliar to us in contemporary philosophy, but they are of great importance to Aquinas. And since, as he often points out, that which can be is that which does not necessarily not be, there are different kinds of necessity that answer to these potentialities. Moreover, there are many other different kinds of necessity and potentiality too. For Aquinas, that which has no tendency to stop existing — as, he thought, the heavenly spheres and animal species had not — can be called a necessary existent. We know better, perhaps: but the concept is a valuable one. Again, for Aquinas, as for Aristotle, as we have seen, there is a sense in which that which is the case and that which has been the case is necessary: it cannot now be the case that it is not the case, since it already is or already has been the case. But what is yet to come is not in this sense — or in any sense — necessary: it is possible, unless, as may happen, it is already determined in its causes.

Passage 3: Existence

Aquinas seems to have taken some time over the *Commentary on the*

Metaphysics. He probably began it in Paris and continued it in Naples. But he seems not to have begun at the beginning and worked steadily through to the end. All the passages from it which are collected here seem to have been among the earlier parts of the work commented on. Even so we cannot date them any more accurately than between 1269 and 1272. Book V (or Delta) of the *Metaphysics* is Aristotle's philosophical lexicon, in which he gives useful explanations of the key terms he is using. Hence there are no exact parallel passages in the *Summa theologiae*.

Commentary on the Metaphysics, Book V, *lectio* 9 (Aristotle's text: 1017a7 – 1017b9; commentary: Marietti, sections 885 – 97)

1. Here the Philosopher distinguishes the different senses of 'the existent' [*ens*]. First he distinguishes, within the existent, between the *existent in its own right* [*ens per se*] and the *coincidentally existent* [*ens per accidens*]. Then he distinguishes the [different] ways of being coincidentally existent [section 2], and thirdly, the [different] ways of being existent in one's own right [section 5].

He says, then, that one sense of 'the existent' is the existent in its own right, and another is the coincidentally existent. But you should be aware that [despite the similarity between *per accidens*, coincidentally, and *accidens*, accident,] this division within the existent is not the same as the division which is made between substance and accident. This is obvious from the fact that he himself later divides the existent in its own right into the ten categories, of which nine are accidental. The existent is divided into substance and accident by considering it without reference to anything else. In this way whiteness, considered by itself, is said to be an accident, and a human being is said to be a substance. But the coincidentally existent in the sense we are talking about here has to be grasped by making a relation between accident and substance. This making of a relation is signified by the word 'is', when we say e.g. 'A human being is pale'. Hence this whole, that a human being is pale, is an existent coincidentally. So it is clear that the division of the existent into the existent in its own right and the coincidentally existent comes to our notice in virtue of something's being predicated of another, either in its own right or coincidentally. The division of the existent into substance and accident, on the other hand, comes to our notice in virtue of something's being by its own nature a substance or an accident.

2. Then he shows us in how many ways the coincidentally existent is expressed. There are three ways, he says: the first is when an accident is predicated of an accident, as in the sentence, 'Someone honest is musical'. The second is when an accident is predicated of a

subject, as in the sentence, 'A human being is musical'. The third is
when a subject is predicated of an accident, as in the sentence,
'Someone musical is a human being'. Since he has already distinguished [earlier in this book of the *Metaphysics*] between something's
being a cause coincidentally and its being a cause in its own right, he
uses here the notion of being a cause coincidentally to make clear the
notion of being an existent coincidentally.

3.   He says that we assign a cause coincidentally when we say that
[e.g.] someone musical is building. This is because being someone
musical coincides in a builder, or vice-versa. (It is clear that 'so-and-
so is such-and-such', [e.g.] that a musical person is building, just
means that such-and-such coincides in so-and-so.) It is just the same,
too, with the different ways of being coincidentally existent, which
we mentioned above. We say, then, that a human being is musical,
predicating an accident of a subject; or that someone musical is a
human being, predicating a subject of an accident; or that someone
pale is musical, or vice-versa, that someone musical is pale, predicating an accident of an accident. In all these sentences the word
'is' just means 'coincides in'.
     This last, — when an accident is predicated of an accident —
means that both accidents coincide in the same subject. The former
— when an accident is predicated of a subject — is said to exist
because the accident coincides in an existent, that is in the subject.
But we say that someone musical is human because the predicate is
the person in whom being musical coincides, though being musical is
put in subject-position.
     It is much the same kind of predication when a subject is pre-
dicated of an accident, and when an accident is predicated of another
accident. For a subject is predicated of an accident in the following
way: the subject is said to be that in which the accident mentioned in
the subject-position coincides. In the same way an accident is predicated of an accident, because it is predicated of the subject of the
accident. Hence, when we say that something musical is a human
being, it is like saying that something musical is pale, since that in
which being musical coincides — i.e. the subject — is pale.

4.   It is clear, then, that the things that are said to be existent coincidentally are said to be so for three reasons. It may be that both the
subject and the predicate belong to the same thing, as when an
accident is predicated of an accident. Or it may be that the predicate
— such as 'musical' — is in an existent, i.e. the subject which is said
to be musical. This is the case when an accident is predicated of a
subject. Or it may be that the subject, which is put in predicate
position, is that in which the accident exists: that of which that
accident, used as a subject-term, is true. This is the case when [what
is really] a subject is [grammatically] predicated of an accident, as
when we say, 'Someone musical is a human being'.

5.   Then he makes distinctions within the [different] ways of being

existent in one's own right. First he distinguishes the existent which is outside the mind into the ten categories or predicaments. This is what is completely existent. Then he puts forward another kind, the existent which is only in the mind [section 11]. Thirdly he divides the existent into the potentially existent and the actually existent [section 13]. The existent divided up in this way is more general than the completely existent, since the potentially existent is only relative and incompletely existent.

First, then, he says that the things which signify the figures of predication are said to be existents in their own right. You should be aware that the existent cannot be broken up in a determinate way in the way that a genus is broken up into its species, by specific differences. This is because a specific difference is not itself a member of the genus, and thus it does not fall within the essence of that genus. But there is nothing that can fail to fall within the essence of the existent, so as to be capable of specifying it. This is because that which does not fall within the existent is nothing, and so cannot make a specific difference. This is how the Philosopher proved in the third book of the present work that the existent cannot be a genus [998b21].

6.   Hence the existent should be specified according to different ways of predicating, which follow on from different ways of existing. As he says, ' "Is" signifies in the same number of ways as there are ways of saying', i.e. there are as many ways of expressing the existence of something as there are ways of predicating something. That is why the first division of the existent is into what are called the categories or predicaments: because they are distinguished by different ways of predicating. This is because some of the things which are predicated signify what a thing is, others how it is, others how big, and so on. So within each of the different ways of predicating, existence or being should signify the same thing. When we say 'A man is an animal', for example, the 'is' signifies [the existence of a] substance. But when we say 'A man is pale', it signifies [the existence of a] quality, and so on.

7.   You should know that the predicate can be related to the subject in three ways. In one way, it is what the subject is, as when I say 'Socrates is an animal'. This is because Socrates is that which is an animal. This predicate is said to signify first substance, i.e. an individual substance, that of which everything [else] is predicated.

8.   In the second way, the predicate is taken from something that is in the subject [i.e. an accident]. This predicate can be in the subject in its own right and without reference to anything else. This may be either as following from its matter, as it is in the case of *quantity*, or as following from the form, as it is in the case of *quality*. Or, on the other hand, it can be in the subject, not [without reference to anything else] as the above are, but with some reference to something else: this is the case of *relation*. In a third way, the predicate is taken from

something outside the subject. This can be sub-divided: it may be completely outside the subject or not. If it is, then if it is not some measurement of the subject, then it is a predicate of *having*, e.g. Socrates has shoes on, or has clothes on. But if it is the measurement of the subject, then since extrinsic measurement is either time or place, the category is taken either from the side of time, i.e. *when*; or from the side of place, in which case it will be *where*, provided that the arrangement of its parts in the place is not considered. If it is considered, it will be *posture*. There is another kind of category if that from which the predicate is taken is in the subject of which it is predicated in some relative way. If it is in the subject as its origin, then it will be a predication of *acting*. This is because the origin of an acting is in the subject of the acting. But if it is in the subject as its terminus, then it will be a predication of *being acted on*. This is because being acted on has its terminus in the subject which is acted on.

9.   But there are predications in which the word 'is' [which is the same as 'exists' in Latin] is clearly not used. You should not think, however, that such predications do not belong to the predication of existence. For example, take 'A man walks'. Aristotle dismisses this by saying that all predications of this kind signify that something exists. This is because any verb can be analysed into the verb 'is' [or 'exists'] and the participle. It makes no difference whether you say a man is convalescent, or convalesces; and similarly for the others. Hence it is clear that there are as many ways to express existence as there are ways of predicating.

10.   What Avicenna said is false: he said that the predicates which fall within the accidental categories, e.g. 'pale' or 'musical', principally signify substance, and only signify accident secondarily. 'Pale', as it is said in the categories, signifies a quality alone. But [it is true that] the word 'pale' does signify a subject; not principally, however, but consequently, since it signifies whiteness in a manner of signification appropriate to an accident. Hence it should include, consequently, the subject in its description. This is because the existence of accidents is existence in something. The word 'paleness', however, though it signifies an accident, does so in a manner appropriate to a substance. Hence this word does not consignify substance at all. If it did principally signify a subject, then the Philosopher would not have put accidental predicates under the existent in its own right, but rather under the coincidentally existent. For this whole, that a human being is pale, is an existent coincidentally, as has been said.

11.   Then he gives us another sense of 'the existent', according to which *exist* and *exists* mean the composition of a proposition, which is brought about by the intellect when it composes or divides. Hence he says that 'existence' here means the truth of a thing: or rather, as another version has it, that existence means that some sentence is true. Hence the truth of a proposition can be called the truth of a thing through its being so caused. This is because an utterance is true

or false depending on what the thing is or is not. When, then, we say that something exists, we mean that a proposition is true: and when we say it does not exist, we mean that a proposition is not true. This works whether we are making an affirmation or a denial. In making an affirmation, we say that Socrates is pale, meaning that this is true. In making a negation, we say that Socrates is not pale, meaning that this is true, i.e. his not being pale. In the same way we say that the diagonal is not commensurable with the side of a square, meaning that this is false, i.e. the diagonal's being commensurable.

12.   But you should know that this second sense is related to the first as effect to cause. This is because truth and falsehood in a proposition follow from what a thing is in reality. Truth and falsehood are signified by this word 'is', used as the copula. But there are things which are not existents, but which are dealt with by the intellect as if they were: such as negations and the like. Thus sometimes we speak of the existence of something in this second sense and not the first. We say, that is, that blindness exists in the second sense, on the grounds that the proposition is true which says that something is blind. We are not saying that it is true in the first sense. For blindness has no existence in reality: rather it is being deprived of some existent. But it is merely coincidental that anything should have something truly said or thought of it: because reality does not depend on knowledge, but vice-versa. The existence which each thing has by nature is substantial. So if, when we say 'Socrates exists', we take this 'exists' in the first sense, it is a substantial predication. The existent, after all, is a kind which is superior to all existents, as the kind 'animal' is a superior kind to 'human being'. But if we take it in the second sense, it is a coincidental predication.

13.   Then he makes a distinction between actuality and potentiality. He says that 'the existent' and 'exist' signify either that which is said or spoken potentially, or that which is said or spoken actually. That is, in all the terms discussed above, the terms which signify the ten categories, something is said actually, and something said potentially. Hence it happens that each of the categories can be divided into actuality and potentiality. This is true of reality outside the mind: things are said actually and things are said potentially. It is also true within the activities of the mind, and for privations, whose existence is purely dependent on the mind. We say that people know, both because they *could be* using their knowledge, or because they are using it. It is the same with 'resting': one might either be actually in a state of rest, or able to be resting. This applies not only to accidents, but also to substances. For we say that the Mercury — i.e. the statue of Mercury — exists in the stone potentially, and that the half of a line exists in the line potentially. This is because any part is contained within the whole. He gives a line as an example of a substance, using here the opinion of those who thought that mathematical entities were substances. He has not yet rejected that view [see passage 4]. We say that there is corn even when it is not yet

complete, and the corn is only sprouting: and this is there potentially. But when there is something potentially and when there is not
yet anything potentially is a subject he leaves to be discussed elsewhere, in Book Nine.

Passage 4: Existence and substance

This passage serves to connect the last passage with the later discussions of substance, form and matter. Why he says 'the form
and species of each thing are also called substance' (section 6) will
be explained in the following passages.

Commentary on the Metaphysics, Book V, *lectio* 10 (Aristotle's text: 1017b9–25; commentary: Marietti, sections 898–905)

1. Here he shows how many senses there are of 'substance'. He
does two things on this: first of all he shows how many senses there
are, then he brings them all back to two [section 5].
   On the first he gives us four senses of 'substance'. The first of
them is the sense in which individual substances are said to be substances: e.g. non-complex bodies, such as earth, fire, water etc. Also,
all bodies, even if they are complex, but mixtures of like parts: e.g.
stone, blood, flesh, etc. Then again, animals, which are made up of
this sort of sensed bodies, and their parts, such as hands and feet and
the like; and 'demons', i.e. idols, which were put up in temples and
worshipped as gods. (Or perhaps 'demons' means certain rational
animals in the Platonic system, which Apuleius defines in this way:
'Demons are animals with an airy body, rational mind, a soul that
can be acted on, and eternal duration.') All of the above are said to
be substances, because they are not said of any other subject, but
instead other things are said of them. This is the description given of
first substance in the *Categories* [2a11].
   Then he says that there is another sense of 'substance' in which
substance is the cause of the existence of the substances mentioned
above, which are not said of a subject. Not an extrinsic cause,
though, like the efficient cause, but an intrinsic cause, i.e. the form.
This is as when we say that the soul is the substance of the animal.

2. Then he gives a third sense which follows the view of the
Platonists and the Pythagoreans. In this sense all the little particles
which are the limits of the substances mentioned above are substances; they signify 'this something', as they would say, and are
such that when they are destroyed the whole is destroyed. This is
because, some would say, the body is destroyed when the surface is

81

destroyed, and a surface is destroyed when the line is destroyed. It is clear that the surface is the limit of a body, and the line is the limit of a surface. According to this view, then, the line is a part of the surface, and the surface is a part of the body. They claimed that a body is made up of surfaces, and a surface of lines, and a line of points. So it would follow that the point is the substance of the line, and the line of the surface, and so on. According to this view numbers seem to be the substance of the whole universe: take away number and nothing real remains, since that which is not one thing does not exist. Equally, things that are not many things do not exist [as many separate individuals] either. Number is seen as the limit of everything, since it is used to measure everything.

3.   This sense is not a genuine one. What is generally found in everything, and without which nothing can exist, does not have to be the substance of things: it could be some inseparable property that follows on from the substance of things or the originating principles of substance. They were particularly prone to this error with regard to 'one' and 'number', since they did not distinguish between 'one' in the sense in which it is convertible with 'existent' [i.e. 'one and the same thing'], and the sense in which it is the originating principle of numbering.

4.   He gives a fourth sense: the essence of a thing, which is signified by the definition, is also called the substance of each thing. Now, this essence of a thing, whose description is the definition, is different from the form, which was said to be the substance in the second sense. Humanity is different from the soul. The form is a part of the essence of a thing. The essence of a thing includes all its essential originating principles. So the genus and the species are said to be the substances of the things of which they are predicated in this last way. Genus and species do not signify the form alone, but the whole essence of the thing.

5.   Then he brings these senses back to two. He says that we can gather from the above senses that there are really two senses of 'substance': one is that in which a substance is ultimately the subject in a proposition, since it is not predicated of anything else: i.e. first substance. This is what is a 'this something', that which exists in its own right, and is separable from other things, since it is distinct from all of them and cannot be communicated to many. With reference to these points there are three differences between the individual substance and the universal. The first is that the individual substance is not predicated of anything that falls under it, as the universal substance is. The second is that the universal substance does not exist except in virtue of the individual that exists in its own right. The third is that the universal substance exists in many things, while the individual does not, but is separate from everything else and distinct from them.

6.   But the form and species of each thing are also called substance.

This includes the second and the fourth sense. Essence and form are akin in that each is said to be that in virtue of which a thing exists. But form has a reference to matter, which is what it makes to actually exist. Essence has a reference to the individual existent, which is spoken of as what has such-and-such an essence. So both form and species are included under one sense, i.e. the sense of the essence of a thing.

7. The third sense is left to one side, as it is not genuine: or, perhaps, because it can be brought back to that of form, which also falls under the description of being a limit. Matter is also said to be substance, but it is passed over here, as it is not actually a substance. But it is included in the first sense, since an individual substance cannot be a substance and an individual among material things except by its matter.

Passage 5: Substance

The claim at section 13 that substance is temporally prior to accident would seem to be a mistake. The discussion at section 15 is relevant to the understanding of the latter part of passage 6. There is a discussion of substance in the *Summa theologiae* at I q.29 a.2.

Commentary on the Metaphysics, Book VII, *lectio* 1 (Aristotle's text: 1028a10 – b35; commentary: Marietti, sections 1245 – 1269)

1. The Philosopher has refused to admit the coincidentally existent and the existent in the sense of the true as being principal objects of this study. Here he begins to establish the truth about the existent in its own right, which is outside the mind. This is the principal object of this study.

This section is divided into two parts. This study establishes the truth about the existent as such, and about the first originating principles of the existent, as was claimed in Book Six. In the first part, then, he establishes the truth about the existent [in Books VII – XI of the *Metaphysics*]: in the second part, he deals with the first originating principles of the existent, in Book Twelve.

The existent and the 'one and the same' follow one from the other, and fall under the same investigation, as was claimed at the start of the fourth book. So the first part of this investigation is divided into two. In the first part he lays down the truth about the existent; in the second, about the 'one and the same', and what follows from it, in the tenth book.

The existent in its own right, outside the mind, is divided up two different ways, as was said in the fifth book. One way is to divide it into the ten categories, another is to divide it up according to potentiality and actuality. So the first of the above two parts is itself divided into two parts. In the first part [which starts here] he establishes the truth about the existent, as it is divided up into the ten categories; in the second, as it is divided up according to potentiality and actuality. He does this latter in the ninth book.

2. The first of these parts is divided, again, into two parts. In the first, [in this passage] he shows that in order to establish the truth about the existent, as it is divided into the ten categories, we must establish the truth about substance on its own. In the second part he begins to do this [in *lectio* 2].

On the first of the above he does two things. First he shows that we have to establish the truth about substance [section 3]: then he shows us what we should deal with in this treatment [section 19].

On the first he does two things. First he shows that when we intend to deal with the existent, we should deal with substance on its own according to rational argument [section 3]. Then we should deal with it in the way that other thinkers usually do [section 16].

So in the first part he intends to give us the rational argument. That which is first among existents, that which is, as it were, just the existent without qualification, without any relation to anything else, reveals sufficiently clearly what the nature of the existent is. Substance is like this: so to be aware of the nature of the existent it is enough for us to establish the truth about substance.

On this he does two things. First he shows that substance is the first existent; then he shows in what ways it is said to be first [section 13].

3. But he does two things on this [first] point. First of all he lays down what he plans to do: 'the existent' has many senses, as it said in the fifth book [Book V, *lectio* 9: passage 3 above]. There he distinguished all the different senses of this kind of name: 'the existent' sometimes signifies what a thing is, and this something, i.e. substance. ('What' means the essence of a substance, and 'this something' the individual subject: and all the different ways of being a substance can be brought back to these two, as was said in the fifth book [Book V, *lectio* 10: passage 4 above].) But sometimes it signifies a quality or quantity, or something in one of the other categories. Since there are so many senses of 'the existent', it is clear that the first among all the existents is that which exists, i.e. 'the existent' in the sense of substance.

4. Then, he proves what he has put forward. The argument he uses is as follows. That which exists in its own right, without qualification, in any category, is prior to that which exists in virtue of something else, and in a relative way. But substance is existent without qualification, in its own right: all the other non-substantial

categories are existent in a relative sense, and in virtue of a substance. So substance is the first of all existents.

5.   He proves the minor premiss in two ways. First, from our way of speaking, or predicating. He says it is clear that substance is the first of existents from the fact that when we ask what something is like we say it is either good or bad. These words signify quality, which is something different from substance and quantity. 'Six feet high' signifies a quantity, and 'human being' signifies a substance. So when we say 'Something is like this', we are not saying that it is six feet high or a human being. But when we say what a thing is, we do not say that it is pale, or hot — which signify qualities — or that it is six feet high, which signifies a quantity: we say it is a human being, or that it is God; and these signify substances.

6.   So it is clear that the words that signify substances say what a thing is without qualification. The words that predicate a quality do not say what, without qualification, the thing is of which they are predicated, but what it is like. And the same sort of thing is true of quantity, and of the other categories.

7.   So it is clear that a substance is said to be an existent in its very own right: the words which signify a substance without qualification signify what this is. Other things are said to be existents, but not because they have some essence in their own right — as if they were existents in their own right — because they are not said to be what a thing is without qualification. It is because they are of such-and-such an existent, i.e. because they have some relation to a substance which is an existent in its own right [that they are said to be existents]. They do not signify an essence. Some are qualities of such-and-such an existent, i.e. a substance, others are quantities, others ways of being acted on, or some other such thing which is signified by the other categories.

8.   Then he proves this by an example. Other existents are only existents in so far as they are related to a substance. So there can be doubt about other existents when they are signified in an abstract way, i.e. without any reference to a substance being signified. We can wonder whether they are existents or not. For example, walking, getting well, sitting down, and all such things signified in an abstract way: are they existents or not? It is the same with all other such things that are signified in an abstract way, whether they are signified in the way that actions are, as the examples above were, or not, e.g. paleness or darkness.

9.   Accidents signified in an abstract way do not seem to be existents, to this extent: none of them is by nature such as to exist on its own. Rather, the existence of each of them is to exist in something else, and none of them can be separated from a substance. So when they are signified in an abstract way — as if they were existents in

their own right and separate from substances — they look as if they are not existents. But it is true that the way in which utterances signify does not follow immediately on the way in which things exist: it follows mediately, through the way in which they are thought of. This is because thoughts are the likenesses of things, while utterances are the likenesses of thoughts, as it says in the first book of the *De interpretatione* [16a3].

10.   But though the manner in which accidents exist is not such that they exist in their own right, but only such that they exist in another, the intellect can think of them in their own right. This is because the nature of the intellect is such that it can put apart the things that are joined together by nature. So the abstract names of accidents signify existents which inhere in another, even though they do not signify them in the manner which is appropriate to things that inhere. The things which are signified by such names would be non-existents if they did not exist in a thing.

11.   So, while the things which are signified in this abstract manner seem to be non-existents, the concrete names of accidents seem to signify existents rather more. 'Some existent is walking and sitting down and getting better' seems more to signify an existent, since it determines some subject by the very signification of the name: in so far, that is, as the accidents are signified in a concrete manner, related to a subject. But this subject is a substance. So every name of this kind that signifies an accident in a concrete manner 'appears in that category', as Aristotle says: i.e. it seems to convey the category of substance. It is not that the category of substance is a part of the signification of such a name: 'pale', as was said in the *Categories* [?9a29 ff], only signifies a quality. Rather it is in so far as such names signify accidents as things inhering in a substance [that they convey the category of substance]. 'Good' or 'sitting down' is not said without a substance. This is because it signifies an accident as it is made concrete in relation to a substance.

12.   Accidents, then, do not seem to be existents in so far as they are signified in themselves, but only to the extent that they are signified as being made concrete in relation to a substance. So it is clear that each of the other kinds of existent is existent because of substance. From this it is further clear that substance is the first existent, and the existent without qualification, and not an existent in relation to something else, as the accidents are. To be pale is not just to be or exist, but to exist relative to something else. This is made clear by the fact that when something comes to be pale, we do not say that it comes to be or exist without qualification, just that it comes to be pale. But when Socrates comes to be a human being, we say that he comes to be or exist, without qualification. So it is clear that to be a human being signifies to exist without qualification; to be pale signifies to exist relatively.

13.   Then he shows in what way substance is said to be first. He

says that this word 'first' has many senses, as was said in the fifth book [1018b8 – 1019a14]. But substance is first among all the other existents in three ways: according to the awareness we have of it, according to its definition, and according to time. Its being temporally prior to the others is proved in this way: nothing in the other categories can be separated from substance: only substance is separable from the others. No accident is to be found without a substance, while some substances are to be found without accident. So it is clear that we do not always have accidents when we have a substance, but not vice-versa. So substance is temporally prior.

14. Its priority according to its definition is clear from the fact that we have to put the definition of a substance in the definition of any accident. We put 'nose' into the definition of 'snub': and in the same way we put any accident's proper subject into its definition. So just as 'animal' is prior to 'human being' by its definition, since the definition of animal is put into the definition of human being, by parity of reasoning substance is prior to the accidents by its definition.

15. That it is also prior in the order of our being aware of it is clear too. What is prior in the order of our awareness is what is better known and more clearly reveals a thing. We are aware of a thing more when we know its substance than when we know its quality or quantity. We think that we know an individual thing best when we know what it is, a human being, or a fire, rather than when we know what it is like, or how big it is, or where it is, or anything else about it that comes into some other category. That is why we know individual things that are in the accidental categories when we know of each of them what it is. When we know what 'what like' itself is, we know quality, and when we know what 'how big' itself is, we know quantity. The other categories do not exist except in so far as they are in a subject, and in the same way we are not aware of them except in so far as they share to a certain extent in the way in which we are aware of substances, i.e. knowing what they are.

16. Then he shows the same point, namely that we have to deal with substance alone, from the way in which other philosophers tend to speak. He says that the philosophers have asked and always wondered about what the existent is, both 'once upon a time', in the past, and now, in the present. This is just to ask and wonder about what is the substance of the world.

17. Some said that this existent, i.e. substance, was one and the same, and unchanging: e.g. Parmenides and Melissus. Others said it was changing, e.g. the ancient natural philosophers who claimed that there was only one material originating principle of the world. They thought that only matter was existent substance. So, when they claimed that there was just one existent, because there was one and

the same material originating principle, it is clear that what they meant by 'one existent' was 'one substance'. But others claimed that there was more than one existent: they claimed that there was more than one material originating principle. So they claimed that there was more than one substance in the world. Some of these claimed there was a finite number of them, e.g. Empedocles and his four elements; others said they were infinite, e.g. Anaxagoras and his infinite like parts, and Democritus and his infinite atoms.

18.   So if the other philosophers who dealt with existents paid attention to substances alone, we too should investigate 'this kind of existent', i.e. substance: what it is. We should do so especially because it is the principal goal of our work. This is so, in the first place, because by it 'on its own, so to speak' we get to be aware of other things: by establishing the truth about substance on its own, we get a notion of everything else. So in a way Aristotle establishes the truth about substance on its own, and in another way he establishes the truth about substance *not* on its own. This is what he means when he says 'so to speak', which is what we usually say about things which are not absolutely true.

19.   Then he shows what we have to establish about substance. He does two things on this. First, he puts forward the views of other people about substance, then he says that we have to investigate the truth of these [section 24].
     On the first of these he does two things. First he puts forward what is obvious about substance. He says that it is in bodies that we most obviously find the existence of substances. This is why we say that animals and plants, and their parts, are substances: other natural bodies, too, such as fire, earth and water, and 'individuals like these', i.e. such-like elementary bodies. These would be air, and vapour, according to Heraclitus, and other half-way stages between them, according to others. Also, all the parts of the elements, and also bodies which are composed of the elements, or of parts of the elements, i.e. individual mixed bodies; or out of all the elements, i.e. made up of the whole of the elements, that is the whole sphere of bodies that act on one another and are acted on; or even the heavens, because we say that a natural body which is not made up of the elements is a substance, and so are its parts, e.g. the stars, the moon and the sun.

20.   But there is a question that we need to examine: are these sensed substances the only substances, as the ancient natural philosophers said, or are there also some other substances, as the Platonists said? Or are none of these substances, so that the only substances are different from them?

21.   Then he goes through the views of the philosophers about the substances that are not apparent to us. He says that some thought that the limits of bodies are the substances of the world. I.e. surfaces,

lines, points and units are more substances than are bodies and solid things. This view was taken two ways. Some, the Pythagoreans, thought that none of these limits were separate from sensed things. Others claimed that there were certain eternal existents separated from sensed things, and that there were more of them than there are sensed things, and they were more existent than the latter were. When I say 'more existent' I mean that they are undying and unchanging, while sensed things can cease to exist and can change: and when I say 'more of them' I mean that there is only one order of sensed things, while there would be two orders of separated things. For [as Aristotle says in the text being commented on here] 'Plato said that there were two separate substances', i.e. that there were two different orders of separated substances: Forms or Ideas, and mathematical beings. He claimed that the substances of sensed bodies were a third order.

22.   But Leucippus, who succeeded Plato in his school, and was his nephew (on his sister's side) claimed that there were many orders of substances, and in each of them there was one thing from which they sprang. He claimed, then, that there was an originating principle in each of the orders of substances. One thing was the originating principle of numbers (which he put as the first substances after the Forms), and that was the number one: something else was the originating principle of geometrical extensions (which he put as the next kind of substances). After that he put in the substance of the soul, and so dragged out the order of substances until he got to bodies that can cease to exist.

23.   There were those who disagreed with Plato and Leucippus, and did not distinguish between the Forms and the first order of mathematical beings, i.e. the numbers. They said that Forms and numbers had the same nature, and everything else existed 'as a result', i.e. as a result of their relation to numbers: from lines and surfaces right down to the first substance of the heavens, and other sensed things, which come in the last order.

24.   Then he shows what we should say about the above. He says that we must say what is good in the above and what is not: we should say what are the substances, and whether or not the mathematical beings and Forms mentioned above are anything real, which is apart from sensed things. If those substances do exist apart from sensed substances we should say what is the manner in which they exist; and if they do not exist apart from sensed substances, whether there are any other separated substances, and why and how they exist. Or we should say if there are no substances apart from the sensed ones.

25.   He will establish the truth about this in the twelfth book below. Before we establish the truth about these, though, we should first put down and delimit what substance is among the sensed things, as

substance is most clearly found there. He does this in this book, the seventh, and in the following.

Passage 6: Matter and form

There is some interesting light cast on the notion of matter by q.66 aa.1 and 2 in the *Summa theologiae*. On form, the discussion of the human soul at I q.76, especially a.1, is relevant.

Commentary on the Metaphysics, Book VII, *lectio* 2 (Aristotle's text: 1028b33 – 1029b12; commentary: Marietti, sections 1270 – 1305)

1.   After showing that the chief aim of this study is to consider substance, he begins here to establish the truth about substance. He divides this part into two.

First of all he shows the way of dealing with substance, and the order in which this should be done. In the second he continues with the treatment of substance [in *lectio* 3].

He shows the way of dealing with substance and the order to be followed by dividing substances into their parts, and teaching us which of these parts we should get clear about first, and most principally, and which parts should be put off till later, and in what order we should consider them. So he divides the first part into three, according to the divisions and subdivisions of substance that he makes. [The second part starts at section 7, the third at section 28.]

He says first, then, that 'substance' is said in at least four different ways, if not in more. There are, too, other ways in which some people use the name 'substance'. This is clear from the fact that people said that the limits of bodies were substances. This way is passed over here. The first of these ways is that in which the 'what is it' of a thing, i.e. its essence or nature, is said to be its substance.

2.   The second way is that in which the universal is said to be a substance, according to the view of those who claimed there were Form-ideas, i.e. the universals that are predicated of individuals, and that these are the substances of these individuals.

3.   The third way is that in which 'the first kind seems to be the substance of each thing'. In this way the existent and the one and the same are said to be the substances of everything, as the first kinds [or categories] to which everything belongs.

4.   The fourth way is that in which the subject, i.e. the individual substance, is called a substance. He means the subject of which other

things are said: either as something higher which is said of the lower, as is the genus in relation to the species and the specific difference, or as the accidents are predicated of the subject, whether they be common or proper accidents. For example, we predicate human being, animal, rational, able to laugh, and pale of Socrates. But the subject is not predicated of anything else. This means, it is not predicated in its own right. There is no objection to predicating being Socrates of this pale thing, or of this animal, or of this human being, coincidentally; this is because that in which there is pale, or animal, or human being, is Socrates. He is predicated in his own right of himself when we say 'Socrates is Socrates'. It is clear, then, that what is called 'the subject' here is what was called 'first substance' in the *Categories* [2a11]. It is clear because the same definition is given of subject here as was of first substance there.

5.   His conclusion, then, is that we have to establish the truth about this, i.e. the subject or first substance, since this subject seems most of all to be substance. That is why he says in the *Categories* that this kind of substance is substance properly, principally, and especially so-called [ibid.]. This kind of substance is what in its own right *stands under* [*sub-stat*] everything else, the species and the genus and the accidents. The second substances, i.e. genera and species, only stand under accidents: and they do so only in virtue of the first substance. The human being is pale only in so far as this human being is pale.

6.   So it is clear that the division of substance which he has made here is more or less the same as that which he made in the *Categories*, as 'subject' here means 'first substance'. What he has called the genus and the universal (which seems to have to do with genus and species) falls under second substance. The 'what is it' is put in here, but was passed over there, since it does not fall under the ordering of the categories, except as the originating principle of that ordering. This is because it is not a genus, nor a species, nor an individual, but the formal originating principle of all these.

7.   Then he subdivides the fourth way which was distinguished above, i.e. the subject. He does three things on this.
    First of all he makes the division. Then he relates the different parts so divided to each other [section 9]. Then he shows how we should proceed with regard to each of these parts [section 25].
    He says first, then, that the subject — i.e. the first individual substance — is divided into three: the form, the matter, and that which they make up or compose. This division is not the division of a genus into its species, but rather of an analogical predicate which is said of the things that fall under it according to a principal sense and secondary related senses. That which is made up by form and matter, and the matter, and the form, are all said to be the particular substance, but as parts of the same ordering. So he will look later at which of these is substance in the principal way.

8.   He gives an example of these parts of the division which he draws from an artificial thing, [a statue of bronze]. The bronze is like the matter, the shape is like the form of the species — i.e. that which gives the species — and the statue is what they make up. This example should not be taken as a literal case of what we are discussing: it should be taken according to the proportional likeness it bears. Shape and other artificial forms are not substances, they are accidents. But the way that the shape is related to the bronze in things made artificially is the way that the substantial form is related to the matter in natural things. So he uses this example, to show what is not known by means of what is obvious.

9.   Then he relates the different parts he has distinguished one to another. On this he does three things.

First he shows that the form is more substance than is the thing made up of form and matter. Then he puts forward the view that matter is substance most of all, which is what some people thought [section 12]: then he shows that both the form and the thing made up are more substance than is matter [section 22].

He says first, then, that the species — i.e. the form — is prior to the matter. Matter is an existent in potentiality, and form is its actuality. But actuality is naturally prior to potentiality. And strictly speaking, it is prior in time too: since potentiality is not changed into actuality except by some actual existent. (This is so, even though in one and the same existent which is sometimes in potentiality and sometimes in actuality, potentiality may precede actuality in time.) So it is clear that form is prior to matter, and is also more of an existent than matter, since that on account of which a thing is *x* is more *x*. Matter does not become an actual existent except through the form. So form has to be more of an existent than is matter.

10.   From this it further follows, by the same argument, that the form is prior to that which is made up of both matter and form. This is in virtue of the fact that there is something of matter in that which is made up: so it has some share in that which is naturally secondary, namely matter. Again, it is clear that matter and form are the originating principles of that which is made up. But a thing's originating principles are prior to it. So if form is prior to matter, it will be prior to that which is made up.

11.   Some might think that since the Philosopher has given us all the ways in which 'substance' is said, this is enough to know what substance is. This is why he adds that now we have said what substance is roughly, i.e. only generally: we have said that substance is that which is not said of a subject, but of which other things are said. But this — a logical and general definition — is not the only way in which we have to be aware of substance, and other things. It is not enough to give us an awareness of the nature of a thing. What is attributed by such a definition is obvious. Such a definition does not touch on the originating principles of a thing, and it is on this that a

full awareness of the thing depends. It just touches on some common characteristic of the thing in virtue of which such a kind of notion arises.

12.   Then he puts forward the view that matter is substance most of all. He does two things on this. First of all he puts forward the argument of the ancients, on account of which they claimed that matter, most of all, and matter alone, was substance. Then he gives a notion of what matter is [section 16].

He suggests first, then, [in expounding the argument of the pre-Socratics] that not only are form and that which is made up substance, as the above argument has it, but matter is too. Indeed, if matter is not substance, then what other substance there can be apart from matter escapes us. For if we remove from sensed things — among which substance is obvious — other things which are plainly not substance, nothing is left, it seems, except matter.

13.   This is because some of the things in these sensed bodies, which everyone admits are substances, are things which happen to bodies, e.g. being hot, being cold, etc. It is clear that these are not substances. There are also in bodies certain becomings, i.e. comings to be and passings away, and changes; and it is clear that these are not substances either. Also there are powers, which are the originating principles of the becomings and changes we have mentioned — i.e. the powers of acting and being acted upon which there are in things. These too are clearly not substances, but rather fall under the category of qualities.

14.   After all these we find in bodies the sensed dimensions, length, breadth and height. These are quantities, not substances. It is obvious that quantity is not substance: rather, that in which the dimensions exist, as their first subject, is substance. So when you take away these dimensions there seems to be nothing left except their subject, that which is made determinate and distinct by them. But this is matter. Measurable quantity seems to exist in matter immediately, since [a lump of] matter is not distinguished by receiving different forms in different parts of it, unless it is [first] distinguished according to this kind of quantity. So it seems necessary, by this train of thought, [to conclude] that not only is matter substance, but even that only matter is substance.

15.   When the ancient philosophers brought in this argument they were led astray by their ignorance of substantial form. They had not yet got so far as to raise their minds to anything which is beyond what can be sensed. Hence they only consider those forms which are sensed in a proper or common way. It is clear that such things — e.g. black and white, large and small — are accidents. But the substantial form is only sensed coincidentally: so they did not reach an awareness of it which would enable them to distinguish it from matter. Rather they said that the whole subject — which we say is made up

93

out of matter and form — was some first matter, e.g. air, water, etc. What they called forms are what we call accidents, e.g. quantities and qualities. Their subject is not first matter, but the made-up substance, which is a substance in actuality. After all, every accident exists because it exists in a substance, as we have said.

16.   Then: the above argument which 'shows' that only matter is substance seems to arise from an ignorance of what matter is, as we have said: so Aristotle goes on to say what matter really and truly is, as is set out in the first book of the *Physics* [190b25 ff]. We cannot be properly aware of matter in itself, except by considering change, and the investigation of change seems to belong to natural philosophy. So the Philosopher here picks up what was investigated in the *Physics*, and says: 'I say that matter is that which in its own right' — i.e. considered according to its own essence — 'exists in no way: it is neither a "what", i.e. a substance, nor a quality, nor anything else of the other categories by which the existent is divided up or determined.'

17.   This is particularly clear in change. The subject of change and motion has to be something strictly different from either of the termini of the change. This was proved in the first book of the *Physics* [189b30 ff]. Now, since matter is the first subject that underlies change — not only changes of quality, quantity, and other accidents, but also substantial changes — it has to be essentially different from any substantial form or the privation of it. These are the termini of coming-to-be and passing-away. It has to be different from these, not only from quantity and quality and the other accidents.

18.   But the Philosopher does not prove that matter is different from all forms by an argument from change. This proof is an argument from natural philosophy. Instead, he uses an argument from predication, which belongs to logic: in the fourth book we said that logic and metaphysics are akin. He says, then, that there must be something of which all the above are predicated. But it must be different in such a way that the subject of which they are predicated, and each of those things that are predicated of it [i.e. the substance and its accidents], are of a different essence.

19.   You should notice that what is said here cannot be understood as true of univocal predication, according to which a genus is predicated of the species in whose definition it occurs. There is no difference of essence between animal and human being [in that context]. We should instead understand Aristotle to be speaking of 'denominative' predication, i.e. as when 'white' is predicated of a human being. Here there is a difference of essence between white and human being. So he adds that the other categories are predicated in this denominative way of a substance, and being a substance is predicated denominatively of matter.

20.   We should not understand, then, that an actually existent

substance, which is what we are talking of here, is predicated of [a lump of] matter with univocal (or essential) predication. We have already said above that matter is not a 'what' [i.e. a substance], nor is it anything in the other categories. We should understand that we are talking of denominative predication, which is the way in which accidents are predicated of a substance. For example, 'A human being is pale' is true, but 'A human being is paleness' is not. Nor is 'Humanity is paleness'. In the same way, 'This material thing is a human being' is true, while 'Matter is a human being' and 'Matter is humanity' are not. The very fact, then, of using denominative (or 'concretive') predication shows that matter and substantial forms are essentially different, just as substance is essentially different from the accidents. So it follows that in the end the subject, strictly speaking, is not a 'what', i.e. a substance, nor a quantity, nor anything else that falls under any category of the existent.

21.   Not even negations can be essentially predicated of matter. Forms are outside the essence of matter, and so are related, as it were, coincidentally to it. In the same way, the denials of form — which is what privations are — exist in matter coincidentally. If they existed in matter in their own right, then a form could never be received by matter so long as the matter existed. The Philosopher says this to dismiss the view of Plato. He did not distinguish between matter and privation, as we read in the first book of the *Physics* [187a18, 192a11]. Aristotle concludes, finally, that people who consider this question according to the foregoing arguments alone end up believing that matter alone is substance. This was the conclusion of the earlier argument, too.

22.   Then he shows that the contrary of this conclusion is true. He says that it is impossible that matter alone should be substance, or even that it should especially be substance. There are two things that seem to belong especially to substance. The first is that it should be separable, since an accident cannot be separated from a substance, while a substance can be separated from an accident. The other is that substance is 'this something I am pointing to'. The other categories do not signify a 'this something'.

23.   These two things — being separable and being a 'this something' — do not fit matter. Matter cannot exist in its own right without a form, in virtue of which it is an actual existent. This is because in its own right it exists only potentially. And matter is not a 'this something' except in virtue of a form, in virtue of which it comes actually to exist. So being a 'this something' belongs especially to the thing made up [of matter and form].

24.   So it is clear that the species, or form, and that which is made up of both [matter and form] are more obviously substance than is matter. The thing made up of both [matter and form] is separable, and is a 'this something'. Form is not separable, nor is it a 'this

something'; nevertheless it is in virtue of form that the thing made up becomes an actual existent, and hence something separable, and a 'this something'.

25.   Then he shows how we need to work with regard to the parts of the division of substance we have been following, i.e. into form, matter, and that which is made up [of them]. He says that although both the form and the thing made up [of matter and form] are more substance than is matter, we still have for the present to put aside substance as made up of both form and matter. There are two reasons for this.

26.   One is that it is in fact naturally secondary to both form and matter, in that that which is made up is secondary to the simple elements which make it up. So an awareness of matter and of form comes before an awareness of the substance which they make up.

27.   The other is that this kind of substance is open to view, or obvious, since it falls under the senses. So there is no need to dwell on acquiring an awareness of it. Matter, meanwhile, though it is not secondary but in some way prior is also in some way obvious. He says 'in some way obvious' because by its essence there is no way to get to know it: the originating principle of getting to know something is form. But matter is known through a kind of proportionate likeness [or analogy]. The relation between sensed substances and artificial forms — e.g. that between timber and the form of a bench — is the same as that between first matter and sensed forms. That is why the first book of the *Physics* says that first matter can be known by means of an analogy [191a9]. So we are left to look at the third, i.e. form, since it is most questionable.

28.   Then he shows the manner and the order to be followed in pursuing the parts of the third division of substance: i.e. substance as divided into sensed and non-sensed substances. He does three things on this.

29.   First, he shows that we have to deal with sensed substances first, since they are universally admitted: everyone admits that sensed substances are substances, but not everyone admits that non-sensed substances are. So we have to look into sensed subjects first, as they are better known.

30.   Then he shows us what we have to establish about sensed substances. He says that when we made our earlier division — the ways in which substance is said — one of those ways was substance as the 'what-is-it', i.e. the essence. So we have to discuss this first, i.e. showing the essences of sensed things.

31.   Thirdly, he gives a reason for the above ordering: he says that we have to speak of sensed substances first, since this is a preamble,

or preparatory task to our main task. This is because from these sensed substances, which are more obvious to us, we can pass to something that is more easily known in itself and by nature, i.e. substances which are only thought of. These are what we are principally interested in. This is the way to teach any subject to anyone: to start from those things that are by nature less easily known, and pass to those things that are by nature easily known

32. This is because all teaching is done by means of what is better known by the learners, who have to be previously aware of some things if they are to learn. So our teaching here has to go from what is more easily known to us, which are often the things that are less easily known by nature, to the things that are more easily known by nature, but are less easily known by us.

33. This is because our awareness starts with the senses: so we are more easily aware of the things that are more available to the senses. But by nature things are more easily known which are by nature more fit for our awareness. These are the things that are most existent, and most actual. But these are less available to our senses, while sensed forms are forms in matter.

34. So in teaching we have to go from what is less easily known by nature to what is more easily known. We have to do in this as we do in the arts and active powers, in which the whole or universal good — and hence each one's good — comes about through the individual good, the good for this character or that character. The art of warfare brings it about that the whole army wins — a sort of common good — from the individual winning of this soldier and that soldier. And similarly the art of building brings about the putting together of a whole house from the putting together of this stone and that stone. The same thing should happen in philosophy: from what is more easily known to the pupil we should get through to what is easily known by nature, which at last gets known even by the pupil.

35. The reason for this is not that what is more easily known by this character or that character is just more easily known, without qualification: the things which are known to the individuals — this character or that character — and are known by them earlier, are often things which are more feebly known by nature. This is because they have little or no degree of existence, and a thing can be known in so far as it exists. It is clear that accidents, and changes, and privations have little or no degree of existence: but nevertheless we know them better than we do the substances of things, because they are more available to the senses. This is because they fall under the senses in their own right, as being sensed as proper or common objects of the senses. But substantial forms are sensed only co-incidentally.

36. He says 'often' because sometimes what is more easily known

by us and what is more easily known by nature are the same. This happens in mathematics, which abstract from sensed matter. So in mathematics we always work from what is naturally more easily known, which is the same as what is more easily known by us. And though the things which are more easily known to us are more feebly known by nature, nevertheless, we have to try to get to know what is wholly or universally and completely knowable from those things which are badly known by nature, but more easily knowable by the pupil. We do this by getting to know them by means of things that are weakly known in their own right, as we have said.

4

Aquinas on God

An introduction to Aquinas on God

The existence of God

The crown of the study of metaphysics is the study of the supreme existent, God. Aquinas holds that something can be known of God even by the natural light of human reason, unaided by grace, by analogy with what is known of the world and its constitution. It can be known that there is a God: i.e. that there is something that answers to the description 'maker of the world'. One of Aquinas's arguments to demonstrate that this is the case is given below. Aquinas's best-known arguments for the existence of God are to be found at *Summa theologiae* I q.2 a.3, the famous 'five ways': passage 7 is taken from the earlier work, the *Summa contra gentiles*.

The desire to bring to the reader a less well-known text is not the only reason for choosing this passage. This passage has the merit of being more fully worked out than the parallel arguments in the five ways, and far more carefully articulated. It is hoped that this articulation will help the reader to understand the rather briefer arguments of the five ways. Another reason is that this passage seems to depend on Aristotelian physics and astronomy — the picture of the cosmos as a nest of concentric spheres — far more than do the five ways. It has been alleged in recent years that the five ways in fact do rely tacitly on a background of Aristotelian physics and astronomy, and that they thus are not anything like conclusive arguments for the existence of God if one does not accept these dated and false views. In this passage, in contrast, Aquinas's Aristotelian views of the cosmos are brought out much more. It is hoped that the reader will be able to judge how far these beliefs affect the argument. Parts of it may have to be rejected: but it is arguable that we are left with at least the sketch of a genuinely interesting, and arguably valid, proof of the existence of God. Indeed, careful reading of this passage will reveal that at one point at least the Aristotelian cosmology is a serious liability for Aquinas's argument.

Two doubtful premisses

Aquinas makes the structure of the argument very clear: we can thus concentrate on the premisses. As he himself points out, the two most doubtful premisses are 'everything that is in process of change has that change initiated in it by something else' and 'we cannot go on to infinity in the line of initiators of change and things in process of change' (section 4). It is important to notice that the changes being discussed are explicitly said to be changes in what is divisible or material, i.e. what we would call physical changes (section 10). Changing one's mind is not considered. The key concepts translated 'initiating change' and 'being in process of change' are expressed in Latin by the active and passive voices of the transitive verb *movere*, to move. Kenny, in his book on the five ways, thinks that Aquinas is misled by the fact that he must use the same expression for 'being in process of change' and 'to have one's process of change initiated by something else'. The reader should be alive to the possibility of this equivocation in the Latin: in this more articulated version of the argument it should be easier to pick out this kind of error if it occurs.

Everything in process of change has its change initiated by something else

Some of the arguments Aquinas gives to prove these two premisses clearly depend on the Aristotelian cosmology: but some do not, or can be separated from them. It is true that we can make little of the distinction between natural change and forced or violent change, which he uses at section 8. But other arguments are less affected by our rejection of Aristotle's physics. We have already seen, for example, in the introduction to the section on metaphysics, that Aquinas will not admit that any material thing initiates change in itself 'in the principal sense': it must be that one part or aspect of it initiates change in another part. Aquinas argues for this here in three ways (sections 5–10). We might sum them up by claiming more modestly that no change is initiated by that which is in process of change in the respect in which it is in process of change.

This admits the existence of things that initiate change in themselves 'in a secondary sense', though: will this give us the interconnectedness of cause and effect which Aquinas sees as encompassing the whole material world? If a thing — an animal, say — initiates change in itself, even if in a secondary sense, do we not have to take that as a basic fact? Do we need to ask whether anything initiates change in the part that initiates change in another part?

Clearly there is no logical requirement to investigate further: only the philosophical one of wanting to find out. Does the part of an animal that initiates change in another part initiate change in virtue of being itself in process of change or not? Aquinas's answer would have been that what initiates change in bodily parts of an animal is its soul, and this is certainly in process of change: a change which is initiated by things outside the animal that are desirable or to be avoided, by means of the senses (sections 23, 28). (We should notice that such a change brought about in a human being is not entirely a physical change, as the human intelligence is not material.) Our more detailed knowledge of the mechanisms on which this sort of thing depends gives us no reason to doubt this. Thus, even without the Aristotelian picture of one sphere whirling round another, we already have the beginnings of an inter-connected web of things that initiate changes in others in virtue of being in process of change themselves. Aquinas's aim, it is to be remembered, is to prove that there is at least one thing that initiates change in others that is not itself in process of change at all.

We cannot go on to infinity in this line

He pursues this by means of the other premiss, that we cannot go on for ever in such a line of initiators of change and things in process of change. This is supported by three arguments. The first (sections 12–13) depends on the idea that the initiator of change and the process of change must exist simultaneously. This is clearly all right: but then Aristotelian physics seems to come in and insist that an initiator of change must act all the time that the subject of change is in process of change. We do not accept this. Aquinas claims that if something is an initiator of change in virtue of its being itself in process of change, then according to the hypothesis of an endless series of initiators of change which are themselves in process of change we must have an infinite number of initiators of change acting all at once, in a finite time. He regards this as impossible. This argument seems to be genuinely vitiated by the archaic science.

But the second and third arguments in favour of the principle — which, as he points out, are the same argument running in opposite directions — look a little better (sections 14 – 15). They are also the same argument as he uses in the *Summa theologiae*: that if each process of change in the whole series is derivative — if it is initiated by something which initiates change in virtue of being in process of change itself — then the whole system of processes of change, however long it may be, is only derivatively an initiator of change. That is, it only initiates change in virtue of being itself in process of change. So the same question arises for the whole system as for any part of it: why is it in process of change? We must then postulate some initiator of change that is not itself in process of change: some first initiator of change, as Aquinas says. To say that a system of derivative initiators of change is not itself derivative — which is the only other way out — is surely absurd.

It should be clear that this argument does not depend, as Kenny suggests, on an ambiguity in 'first', a confusion between 'temporally prior' and 'uncaused'. In Borges's story 'A lottery in Babylon' the whole state is involved in a massively complex lottery which affects all aspects of life and doles out penalties as well as prizes. This gives the Babylonians a beneficial sense of terror and apprehension in their everyday life. But, Borges claims towards the end, everything is submitted to the lottery; even the working-out of the penalties or prizes. You may win a death sentence: but there are then innumerable drawings of the lottery to determine the manner of death, in all its details, the list of possible executioners, the date . . . and in many of these drawings one possible outcome is the revoking of the original sentence. Thus nothing in fact is ever carried out as the result of drawings of the lottery — except, of course, other drawings. Are we to believe that the Babylonians will really be kept by this means in a beneficial state of apprehension? No doubt opinions will be divided on this, as they are divided on whether there is a God.

Aquinas then goes on to show that it is not true that every initiator of change is so in virtue of being itself in process of change: thus that there is something that initiates change without being itself in process of change (sections 21 – 7). This argument, again, depends on the notion of physical change. Hence its immediate conclusion is not to the existence of God, but to the existence of Aristotle's unmoved heaven: the intelligence of the outermost sphere of the material universe, that is not in process of physical change but initiates change of place in its own sphere and all the lower spheres (section 27). It does so out of love of God: this change is not a physical one (section 28). It is important to notice that St Thomas finds the Aristotelian cosmology a positive handicap here, as he himself points out. We have no tendency to take the unmoved heaven seriously, so we should be able to conclude more immediately to the existence of God (section 32).

The nature of God

The fact that there is one is not all we can know about God. Although a complete knowledge of God's nature is impossible to acquire in this life, we can gain some understanding of it by seeing what are the defects in created things that must be denied to it, and what are the perfections in created things that must be attributed to it in a super-eminent degree. We find, then, that the divine nature must be altogether simple: there can be no division or composition in it. Thus there can be only one God: in contemporary terms, for any x and for any y, if x is God and y is God, then x is the same God as y. This leaves open the possibility of there being an x and a y that are both one and the same God, but not one and the same person. Aquinas naturally wants to leave this possibility open, as his faith tells him that there are three different persons that share in the unique divine nature. But he claims that philosophy can tell us nothing about whether this possibility is realised.

Naturally, also, God has no accidents: God is not composed of form and matter: there is no distinction between God's essence and powers and God's activities, nor any distinction between God's activities. God's thought is the same activity as God's love, and both are the same as God's existence. The different terms we use to express this reflect distinctions in our manner of thought, not in God. Lastly, and most famously, there is not even any distinction between God's essence, that in virtue of which God is what God is, and the act of existence in virtue of which God exists. God just is God's own act of existence: in all creatures, even nonmaterial ones, we can make this distinction which we are denying of God.

God and the world

God made the world and keeps it in being: or perhaps one should say that God is continually making the world. There is no difference between the act by which God first created the world long ago in time, and the act by which God continues to keep the world in being. The world is something that God is doing, rather than something that God has made. This is one reason why Aquinas is not bothered by the fact that he thinks that there is no philosophical reason to suppose that the world began in time, rather than has been going on for ever. Even if the world were eternal — as Aquinas's faith teaches that it is not — that would not take away the world's dependence on God for its existence from moment to moment. Aquinas's proofs of the existence of God have nothing to do with a claim that some time, long ago, the chain of causes in this world had a start: he does not think that philosophy can tell us anything about this.

From the fact that the world is something that God is doing follows God's providential care of the world. Nothing can happen in the world that God is not aware of, and does not in some sense desire, since nothing can happen in the world without God in some sense bringing it about. This thought has important consequences in the field of practical ethics, as Aquinas is aware.

Passage 7: The existence of God

The *Summa contra gentiles* is quite an early work of Aquinas's. The early parts of it probably date from around 1258–9, and it was written in Paris. The reasons for choosing this passage, rather than the much better-known parallel at *Summa theologiae* I q.2 a.3, are explained in the introduction to this section.

Summa contra gentiles, Book I, chapter 13 (commentary: Marietti, sections 81–115)

Arguments to prove that God exists.

1. Now that we have shown that it is not pointless to try to give a demonstration of God's existence, let us give the arguments with which both philosophers and doctors of the universal Church have proved that he exists.

2. First we will give the arguments that Aristotle used to prove the existence of God. He tries to prove it from the process of physical change, in two different ways.

3. The first is this: everything that is in process of change has that change initiated in it by something else. Now it is clear to the senses that some things are in process of change; for example, the sun. So they have change initiated in them by something else that initiates it.

Now, that which initiates this process of change is itself either in process of change or not. If it is not, then we have reached the desired conclusion, which is that there is something that initiates change without itself being in process of change. This is what we call God.

But if it is itself in process of change, then this change is initiated in it by something else. So we must either go on to infinity in this line, or come to something that initiates change without itself being in process of change. But we cannot go on to infinity in this line, so we must posit some first initiator of change that is not itself in process of change.

4. In this proof there are two propositions which themselves stand in need of proof, namely 'everything that is in process of change has that change initiated in it by something else' and 'we cannot go on to infinity in this line of initiators of change and things in process of change'.

5. The Philosopher proves the first of these in three ways. The first is this: if something initiates its own process of change, it must have in itself an originating principle of its process of change. If not, then clearly its process of change would be initiated by something else. Also this should be an initiation of a process of change in a primary sense: i.e. the process of change should be initiated in virtue of the thing itself, not in virtue of some part of it; [i.e. *not*] as the change of place of an animal is initiated by a change of place initiated in its foot. In this case, it is not the whole which has its change initiated by itself, but rather one part that has its change initiated by another part. The thing in question should also be a divisible [i.e. material] whole, and have parts. Everything that is in process of physical change is divisible, as is proved in the sixth book of the *Physics* [234b10 – 20].

6. On this basis he argues as follows. That which is put in process of change by itself is something that is in process of change in a primary sense [see section 5, above]. So when one part of it ceases to be in process of change, then the whole of it does. This is because if, when one part of it ceased to be in process of change, another part continued to be in a process of change, then the whole would not be something whose process of change is initiated in a primary sense; rather it would be the part which continues in process of change while the other part ceases that would be that whose process of change is initiated in a primary sense. This is because nothing that

ceases to be in process of change when something else does initiates its own process of change: if its ceasing follows from the ceasing of something else, then its changing follows from the changing of something else, and so it does not initiate its own change. So the thing that is supposed to initiate its own process of change does not do so: so necessarily everything that is in process of change has that change initiated in it by something else.

7.   It is not an objection to this argument to say that the thing which is supposed to initiate its own process of change cannot have one part whose change ceases, or to say that a part is in process of change or ceases to be in process of change only in a coincidental sense (as was erroneously suggested by Avicenna). The force of the argument is that if a thing initiates its own change in a primary sense and in its own right, and not in virtue of its parts, then its process of change should not depend on something else; but the process of change of something divisible depends on that of its parts, just as its existence does. So something divisible cannot initiate its own change in a primary sense and in its own right. For this conclusion to be true you do not have to suppose that 'a part of what initiates a process of change in itself has ceased to be in process of change' is true in an absolute sense: what must be true is this conditional, that *if* the part ceases to be in process of change, the whole ceases to be in process of change. This conditional can be true even if the antecedent is impossible, just as the following conditional is true: 'If human beings are donkeys, then they are irrational'.

8.   He proves it in a second way by induction [by eliminating all the different species of change] as follows. That which is in process of change in a coincidental sense does not initiate its own process of change, since it is in process of change because something else is. Nor does what is in process of change through force or violence initiate its own process of change: this is obvious. Nor do things that are in process of change by nature, (e.g. things whose change is initiated from inside them such as animals): they clearly have their processes of change initiated by the soul. Nor, again, do things that are in process of change by nature in the way that heavy and light things are: these have their processes of change initiated by what brings them into existence and what removes obstacles [to their change]. But everything that is in process of change is so either in its own right or in a coincidental sense. If it is in process of change in its own right, then it is in process of change either through force or by nature. If by nature, then either it has its change initiated from inside, as the animal has, or not, as heavy and light things have. So everything that is in process of change has that change initiated in it by something else.

9.   The third way of proving it is as follows. One and the same thing is never in actuality and in potentiality with respect to the same characteristic. But everything that is in process of change is in

potentiality in so far as it is in process of change, since process of change is 'the actuality of something that is in potentiality in so far as it is in potentiality'. But everything that initiates change is in actuality in so far as it initiates change: nothing acts except in so far as it is in actuality. So nothing both initiates change and is in process of change with respect to the same process of change.

10. You should be aware, though, that when Plato said [in the *Phaedrus*] that everything that is in process of change has its change initiated by something else, he was using 'process of change' in a wider sense than did Aristotle. Aristotle took it in the sense of 'the actuality of something that is in potentiality in so far as it is in potentiality', and this applies only to divisible things and bodies, as he proves in the sixth book of the *Physics* [234b10–20]. But according to Plato that which initiates its own process of change is not a body: he took 'process of change' to mean any performance, so that thinking and having an opinion would be processes of change. Aristotle touches on this way of speaking in the third book of the *De anima* [?431a7]. This is why he said that the first initiator of change initiates its own change because it thinks of itself and wants or loves itself. This is not totally contrary to the arguments of Aristotle: there is no difference between getting back to some first thing that first initiates change in itself, as Plato did, and getting back to some first thing that is not subject to any change, as Aristotle did.

11. Aristotle proves the other proposition, 'we cannot go on to infinity in this line of initiators of change and things in process of change', by three arguments.

12. The first is as follows. If we do go on to infinity in this line of initiators of change and things in process of change then there must be an infinite number of bodies of this kind, since everything that is in process of change is a divisible body, as he proves in the sixth book of the *Physics* [234b10–20]. But every body that initiates a process of change in something that is in process of change is itself in process of change while it is initiating the process of change. So all this infinite number of bodies would be in process of change while any of them is. But any one of them, being finite, is in process of change during a finite time; so an infinite number of them are in process of change in a finite time. But this is impossible: so it is impossible that we should go on to infinity in this line of initiators of change and things in process of change.

13. He proves that it is impossible that the infinite number of things mentioned above should all be in process of change in a finite time as follows. That which initiates a process of change and that which is in process of change have to co-exist in time. (He proves this by induction from each of the different kinds of change.) But bodies can only co-exist in time if they co-exist over a period or at a point of time. But since all the initiators of change and things in process of

change that we are talking about are bodies, as we have proved, then they have to be like one single thing in process of change over a period of time or at a point of time. So one infinite being would be in process of change over a finite time, and this is impossible, as is proved in the sixth book of the *Physics* [238a32 – b16].

14.   The second argument to prove the same point is the following. In things that initiate change and are in process of change that form an ordered series — i.e. such that one thing in the series has its process of change initiated by another in order — we must find that if you take away the first initiator of change, or if it ceases to initiate change, then none of the rest will initiate change or be in process of change. This is because the first is the cause of the initiation of change of all the rest. But if there is an ordered series of things initiating changes and in process of change that goes on for ever, there will be no first initiator of change: they will all be mediate initiators of change. So none of the others can be in process of change, so nothing will be in process of change in the world.

15.   The third proof comes to the same thing, except that the order is reversed, i.e. he starts from the top end. It goes as follows. That which initiates change in another as an instrument of something else cannot initiate any change unless there is something that initiates change in a [non-instrumental,] principal way. But if we go on for ever in a series of initiators of change and things in process of change, then all the initiators of change will be like instrumental initiators of change, since we have assumed that they are initiators of change that are themselves in process of change, and there will be nothing that initiates change in a principal way. So nothing will be in process of change.

16.   So it is clear that both propositions that were used in the first way of demonstration — which Aristotle uses to prove that there is a first unchanged initiator of change — are proved.

17.   The second way is the following. If everything that initiates change is in process of change, then this proposition is true either in its own right or coincidentally. If it is true coincidentally, then it is not necessary, since things that are true coincidentally are not necessary. So it is a possibility that no initiator is in process of change. But *ex hypothesi*, if it is not in process of change, it is not initiating change, either. So it is a possibility that nothing is in process of change, since if nothing initiates change, nothing is in process of change either. But Aristotle holds that it is impossible that at some time there should be no process of change. So the former was not a possibility, since a false impossibility cannot follow from a false possibility. [That is, 'p and possibly not p' is inconsistent with 'necessarily not p'.] So the proposition 'everything that initiates change is in process of change initiated by something else' is not coincidentally true [but either false or necessarily true].

18.   Also, if two things happen to co-exist coincidentally in one subject, but one of them can be found without the other, it is probable that the other one can be found on its own too. So, e.g., if pale and musical are found in Socrates, and musical without pale in Plato, then it is probable that in some other person you could find pale without musical. If, then initiating change and being in process of change co-exist coincidentally in one subject, and being in process of change is found in something without it initiating change, then it is probable that something initiating change will be found without being in process of change.

It is no counter-example to bring against this a pair in which one depends on the other, because the things we are talking of co-exist coincidentally, not in their own right.

19.   But if the proposition under discussion is true in its own right [not coincidentally], then there also follows an impossible or unsatisfactory conclusion. This is because that which initiates change and is itself in process of change is either in the same kind of process of change as that which it initiates, or in a different kind.

If it is the same kind of process of change, then it will have to be that what initiates qualitative change is in a process of qualitative change, and that what initiates a curing is itself being cured, and what teaches is itself being taught, and indeed being taught the same subject. But this is impossible: the teacher needs to know the subject, while the learner has to be ignorant, so the same person will be in possession of and ignorant of the same knowledge. This is impossible.

But if the initiator of change is in another kind of process of change, e.g. if what initiates qualitative change is in process of change of place, and that which initiates change of place is growing in size, and so on, then since there is a finite number of kinds and types of processes of change, we cannot go on to infinity like this. So there will be some first initiator of change that is not in process of change initiated by something else.

But someone might suggest that the thing turns back on itself, so that when we have gone through all the different kinds and types of processes of change we should go back to the first again. For example, that which initiates change of place is in process of qualitative change, and that which initiates qualitative change is growing, and that which initiates growth is in process of change of place. But this leads to the same conclusion as before: we would have something which initiates change of one kind being in process of change of that kind, though mediately and not immediately.

20.   So we are left with the conclusion that we have to posit some first thing that is not in process of change initiated by anything outside it.

21.   But though we accept this, that there is a first initiator of change that is not in process of change initiated by anything outside it, it does not follow that this first initiator is completely unchanging.

So Aristotle goes on to say that there are two ways in which there can be a first initiator of this kind.

In one way, that first initiator will be completely unchanging. If we grant this, then we have what we set out to prove, i.e. that there is some first initiator of change that is completely unchanging.

In the other way, that first initiator of change will be in process of change, but in a process of change that it itself initiates. This is quite plausible: that which is so-and-so in its own right always comes before that which is so-and-so in virtue of something else. So it is reasonable that among things in process of change the first thing in process of change should have its process of change initiated by itself, not by something else.

22. But, even if we grant this, the same conclusion follows. We cannot say that in the initiator of its own process of change the whole initiates the process of change of the whole: if we did, the former unsatisfactory conclusions would follow, e.g. that someone could be taught and teaching at the same time, and so on for other kinds of change. [Generally, this means that] something could be in potentiality and actuality at the same time, since that which initiates change, in so far as it does initiate change, is in actuality, while that which is in process of change is in potentiality. We are left, then, with the conclusion that one part of it initiates change and the other part is in process of change. So we come to the same thing: that there is some unchanging initiator of change.

And one cannot say that both parts are in process of change, a process initiated in either part by the other; nor that one part initiates change in itself and in the other, nor that the whole initiates change in the part. If one did, the former unsatisfactory conclusions would follow, i.e. that something will be at the same time in process of change and initiating the same kind of process of change, and so that it would be at one and the same time in potentiality and in actuality. Moreover, the whole would not be initiating change in itself in the primary sense, but only in virtue of a part. So we are left with the conclusion that what initiates a process of change in itself must have one part that is unchanging and initiates change in the other part.

23. But in the things which initiate change in themselves that we have around us, i.e. in animals, it is one part, the soul, that initiates change. And though the soul is unchanging in its own right, it is in process of change coincidentally. So Aristotle goes on to show that the part that initiates change in the first initiator of change is not in process of change, either in its own right or coincidentally.

24. The things that initiate change that are around us, i.e. the animals, can cease to exist. So the part in them that initiates change is itself in process of change in a coincidental sense. But the things that initiate change in themselves and can cease to exist need to be brought back to some first initiator of change that goes on for ever. So there must be some initiator of change in that which initiates

change in itself, which is not in process of change either in itself or coincidentally.

25.   So it is clear that according to the view of Aristotle there must be some everlasting thing that initiates change in itself. Now, if the process of change goes on for ever, as he claims, then there must for-ever be coming into existence things that initiate change in them-selves but come into existence and cease to exist. But the cause of this happening forever cannot be any one of the things that initiate change in themselves, because none of them exist all the time. Nor can it be all of them together: firstly, because there are infinitely many of them, and secondly because they do not all exist at the same time. So we are left with the conclusion that there must be something that is forever initiating change in itself, which is forever causing the things that initiate change in themselves down here to come into existence. And so what causes the process of change in this is not in process of change either in itself or coincidentally.

26.   Again, in the things that initiate their own process of change we see that some of them begin to be in process of change on account of some process of change which is not initiated by the animals them-selves: e.g. on account of food being digested or the air changing its quality. The thing which initiates change in itself is here in a process of change that is coincidental. We can gather from this that nothing that initiates change in itself is always in process of change if its initiating part is itself in process of change, either in its own right or coincidentally. The first initiator of change is always initiating change in itself; if it were not, then processes of change could not go on for ever, since every other process of change is caused by the process of change of the first thing that initiates change in itself. So we are left with the conclusion that the first thing that initiates change in itself has its process of change initiated by some change-initiating element that is not itself in process of change either in its own right or coincidentally.

27.   It is no counter-argument to say that the things that initiate change in the lower spheres [of the heavens] are for ever initiating change, but are nevertheless said to be in process of change in a co-incidental sense. This is because they are said to be in process of change in a coincidental sense not under their own proper descrip-tion [as initiators], but under the description of being the things in which they initiate change, and the things in which they initiate change follow on from the process of change in the higher sphere.

28.   But God is not any part of anything that initiates its own process of change: Aristotle goes on to work out in the *Metaphysics* [1072a26 – 30], from a consideration of the change-initiator that is a part of that which initiates its own process of change, that there is another change-initiator that is completely separate, i.e. God. Every-thing that initiates its own change is in a process of change that is

initiated by desire, so the change-initiator that is a part of that which initiates its own change must initiate change on account of something desirable. And this will be higher up in the order of initiating of change, since that which desires is in some senses an initiator of change that is in process of change, while that which is desired is something that initiates change and is not in any process of change. So there must be a first initiator of change that is completely unchanging, and this is God.

29.   There are two weak points about the above arguments. The first is that they presume that processes of change go on for ever, and this is presumed to be false according to the Catholic faith.

30.   The answer to this is that the most effective way to prove the existence of God is to suppose that the world lasts for ever, since if you do suppose this it looks less obvious that there is a God. If the world and the processes of change had a start, then it is clear that you have to suppose some cause to bring them suddenly into existence. Everything that has a sudden start must draw its origin from some starter, since nothing can bring itself from potentiality into actuality or from non-existence to existence.

31.   The second weak point is that in the above arguments we have supposed the existence of a first thing in process of change that initiates its own change, i.e. the heavens. It follows from this that it has a soul, and there are many who would not grant this.

32.   The answer to this is that if we do not suppose that the first initiator of change initiates its own change, then it must have its process of change directly initiated by something completely unchanged. So Aristotle comes to a disjunctive conclusion: i.e. that we either immediately reach a first initiator of change that is separate and unchanging, or we reach something that initiates its own process of change, and from this we get back to some first initiator of change that is separate and unchanging.

33.   The Philosopher gives another way in the second book of the *Metaphysics* [994a1 – 19], to prove that we cannot go on for ever in the series of efficient causes, but must get back to some first cause. This is as follows. In every ordered series of efficient causes the first cause is the cause of the cause in the middle, and the cause in the middle is the cause of the last. It does not matter whether there are many causes in the middle or only one. If you take away a cause, then you take away what it causes. So if you take away the first cause the one in the middle cannot exist. But if there is an infinite series of efficient causes, none of the causes will be first: so all the other causes in the middle will disappear. This is clearly not the case. So we must posit that there is a first efficient cause, which is God.

34.   One can gather another argument from what Aristotle says. In

the second book of the *Metaphysics* [993b21 ff] he says that the things which are true to a higher degree exist to a higher degree as well. In the fourth book of the *Metaphysics* [1008b31 – 1009a5] he shows that there is something true to the highest degree, from the fact that we see that of two falsehoods one is falser, and so the other is truer. And it is truer by being nearer to what is true in the highest degree, true without qualification. We can conclude further from this that there is something which exists in the highest degree, and this is what we call God.

35.   On this point Damascene brings in another argument which comes from the government of the world. The Commentator hints at this too in his commentary on the second book of the *Physics*. It goes as follows. It is impossible for things that are contrary and discordant to agree either always or in the majority of cases without some government, which makes each and every one of them tend to a certain end. But in the world we see that things of different natures agree in one ordering, not every so often or by chance, but always, or in a majority of cases. There must then be something that governs the world by its foresight: and this we call God.

5
Aquinas on Truth, Knowledge and the Mind

An introduction to Aquinas on truth, knowledge and the mind

The transcendentals

In 'An introduction to Aquinas on metaphysics' we linked the explanation of the notions of 'existent in its own right' and 'existent coincidentally' with the notions of 'one and the same in its own right' and 'one and the same coincidentally'. We also drew attention to the connection in St Thomas's mind between truth and existence. St Thomas in fact holds that all these notions — being existent, being one and the same, and being true — are 'convertible'. It is not clear quite what he means by this label. Geach suggests that attention to the metaphor of *convertibile* — i.e. 'turning together' like a train of gears — may be helpful (in 'Ontological relativity and relative identity', in Milton K. Munitz (ed.) *Logic and Ontology*, New York: New York University Press, 1973, p. 288). The metaphor can be applied a long way. St Thomas does not think that these expressions are synonymous: in fact he explicitly denies this, claiming that they apply to what they apply to in different senses, or under different descriptions: *sub diversas rationes* (passage 8, article 1). Many of the objections and counter-objections that he makes to his own doctrine that existence and truth are convertible, in passage 8, article 1, are in fact outright objections to this logical notion, on the part of those who will not admit any middle ground between synonymy and heteronymy: between two words signifying one and the same thing in the same way, or signifying two quite different things.

The matter is complicated by the distinction Aquinas draws at a. 2 ad1 of passage 8, between being convertible *secundum praedicationem*, according to predication, and being convertible *secundum convenientiam*, according to fittingness. There does not seem much more to this distinction than that the former is in some sense stricter convertibility, closer to synonymy, while the latter is looser, and only entails a close correspondence between the two expressions that are 'convertible'.

Be that as it may, it is clear that St Thomas has a point here. Only that which is one and the same thing can be an existent: and only that which is existent can be one and the same. Moreover, the different aspects of each notion turn together too: only that which is one and the same in its own right can be existent in its own right, as we saw above: that which is one and the same thing only coincidentally can only be existent coincidentally. These convertible terms, together with a few others, such as 'thing', 'this something', 'true' and 'good' are called 'transcendentals': they apply indifferently to anything in any of the categories of the existent.

Logical transcendentals and metaphysical transcendentals

It will be remembered that within the notion of the existent Aquinas also distinguished between a metaphysical notion, the actually existent, and a logical one, the existent in the sense of the true. It is very tempting to wonder whether the same distinction between a logical sense, which applies to everything of which one can make a true proposition, and a metaphysical sense, which applies only to actual existents, can be made with regard to all the transcendentals.

It certainly looks as if this distinction can be carried across at least to 'one and the same'. The connections between existence and identity are well known: we alluded to them in 'An introduction to Aquinas on metaphysics' when discussing Aquinas's rejection of the idea that mathematical beings are substances. These connections apply to everything that there is, not merely to actual existents. If there is a dead cat, then it is one and the same dead cat: and likewise, if a dead cat is one and the same dead cat as itself, then there is a dead cat. The same kind of consideration applies to numbers, as we have seen, and to anything else that may be said to exist in the 'existence in the sense of the true' sense. 'No entity without identity', as Quine's slogan has it: and no identity without entity, either.

'Thing' and 'this something' are also clearly logical transcendentals as well as metaphysical ones, provided that we take 'thing' in its more general sense — for it also has a sense in which it means a material individual. Indeed, it is hard to say just how the sense of 'thing' and 'this something' differ from the senses of 'one and the same' and 'existent'. All these terms would be taken, in modern terminology, as formal or topic-neutral: they can apply to any kind of object. We can thus claim that they are logical transcendentals.

When we come to 'true' things begin to be more difficult. The difficulty here, however, is not in claiming that there is a logical transcendental as well as a metaphysical one, but rather in claiming that there is a metaphysical transcendental as well as a logical one. But even before we get to that stage we have another difficulty to face. The transcendentals are thought of as applying to existents of all kinds, or at least, in the case of logical transcendentals, to objects of all kinds. How can a thing — especially if it is not an actual existent — be true? Aquinas gives some kind of an answer in articles 2 and 3 of passage 8. A thing is 'true' in so far as it exists, and is related to some mind: or, by extension, is such as to be related to some mind. That will be true, then, which can be thought of correctly. We can surely begin to understand something of what 'convertibility' means here: a thing cannot be thought of correctly unless it is one and the same existent this something. There may even be a difference here between the true in its own right and the coincidentally true: that which is true in its own right will be expressed by other kinds of word, or at least by other kinds of conception, from that which is true only coincidentally. Aquinas has dealt with the difference between simple and complex expressions, and simple and complex conceptions, in passage 1, *lectio* 4, sections 9–10.

But, even if we grant the validity of the notion of the truth of a thing, we are still faced with the problem of whether there could be a difference between a logical transcendental truth and a metaphysical transcendental truth. Among later Thomists a distinction is made between two notions which they label 'logical truth' and 'metaphysical truth' in the following way: 'logical truth' depends on the relation between a thing and the human mind, in which truth is caused by the thing, and 'metaphysical truth' depends on the relation between the thing and the divine mind. Here the truth of the thing is its correspondence to God's creative idea which brings it into existence. It is not clear at all that this distinction — which is indeed one that Aquinas makes, though not with those labels — is the one we are looking for here. We want a 'logical truth' that is possessed by everything that exists in any way — even numbers, even the dead — while 'metaphysical truth' would be possessed only by actual existents. This search must be left for another occasion.

The transcendental 'good' is even more problematic. Just as 'true' expressed the relation of each and every existent to some mind, 'good' is supposed to express the relation of each and every existent to some will. It is true that 'good' can be said of things in every different category of the existent, just as the other transcendentals can: it is true, as well, that it looks as if we should be able to make sense of the notion of 'the good in its own right' as opposed to 'the good coincidentally'. Also, a thing has to exist and be one thing for it to be good: so we can perhaps divine some reason for making these terms to some extent 'turn together'. Evil, after all, is a privation of some existent that should be there, rather like blindness: up to this point we can make some sense of including it under the transcendentals. But beyond that — when it comes to making a distinction between 'metaphysical' and 'logical' goodness — we are surely lost. We can go no farther here, either.

Nevertheless, we have managed to establish some rationale for these traditional transcendentals, and we succeeded in relating at least the 'logical' forms of some of them with key concepts in contemporary philosophical logic: with existence, identity, truth, and perhaps even reference and definition. These basic concepts of philosophical logic are notoriously said to form part of a 'seamless web': a notion which is close to Aquinas's notion of convertibility. This is surely enough to make us look more favourably on the others: and perhaps, also, to look favourably on their 'metaphysical' parallels, which are of such importance to Aquinas.

This notion of the transcendentals ranges widely in St Thomas's thought: at least from logic to metaphysics, as we have seen. It is also of great importance here, in the theory of truth and knowledge. Aquinas thinks that it is necessary to explain the notion at length when answering the question 'What is truth?'. This is yet another instance of the connectedness of Aquinas's thought. We shall be seeing other examples continually in this essay.

Theory of knowledge

One place in which this connectedness comes out particularly clearly is in Aquinas's theory of knowledge. Aquinas follows Aristotle here in applying the analogy of sense-knowledge: they claim that thought consists in the existence in the thinking subject of a likeness (*species*) of the thing thought of. This is a fairly familiar notion to readers of the ancient philosophers. Also fairly familiar may be the account given of the way in which this comes about. For Aquinas, as for the empiricists, all our thought and knowledge has its origins in our senses: he rejects the notion of innate knowledge. We see or in some other way sense a thing, receiving different sensations from it in our different senses, according to their different natures and capabilities. This is something we have in common with the non-rational animals: as is the fact that we are able to make up out of the diverse information coming from the senses a sense-image (*phantasma*) of what is sensed. This is in virtue of the 'imaging faculty' (*phantasia*), which all sensitive creatures possess. The next step in the process is one that is proper to human beings. Our intellect has two aspects: an aspect in which it is an active power, that effects a change in the information received and collected in the sense-image, and an aspect in which it is a passive power, in which that information so changed is received. The intellect, then, in so far as it is an active power, one that acts on the object of thought, makes the sense-image the object of its consideration (passage 9, article 4).

Aquinas often speaks as if the active intellect abstracts what is intelligible — what can be an object of thought — from the sense-image, and many later Thomists follow him in this. This is rather a crude picture, which makes one inevitably think of the sense-image as being like a walnut, which carries within a useless shell a certain intelligible core or kernel. This picture, in turn, leads us to ask what this intelligible kernel is, what is its nature, and how the devil it got through the barrier of the senses into the sense-image in the first place. All the problems of empiricism begin to loom up.

But there is another, quite different, analogy which Aquinas uses at least as often. This is to compare the active intellect to a light that shines on the sense-image and reveals what is intelligible in it. The analogy is to this extent clear: there is no apprehension of colour where there is no light, and there is no apprehension of the object of thought without this contribution of the active intellect. The intellect, after all, is active in this aspect: it actually modifies the nature of what it is brought to bear on, in a stronger way than the nutcracker modifies the nature of the nut. There is more to it than that, even: Aquinas says that the analogy breaks down in that light is normally thought of as merely revealing the colours of a thing that were already there. There is no parallel for this with the active intellect: it is more like a light that creates the colours which it makes visible. Thus the object of thought is something that is made by the intellect: not something hanging around in the world or the imaging faculty waiting to be picked up. (Compare *S. Th.* I q.79 a.3 ad 2, and I q.85 a.2 ad 3.)

When there is a coloured object in good light, its visual likeness can be received by the eye. So when the active intellect, which is the intellect in so far as it affects the object of thought, has acted in this way on the sense-image, there is an intelligible likeness, a likeness that can be and is thought of. This likeness is received by the intellect as far as it is a passive power, one that is acted on by the object of thought. Aquinas calls this the 'passive intellect' or 'possible intellect', but he warns us against thinking that we have two intellects.

This account of the structure of thought helps Aquinas to explain the important fact that thought is unlimited: that we can think of everything that exists or can exist. The connection lies in the fact that the thought-likeness is non-material. The reasons for this are clear: if the likeness were in any way material, then the intellect which acts on it and is acted on by it would have to be material as well. Hence the 'material characteristics' of the intellect — the way in which the matter of the intellect was qualified — would in some way limit what likenesses can be received. Aquinas, following Aristotle, points out that the eye is a fit recipient for all kinds of colour only in virtue of its being transparent: i.e. its being devoid of all colour. If it were coloured, it would be incapable of receiving, of sensing, the sense-likenesses of all colours. In the same way, the intellect, which can grasp all kinds of material things, whatever their qualifications or conditions may be, cannot itself be qualified in any way in which any material thing is (passage 10). Hence the intellect is non-material: and hence the likenesses which it produces and receives cannot be material either. In such contexts Aquinas frequently appeals to the principle *Quidquid recipitur, ad modum recipientis recipitur*: whatever is received exists in the recipient according to the manner of existing that belongs to the recipient (passage 9, article 4). He would illustrate this principle by using the example of a seal and wax: the form of the seal, in the seal, is hard and durable, while in the wax it is softer and more easily destroyed. It is easy to see how this principle applies at the level of thought.

From the non-materiality of the likeness received in the mind, it follows that it is purely formal. It is the form of a cat, say, not its matter, which is received in the mind. The thought of a cat is precisely the existence of that which makes a cat to be a cat, in a thinking subject. Were the intellect a material being, then an intellect so informed — having this thought — would be a cat, since that which makes my thought of a cat to be a cat is precisely the same form which makes a cat a cat. Since, however, the form is received in a non-material subject, it is received 'according to the manner of existence of the recipient': in a non-material way. It is said to exist with 'intentional existence', *esse intentionale*: the manner of existence of an object of thought.

The form I receive in my intellect, then, when thinking of Ludo the cat, the form in virtue of which my thought is the thought of a cat, is the very form in virtue of which Ludo is a cat. It is not, however, the form as made individual in Ludo: the form in my mind is made individual only by its occurrence in me, with this different non-material or 'intentional' manner of existence. Thus when my thought has a match (*adaequatio*) with the world, it is in virtue of two different individualisations of the same form, in two different subjects, with two different manners of existing (passage 7, article 1).

Theory of truth

Two important corollaries follow from this. One is that St Thomas manages to avoid the stock objection to what is called the 'correspondence' theory of truth. Many philosophers have held — with, probably, the mass of mankind — that a thought is true when it corresponds to what is in the world. The stock objection to this is that it involves an infinite regress: if thought and reality are to correspond, we need to be able to compare them. Since a thought and a thing cannot be put out before us as two bank-notes can, we can only effect this comparison by means of a medium. But this must itself be a thought: so we need to compare this mediate meta-thought with the world again, in order to establish the correspondence . . . and so on. Very often, the way to avoid an infinite regress is to dodge taking the first step: and this is what Aquinas manages to do here. There is no question of there being a correspondence of two disparate things, an object and a representation: the object thought of and the thought just are the same form in different subjects and different manners of existing.

Thought and individuals

The second corollary is that thought is essentially universal. The thought to which seeing Ludo first gives rise is a thought of a cat, not of Ludo. It is true that my awareness of the form of a material thing — which is, as we have seen, the presence in the mind, in the appropriate manner, of that form — is an awareness of the form of a material thing *as* the form of a material thing (passage 9, article 4). Aquinas's example in this context is that knowing what snubness is entails knowing that it is a quality of noses. But though my thought of a cat is a thought of a material thing, it is not a thought of this material thing, this cat, Ludo. (We see from passage 9, article 5 that when we think of a human being we are not thinking of *this* matter.) To become a thought of Ludo, Aquinas tells us, the thought has to be put in the context of the sense image, by a 'turning-back' or 'turning again' to that sense-image (*conversio ad phantasmata* or *reflexio ad phantasmata*). This important concept is dealt with rather sketchily (passage 9, article 5). Some, as a result, have thought that we cannot be thinking of an individual cat without having a sense-image of the cat present to our imagination. This seems implausible, or downright mistaken. This *conversio* is supposed to be an operation of the intellect, not a concomitant operation of the imagination. We should rather fill out this notion in some such way as the following.

What makes a thought of Ludo a thought of Ludo and not just a thought of a cat is its being a thought of, say, the one-and-only cat I saw with such-and-such coloration in such-and-such a place at such-and-such a time. This gives us a perfectly good thought of Ludo, though it is one specified in general terms. It is also clearly produced by an intellectual activity: no image need be arising in us when we have this thought. The thought of a black and white cat need be accompanied by no image at all. Nevertheless, the information from which we produce this thought comes from our sense-image of Ludo at some time that we saw him. We have to have returned at some time and in some way to a consideration of our sensing of Ludo, as presented to us in our sense-image. This, it is suggested, is a perfectly possible account of producing a thought of an individual by a turning-back or reflecting on our sense-image.

This is not, for Aquinas, the only way in which our intellect comes to grips with the individual. We act in virtue of our intellect as well as merely thinking. He claims that the way in which our intellect comes to grips with individuals that it wants to affect is in virtue of another faculty, allied to the imaging faculty, and, like it, common to us and to the brute animals (passage 9, article 5). This faculty is called the *cogitativa* or 'cogitative' faculty: the faculty in virtue of which, for example, the pig is more intelligent than the horse. Other translations are 'animal intelligence' or 'instinct': though both are more normal English than 'cogitative faculty' both are perhaps more misleading than the simple transverbalisation. It is impossible here to enter into a discussion of Aquinas's views on this.

In this discussion the systematic and connected nature of Aquinas's thought has again been made plain. It is not merely that his theory of knowledge depends on his metaphysical doctrines on form and matter. This theory of knowledge fits perfectly with his essentialist, non-empiricist point of view. The great challenge of the empiricists to the conception of essence is an epistemological one: it consists in asking how we can be aware of essences, since there is nothing of the kind to be observed with the senses. Aquinas's answer to this problem is not a complete one, but it is surely a correct sketch of what a complete answer should be like.

The same attitude of mind also goes to explain the interest Aquinas, like Aristotle, shows in his logic in unquantified propositions such as 'The human being is rational'. This is supposed to hold good of every human being, but it is not about every human being: it is about any human being in so far as he or she is a human being: or, if you like, about human nature. This is also the reason why the system of the syllogism has more value than that which Russell, for example, was willing to attribute to it. Russell claimed that 'All human beings are mortal; Socrates is a human being; ergo Socrates is mortal' was uninformative, since in order to know the truth of the premiss 'All human beings are mortal' we would have had to have ascertained that all human beings, including Socrates, were mortal: hence the conclusion of the syllogism has to be known before the first premiss can be. The doctrine that forms or natures are more immediately the objects of intellectual awareness than are individuals begins to make sense of the syllogism.

Truth and propositions

Though a thought-likeness in the mind can match — or, indeed, fail to match, as in the case of the thought of a chimaera — the form of some existing thing in the real world, nevertheless Aquinas holds that truth and falsity are not to be found in merely having a thought of something (passage 8, article 3). The thought of a cat is not true, nor the thought of a chimaera false, as such. It is only in the next operation of the mind, that of forming a proposition, that truth and falsehood first properly arise. This operation Aquinas calls 'the operation of composing and dividing' as opposed to the operation of 'simple apprehension'. By this operation — which is again clearly non-material — we put together a subject and a predicate. It is not till we put together the thought of a cat and the thought of being on the mat, say, that we get something true or false.

The imperishability of the soul

Though St Thomas frequently speaks about 'the will' or 'the intellect', he also frequently warns us against taking this kind of form of words too literally. It is not the intellect that thinks, or the will that desires, but the human being that thinks in virtue of his or her intellect, that desires in virtue of his or her will. This is of importance when considering the soul. Aquinas thinks that there is survival of some human powers and activities after the death of the human being. He does not, incidentally, think that philosophy can show that a person can survive death — this would be on the face of it absurd. He explicitly says that the soul is not the self, 'my soul is not I' (*Commentary on I Corinthians*, 15). It is true, though, that he does think that God will bring it about that human beings will live again. But this belief is a purely supernatural one, based on God's promises.

However, between a person's death and resurrection there is not merely a hiatus: thought, at least, continues. This looks inconsistent with his repeated claim that it is not the intellect or the soul that thinks, but the human being, i.e. a certain animal: how he resolves this problem can be seen in the text from the disputed question *De anima* which is collected below (passsage 10). The argument here is fairly straightforward, and can be left to the reader without much in the way of introduction. It is interesting that he starts out with a recapitulation of Plato's final argument for the immortality of the soul in the *Phaedo*, that what brings existence with it cannot cease to exist. Aquinas believes that this is so in a strict sense: the soul, even of animals, cannot properly speaking cease to exist: it is the animal that ceases to exist. But the soul can cease to exist 'in a relative sense': if it has no activities of its own, then its only existence is that of the animal that it makes such-and-such a lump of matter to be. The crucial claim is that the human being has activities that are not the activities of this body: hence we must attribute them to the soul as their subject. Since activity follows on existence, as we mentioned in the section on Aquinas's metaphysics, that which has activities of its own must have some kind of existence of its own. Hence it can be alleged that it is at least possible that the soul, after death, is a 'this something' with its own existence.

It is clear that the most powerful objections to this argument are those — which Aquinas himself brings — which allege that there are no human activities which cannot be attributed to this body. The claim that there is no thought without images is an example (objection 14). Another difficulty for Aquinas rests on a point of some historical importance. Earlier and contemporary Aristotelians, especially those who looked to Averrhoes, had come to the conclusion that since the intellect was non-material it could not be a power of an individual animal. In each human being, then, the non-material agent intellect was one and the same: God's own intellect, or some created angelic intellect, acting in us. This view was strongly opposed by St Thomas, among other reasons because it would make impossible the continuance of an individual's thought after death, which is what he is trying to defend here.

Passage 8: Truth

The *Quaestio disputata de veritate* is again an early work of Aquinas's, dating from his mastership in Paris. The first question was disputed in the academic year 1256–7. *Quaestiones disputatae* were an academic exercise in the university, in which the students raised difficulties which were partly answered by the bachelor, and finally determined by the master. In the first of these articles we can see that arguments are offered both for and against the thesis that the true and the existent are identical, and some of the bachelor's counter-arguments are recorded.

De veritate, question 1, articles 1 – 3

Article 1

The first question is, what is truth?
It seems that the true is wholly identical with the existent.

1. For Augustine in his book *Soliloquy* says that 'the true is that which is'. But that which is is the existent. So 'true' signifies just the same as 'existent'.

2. But it was said that the true and the existent are the same in the thing referred to, but different as regards their descriptions, [according to the way they are described]. Against this it was objected that the description of a thing is that which is signified by its definition. But 'that which exists' is given by Augustine as the definition of the true, after he has rejected a number of other definitions. Since, then, the existent and the true coincide according to the description 'that which exists', they do not differ as regards their descriptions.

3. Moreover, when two things are different as regards their descriptions, they are related in such a way that the one can be thought of without the other. This is why Boethius says in the *De hebdomadibus* that God's existence can be thought of, if it is separated a little by the intellect from his goodness. But the existent can in no way be thought of if it is separated from the true, since it is thought of precisely in so far as it is true. So the true and the existent do not differ according to different descriptions.

4. Moreover, if the true is not the same as the existent, it must be a qualification of the existent. But it cannot be a qualification of the existent. It is not a qualification that completely destroys its subject, otherwise we would get 'This is true, therefore it is not an existent', just as we get 'This is a dead human being, therefore this is not a human being'. Likewise, it is not a qualification that diminishes its subject, or 'Therefore it exists' would not follow from 'This is true', just as 'Therefore he is white' does not follow from 'He is white of tooth'. Nor is it a qualification that contracts or specifies the existent: if it were, it would not be convertible with the existent. Therefore the true and the existent are wholly identical.

5. Moreover, things that are qualified in the same way are the same. But the true and the existent are qualified in the same way; therefore they are the same. It says in the second book of the *Metaphysics*: 'The way a thing is qualified with regard to existence is the same as the way it is qualified with regard to truth' [993b30]. So the true and the existent are identical.

6. Moreover, things that are not identical differ in some respect. But there is no respect in which the true and the existent differ: they do not differ in essence, as the existent is true by its essence, nor by any other specific differentiation, because then they would have to fall together under some kind. So they are identical.

7. Moreover, if they were not identical, then the true would have

to add some specification to the existent. But the true adds no specification to the existent: it is rather wider than the existent. As the
Philosopher says in the fourth book of the *Metaphysics*, 'When we
define the true we say that what exists exists, and what does not exist
does not exist' [1011b25 ff]. Hence the true includes the existent and
the non-existent. So the true does not add any specification to the
existent, and so they seem to be entirely identical.

But against this:

1. Useless repetition is futile. So if the true were identical with
the existent, it would be futile to say 'true existent'. This is not so: so
they are not the same.

2. Moreover, the existent and the good are convertible terms.
But the true and the good are not convertible: some things are true
which are not good, e.g. that so-and-so is a fornicator. So the true
and the existent are not convertible terms either.

3. Moreover, Boethius says in the *De hebdomadibus*, 'In all
creatures there is a difference between existence and that which
exists'. But the true follows the existence of things: so the true is
different from that which exists, in creatures. But that which exists is
the same as the existent: so the true in creatures is different from the
existent.

4. Moreover, things that are related as primary and secondary
must be different. But that is how the true and the existent are: for as
it says in the *Liber de causis*, the first of created things is existence.
And Averroes says, commenting on the same book, 'Everything else
is said to exist by being informed by the existent'. Hence everything
is secondary to the existent. So the true and the existent are different.

5. Moreover, things that are said alike of that which causes and
that which is caused are more united in the cause than in the caused.
This is especially the case when comparing God with creatures. But
there are 'appropriations' made within God of the set of four:
existent, one, true, and good. Existent belongs to God's essence, one
to the Father, true to the Son, good to the Holy Spirit. But the divine
persons are different not only as regards their description, but also in
reality, which is why one is not predicated of the other. So *a fortiori*
these four should differ in creatures more widely than as regards
their description.

My answer: we must reply that we must bring the investigation of
what something is back to some principles that are known by the
intellect in their own right, just as we should in a demonstration.
Otherwise the investigation would go on *ad infinitum*, as the demonstration would, and we would thus lose all scientific knowledge, and
all acquisition of an awareness of reality.

What the intellect grasps as most obviously known, and what all
conceptions can be brought down to, is the existent, as Avicenna says
at the start of his *Metaphysics*. So all other conceptions of the intellect
must be grasped by specifying the existent. But one cannot specify
the existent by means of something of a different nature to it, in the
way in which the specific difference specifies the genus, or the
accident specifies the subject. This is because every nature is

essentially existent. Hence the Philosopher in the third book of the *Metaphysics* proves that the existent cannot be a genus [998b21]. Things are said to specify the existent by expressing some mode [or sense] of the existent which the word 'existent' does not express.

This can be done two ways. In the first way, the mode which is expressed is some special mode of the existent. For there are different degrees of existence, and it is according to these that the different modes of existing are taken. It is according to these modes that the different genera of things are taken. 'Substance', for example, does not specify the existent by any specific difference, which would signify some nature that specified the existent; rather the word 'substance' expresses a special way of existing, namely being an existent in its own right. And so on for the other categories.

Another way is this: the mode which is expressed is a mode which follows in general on any kind of existent. This can be taken two ways, either as something which follows on any existent taken in its own right, or as something that follows on any existent in so far as it is related to something else.

In the first of these two ways the sense is that something in an existent is expressed either affirmatively or negatively. But there is nothing that is said affirmatively, without any regard to anything else, which can be taken to be in every existent, except for its essence. It is according to its essence that something is said to exist. So it is in this way that we apply the name 'thing', which differs from 'existent' in this (as Avicenna says in the second book of his *Metaphysics*): that 'existent' derives from the act of existence, while the name 'thing' rather expresses the essence of an existent. The kind of negation, on the other hand, which follows on every existent without regard for anything else, is the negation of distinction: this is expressed by the name 'one and the same'. Nothing else is one and the same except an existent which is undistinguished from itself.

But if the mode of the existent is taken in the second of these ways, i.e. as it is related to something else, this can be done in two ways.

The first way is according to the distinction of one thing from another. This is expressed by the name 'something'. The name means something like 'some other thing': so just as the existent is called 'one and the same' in so far as it is undistinguished from itself, so it is called 'something' in so far as it is distinguished from other things.

The other way is according to the fitting of one thing with another. There cannot be this fitting unless we take something which fits every existent by its own nature. The soul is like this: in some way it is all things, as it says in the third book of the *De anima* [431b20].

But in the soul there are two powers, of awareness and of desire. The way the existent fits the desire is expressed by this name 'good', as we read in the first book of the *Ethics*: 'The good is that which all things desire' [1094a2]. The way the existent fits the intellect is expressed by the name 'true'. Awareness of a thing is brought to completion by the likening of the one who is aware to the thing that he or she is aware of. That is why 'likening' [*assimilatio*] is called the cause of awareness: it is the same as the way in which the sight senses colour through being qualified by the likeness [*species*] of colour.

The first relation of the existent to the intellect, then, is that the existent should correspond to the intellect. This correspondence is called the *matching* [*adaequatio*] of thing and intellect. The description of the true is met in a strict sense here. So this is how 'true' specifies 'existent', namely, by adding the conformity or match of thing and intellect; and, as we have said, awareness of a thing follows on from this conformity. So the existence of a thing, and what it is, is prior to its being described as 'true': but awareness of a thing is a sort of effect of truth.

According to this, then, there are three definitions of truth and the true which are given.

The first definition is made with regard to that which comes before the description as 'true', and on which the true is based. Hence Augustine's definition in the *Soliloquy*, 'Truth is that which is', and Avicenna's in the eleventh book of the *Metaphysics*, 'The truth of any thing is that property of its existence which is the foundation of the thing'; and somebody's definition 'The true is the lack of distinction between existence and that which exists.' [This definition was one in common use in the schools, but its origin was unknown.]

The second definition is made with regard to the point at which the description of the true is met in a strict sense. Hence Isaac [Israeli] says 'Truth is the match of thing and intellect', and Anselm, in his book *On truth* says 'Truth is the correctness which only the mind can grasp.' 'Correctness' is said here in the sense of a sort of match, according to what the Philosopher says in the fourth book of the *Metaphysics*, 'When we define the true we say that what exists exists, and that what does not exist does not' [1011b25].

The third definition of truth is made with regard to the effect that follows from it. Hilary [of Poitiers] defines it in this way 'The true is what shows and says that which exists'; and Augustine says in the book *On the true religion* that 'Truth is that by which that which is is shown', and later that 'Truth is that by which we judge of lower things.'

So the answer to the first objection is that that definition of Augustine is a definition of the true in the sense of that which has a basis in reality, not in the sense of that by which the description of the true is completely met, in the match of the thing and the intellect. Or we could say that when he says 'The true is that which is' he does not mean 'that which is' in the sense in which it signifies the act of existence, but in the sense in which it is a name for the composed act of intellect, i.e. in which it signifies the affirmation of a proposition. In this way the sense would be 'The true is that which is, i.e. when we say that a thing that exists exists'. So the definition of Augustine would come down to the definition of the Philosopher which we mentioned above.

The answer to the second objection is obvious from what we have already said.

The answer to the third objection is that 'the one can be thought of without the other' can be understood in two ways. One way is that one can be thought of without the other being thought of: and in this sense things which are different as regards their descriptions are related in such a way that one can be thought of without the other. The other way of understanding 'the one can be thought of without the other' is that it can be thought of without the other existing. In this sense the existent cannot be thought of without the true, since the existent cannot be thought of without its corresponding to or matching the intellect. But it is not the case that someone who thinks of the description of the existent must think of the description of the true: just as not everyone who thinks of the existent has to think of the active intellect, though without the active intellect no one can think of anything.

The answer to the fourth objection is that the true is a qualification of the existent, not in the sense of adding some nature, nor in that of expressing some special mode of existing, but as something which is found quite generally in the existent, which, however, is not expressed by the name 'existent'. Hence it does not have to be a qualification which destroys or diminishes or contracts or specifies.

The answer to the fifth objection is that 'the way they are qualified' there is not used in the sense in which a way of being qualified falls under the category of quality, but in the sense of implying some relation. Those things which cause the existence of another are existent to the highest degree, and those things which cause the truth of another are true to the highest degree. From this the Philosopher concludes that the relations of things in the order of existence, and their relations in the order of the truth are the same, i.e. that where you find that which is existent to the highest degree, there you will find that which is true to the highest degree. This does not mean that the existent and the true are the same thing as regards their description, but rather that a thing is naturally apt to match the intellect according to the degree of existence which it has. In this way the description of a thing as 'true' follows on from its description as 'existent'.

The answer to the sixth objection is that the true and the existent differ as regards their descriptions to this extent: there is something in the description of the true which is not in the description of the existent. It is not that there is something in the description of the existent which is not in the description of the true. Nor are they different according to their essence, nor distinguished one from another by opposed specific differences.

The answer to the seventh objection is that the true is not wider than the existent: for 'the existent' in one sense is said of the non-existent, in so far as the non-existent is grasped by the intellect. This is why the Philosopher, in the fourth book of the *Metaphysics*, says that the negation or privation of an existent is said to exist in one sense [1003b10], and why Avicenna also says at the start of his *Metaphysics*, that an indicative sentence can only be about the existent, since that about which a proposition is formed must be grasped by the intellect. Hence it is clear that everything that is true is in some way existent.

The answer to the first remark against the objections is that it is not futile to say 'true existent', since there is something expressed by the name 'true' which is not expressed by the name 'existent'. It is not because they are really different.

The answer to the second is that although it is bad that so-and-so is a fornicator, it has some existence, and so is naturally something that can match the intellect, and so attain to the description of true. Hence this description does not go beyond the description of existent, nor vice-versa.

The answer to the third is that when he says 'there is a difference between existence and that which is' he is distinguishing between the act of existence and that which such an act fits. The description of 'being an existent' is drawn from the act of existence, not from that which the act of existence fits, so the argument does not follow.

The answer to the fourth is that the true is secondary to the existent in that the description of 'true' is different from the description of 'existent' in the way we have explained.

The answer to the fifth is that there are three things wrong with this argument. The first is that although these three persons are really distinct, the things which are appropriated to a person are not different in reality, but only according to the way they are described.

The second is that although the persons are really distinct from one another, they are not really distinct from God's act of existence. Hence the true which is attributed to the person of the Son is not distinct from the existence which belongs to the side of essence.

The third is that even though existent, true, one and good are more united in God than in created things, this does not mean that what is distinct in God according to the way it is described should be really distinct in created things. This [proportionate distinction] can occur in things which do not have it in their description that they are one in reality. An example is power and wisdom: these are one thing in God, but really distinct in creatures. But existent, true, one and good have 'being one and the same thing' as part of their description; so wherever they are found, they are really one, though this real unity may be more complete in the way in which they are united in God than in the way in which they are united in creatures.

Article 2

The second question is, is truth found more principally in the intellect than in things?

Apparently not.

1.   True and existent, as we have said, are convertible terms. But the existent is found more principally outside the mind; so the true is also.

2.   Moreover, things are not in the mind by their essence, but by their likeness, as it is said in the third book of the *De anima* [431b29]. So if the truth were principally to be found in the mind, truth would

not be the essence of a thing but a likening or likeness, and the true would be the likeness of the thing which exists outside the mind. But the likeness of a thing existing in the mind is not predicated of a thing outside the mind, and so is not convertible with it. So true would not be convertible with existent, which is false.

3. Moreover, whatever is in a thing follows on from that which it is in. If, then, truth is principally in the mind, a judgement of truth is according to the estimate of the mind. This brings back the error of the ancient philosophers, who said that anything that anyone may happen to think is true, and that two contradictory statements are true at the same time; and this is absurd.

4. Moreover, if truth is principally in the intellect, then something which belongs to the intellectual grasp of the truth should be put in the definition of the truth. But Augustine rejects such definitions in his book *Soliloquy*, e.g. 'The true is that which is as it is seen to be'. According to this, that which is not seen is not true. This is shown to be false by the tiny stones that are hidden right away in the bowels of the earth. Similarly, he rejects this definition: 'The true is that which is as it seems to the one who is aware, if he wants and is able to be aware'. According to this a thing cannot be true, unless the one who is aware wants and is able to be aware of it. The same argument applies to any other definition in which something that belongs to the intellect is put in. So truth is not principally in the intellect.

But against this, the Philosopher says in the sixth book of the *Metaphysics*, 'There is no true or false except in the mind' [1027b25].

Moreover, truth is the match of thing and intellect. But this match can only occur in the intellect. So there is no truth except in the intellect.

My answer: when something is said of many things in a principal sense and secondary related senses, that of which the common predication is made in the principal sense does not always have to be the cause of the others. It only has to be that in which the description of that common predication is principally found in a complete way. For example, 'healthy' is said principally of an animal, since in an animal the complete description of health is principally found, even though a diet is said to be healthy in so far as it brings about health. So, when 'true' is said of many things with reference to one principal sense, it should be said principally of that in which the complete description of truth is found.

But the correlative of any change is found in the terminus of that movement. The terminus of a change in the power of awareness is in the soul. So that which one is aware of should be in the one who is aware if it according to the manner of existing of the one who is aware of it. The terminus of a change in the power of desiring is in the thing; hence the Philosopher alleges in the third book of the *De anima* that there is a sort of circularity in the acts of the soul, namely, in that the thing which is outside the soul initiates change in the intellect, and the thing which is thought of initiates change in the desire, and then the desire initiates change towards the thing from which this process of change began [433b15 ff].

Now the good, as we said in the last article, implies a relation to the appetite, while the true implies a relation to the intellect. Hence the Philosopher says in the sixth book of the *Metaphysics* that good and bad are in things, while true and false are in the mind [1027b25]. A thing is not said to be true except in so far as it matches the intellect. So the true is found secondarily in things, principally in the intellect.

But you should know that things are related differently to the practical intellect from the way they are related to the speculative intellect. This is because the practical intellect causes things, so it is the measure of the things which come to exist through it. The speculative intellect, on the other hand, receives from things: so it is in some way changed by them, and measured by them. Hence it is clear that the things of nature, from which our intellect receives knowledge, measure our intellect, as it says in the tenth book of the *Metaphysics* [1053a31 ff]. But they are in their turn measured by the divine intellect, in which there is everything that is created, as everything that is made by a craftsman is in his intellect. So the divine intellect measures, and is not measured by anything: natural things measure and are measured: while our intellect is measured by, and does not measure the things of nature; only artificial things.

So the things of nature stand between two intellects, and are said to be true according to their match with either. They are said to be true according to their match with the divine intellect, in so far as they fulfil what is ordained for them by the divine intellect. This is made clear by Anselm in his book *On truth*, and by Augustine in his book *On the true religion*, and by Avicenna in the definition we have mentioned, i.e. that 'The truth of any thing is that property of its existence which is the foundation of the thing'. But they are said to be true according to their match with the human intellect, in so far as they are by nature such as to have a true estimate formed of them. And vice-versa: things are called false which are by nature such as to seem what they are not, or in some way different from what they are, as it says in the fifth book of the *Metaphysics* [1024b22].

The principal description of the truth is more principally in things than is the second, since the relation to the divine intellect comes before the relation to the human intellect. So even if there were no human intellect, things could still be called true in relation to the divine intellect. But if, *per impossibile*, we were to imagine the absence of both kinds of intellect, then the description of things as true would completely disappear.

The answer to the first objection is that, as is clear from what we have said, 'true' is said principally of the intellect, and secondarily of things that match it. Either way the term is convertible with 'existent', but in a different way in either case. In the way in which 'true' is said of things, it is convertible with 'existent' by predication. This is because every existent matches the divine intellect, and can match the human intellect: and vice-versa [i.e. everything which is true, which matches the divine intellect and can match the human intellect, is an existent]. But if we take 'true' as it is said of the intellect, then it is convertible with the existent outside the mind, but in another way: not by predication, but by correspondence: i.e. in so far as to each true act of the intellect there should correspond some existent, and vice-versa [i.e. that every act of the intellect to which some existent corresponds is true].

This also makes the answer to the second objection clear.

The answer to the third objection is that that which is in something does not follow on from that which it is in, except when it is caused by the originating principles of that which it is in. For example, illumination is caused in the air by some outside originating principle, i.e. the sun: so it follows on from the action of the sun rather than the air. In the same way, truth which is caused in the mind by things does not depend on the estimate of the mind, but on the existence of the thing. Just as an expression is said to be true or false according to whether a thing exists or not, the intellect is said to be true or false in the same way.

The answer to the fourth objection is that Augustine is speaking of the vision of the human intellect, and the truth of a thing does not depend on that. For there are many things which our intellect is not aware of; but there is nothing that the divine intellect is not actually aware of, and that the human intellect cannot be aware of. After all, the active intellect is described as that which can make everything, and the passive intellect as that which can become everything. So in the definition of a true thing we can put its actually being seen by the divine intellect, but not its being seen by the human intellect: only its being able to be seen by it. This has been made clear by what we have said.

Article 3

The third question is, does truth exist in the intellect only when it composes and divides?

Apparently not.

1. 'True' is said according to a relation of an existent to the intellect. But the first operation in which the intellect is related to a thing is the operation in which it forms the essences of things [in itself], by conceiving their definitions. So it is in this operation of the intellect that truth is most principally and most properly found.

2. Moreover, the true is the match of a thing and the intellect. But just as the intellect can match things when it composes and divides, so it can when it thinks of the essences of things. So truth does not exist in the intellect only when it composes and divides.

Against this, we have what the sixth book of the *Metaphysics* says: 'true and false are not in things, but in the mind: but as regards simple things, not even what they are is [true] in the mind' [1027b25].

Moreover, in the third book of the *De anima* it says that the thought of indivisible things is among those things in which there is neither true nor false [430a27].

My answer is that just as the true is found in the intellect more principally than it is found in things, so it is more principally found in the act of the intellect that composes and divides than in the act of the intellect that forms the natures of things [in itself].

The description of the true is 'the match of thing and intellect'. Now a thing does not match itself: 'match' is the equating [*aequalitas*] of two different things. Hence the description of true is found in the intellect principally at the point at which the intellect first has something of its own that the thing outside the mind does not have, but which corresponds to it, so we can notice a match between them.

When the intellect forms natures in itself, it has only a likeness of a thing that is outside the mind, just as the senses have when they receive the likeness of a sensible thing. But when it begins to make a judgement on the thing it has grasped, then this judgement of the intellect is something proper to it, which is not found outside in the thing. But when it matches that which is outside in the thing, the judgement is said to be true.

The intellect makes a judgement about the thing it has grasped when it says that something exists or does not exist. This belongs to the intellect when it composes or divides. Hence the Philosopher says in the sixth book of the *Metaphysics* that composing and dividing is something in the intellect, not in things [1027b30]. Hence also truth is principally found in the composing and dividing of the intellect. The true is said to be in the intellect when it forms definitions, in a secondary sense. A definition is said to be true or false in this way: as falling under the description of a true or false composition. For example, when a definition is said to belong to something that it doesn't, as if one were to assign the definition of a circle to a triangle. Or it could be when the parts of a definition cannot be composed one with another; e.g. if we were to define something as an insensible animal: the composition which is here implied, i.e. that some animal is insensible, is false. A definition is said to be true or false only in relation to a composition, just as a thing is said to be true or false in relation to the intellect.

It is clear, then, from what we have said, that 'true' is said principally of the composing or the dividing of the intellect. It is said secondarily of the definitions of things, in so far as a composition which is true or false is implied in them; and it is said in a third sense of things, in so far as they match the divine intellect, or are by nature apt to match the human intellect. In a fourth sense it is said of a human being. Human beings can choose their expressions, which are true or false, or make a true or false estimate of themselves or of others, by the things that they say or do.

Utterances are said to be true in the same way in which the acts of the intellect which they signify are.

To the first objection, then, we have to say that although the formation of a nature is the first operation of the intellect, the intellect does not by this operation have anything of its own which can match the thing. So truth is not there, properly speaking.

This makes clear the reply to the second objection.

Passage 9: Thought and intellect

This question was disputed by St Thomas in the following year, 1257 – 8. A parallel passage in the *Summa theologiae* is to be found at I q. 84, especially 1 and 6, and q. 86 a.1.

De veritate, question 10, articles 4 – 6

Article 4

The fourth question is, is the mind aware of material things? Apparently not.

1.   For the mind is only aware of things by intellectual awareness. But, as it says in the Gloss on *II Corinthians*, 12,2, 'Intellectual vision is that which reaches those things that have no images that are like them, that are not what they themselves are.' Since, then, material things cannot be in the soul in their own right, but only by means of images that are like them, which are not what they are themselves, the mind is apparently not aware of material things.

2.   Moreover, St Augustine says in *Super Genesim ad litteram* that 'We understand by the mind the things that are neither bodies nor the likenesses of bodies.' But material things are bodies, and the likenesses they have are the likenesses of bodies. Ergo, etc.

3.   Moreover, the mind or intellect is able to be aware of the essences of things, because the object of the intellect is what a thing is, as it says in the third book of the *De anima* [?429b16]. But the essence of material things is not bodiliness: for if it were so, then everything that has an essence would be a body. Ergo, etc.

4.   Moreover, every case of the mind's being aware is according to a form, which is the originating principle of awareness. But the thought-of forms that are in the mind are altogether immaterial. So by them the mind cannot be aware of material things.

5.   Moreover, all awareness is by a likening [*assimilatio*]. But there can be no likening between the mind and material things, because a likeness [*similitudo*] is made by qualities' being one and the same. Now the qualities of bodily things are bodily accidents, and these cannot be in the mind. Ergo, etc.

6.   Moreover, the mind is aware of things only by abstracting from matter and from the characteristics of matter. But material things which are natural cannot be separated from matter even in the way that they are thought of, because matter comes into their definitions. Ergo, etc.

But against this: the mind is aware of the things that are part of natural science. But natural science is about material things. Ergo, we can be aware of material things through our mind.

Moreover, everyone judges well of what they are aware of, and are the best judges of these things, as it says in the first book of the *Ethics*

[1094b23]. But, as St Augustine says in the twelfth book of *Super Genesim ad litteram*, it is by the mind that we judge of things here below. Ergo, we think of material things here below with our mind.

Moreover, through the senses we are aware of material things only. But the awareness of the mind has its origin in the senses. Ergo, the mind too is aware of material things.

My answer is that we must say that all awareness is according to some form, which is the origin of awareness in the one who is aware. Now, this kind of form can be thought of in two ways: first, according to its existence in the one who is aware, and second, according to its relation to the thing whose likeness it is.

According to the first aspect it makes the one who is aware to be actually aware; but according to the second aspect, it determines the awareness towards something determinate of which one can be aware. So the manner of being aware of something is according to the characteristics of the one who is aware, in whom the form is received according to his own manner of existence. But the thing of which someone is aware does not have to exist in the manner of the one who is aware, or according to the manner in which the form (which is the originating principle of awareness) exists in the one who is aware. So there is no obstacle to being aware of material things by means of forms that exist in an immaterial manner in the mind.

This can be different in the human mind, which gets its awareness from things, and in the divine or angelic mind, which get nothing from things.

In the mind of one who gets knowledge from things, the forms exist in virtue of things' acting in some way on the soul. But every acting is in virtue of a certain form: so the forms in our mind have reference to things which are outside the soul first and foremost with regard to their forms.

There are two kinds of form here. Some are such that they do not determine any matter for themselves, e.g. lines, surfaces, etc.; others determine a special matter for themselves, such as all the natural forms.

The awareness of forms which determine no matter for themselves does not leave any awareness of matter. But the awareness of the forms that do determine a matter for themselves, does give rise to an awareness even of the matter itself, in some way. This awareness is in virtue of the disposition the matter has to the form. This is why the Philosopher says in the first of the *Physics* that first matter can be known in virtue of its analogy to form [191a9]. And in this way one can be aware of material things, in virtue of the likeness of their form; just as someone is aware of a snub nose in virtue of being aware of snubness.

But the forms that exist in the divine mind are what the existence of things flows from, and this existence is common to both form and matter. So those forms have reference to both form and matter immediately, not one in virtue of the other.

It is the same for the forms in the intellect of an angel, which are

136

like the forms in the divine mind, although they do not cause things to exist.

So in this way our mind has an immaterial awareness of material things. But the divine mind and the angelic mind are aware of material things in a more immaterial and more complete way.

The answer to the first objection, then, is that the authority cited can be explained in two ways.

In one way, it refers to intellectual vision with regard to the fact that everything can be grasped by it, and so it says 'Intellectual vision is only of those things that have no images that are like them, that are not what they themselves are.' It does not mean the images by which things are seen in intellectual vision, which are a sort of medium of awareness; it means that what one is aware of by intellectual vision are the things themselves, not their images. This does not happen in bodily vision (i.e. sense-vision) or spiritual vision (i.e. the imagination).

For the objects of the imagination and of the senses are certain accidents, from which some outline or image of the thing is set up, while the object of the intellect is the very essence of the thing. It is true that the intellect is aware of the essence of a thing by means of its likeness, but this likeness is a sort of medium of awareness, not an object on which the vision of the intellect is principally bent.

The other way is for us to say that what is said by the authority cited is something that belongs to intellectual vision with reference to the extent to which the intellectual vision goes beyond the vision of the senses or the imagination. Augustine, from whose words the Gloss is taken, means to point out the specific differences of each of these three kinds of vision, and to attribute to the higher vision what goes beyond the lower. Hence he says that spiritual vision [imagination] is when we think of absent things by means of some likenesses. All the same, there is also spiritual or imaginative vision of the things that are seen when they are present; but the imagination goes beyond the senses in that it can also see absent things. So he puts that in as a sort of inseparable property of imagination.

In the same way, intellectual vision goes beyond both imagination and the senses, since it extends to those things that are by their nature objects of thought. So Augustine attributes this to intellectual vision as a sort of inseparable property, even though it can also be aware of material things, which we can be aware of through their likenesses. That is why he says in the twelfth book of *Super Genesim ad litteram* that 'Also by our mind we both judge of things here below, and know the things that are neither bodies nor make forms that are like bodies.'

This makes clear the answer to the second objection.

The answer to the third objection is that if bodiliness is thought of as derived from the body in so far as it is something in the category of quantity, then bodiliness is not the essence of a natural thing, but an accident of it, namely, its three dimensions. But if it is derived from the body in so far as it is something in the category of substance, then 'bodiliness' does name the essence of a natural thing. But it does not follow that every essence is bodiliness, unless we were to say that being bodiliness corresponds to being an essence, precisely as such.

The answer to the fourth objection is that although there are only immaterial forms in the mind, they can nevertheless be the likenesses of material things. It is not necessary that a likeness have the same manner of existing as that of which it is a likeness: they only need to correspond according to their description. The human form in a golden statue does not have the same manner of existence as the human form does in flesh and bone.

The answer to the fifth objection is that though bodily qualities cannot exist in the mind, nevertheless the likenesses of bodily qualities can exist: and it is in virtue of these the mind is likened to bodily things.

The answer to the sixth objection is that the intellect is aware by abstracting from the individual matter and its characteristics, e.g. from this flesh and these bones. It does not have to abstract from matter universally considered. So it can think of the natural form as existing in flesh and bone, though not in this flesh and these bones.

Article 5

The fifth question is, can our mind be aware of material things in their individualness?

Apparently.

1. An individual thing has its existence through its matter: so things with matter in their definitions are called material. But though the mind is immaterial, yet it can be aware of material things. So by the same argument it can be aware of individual things.

2. Moreover, people cannot judge and make arrangements correctly about things unless they are aware of them. But wise people use their minds to judge and make arrangements correctly about individual things: e.g. about their family and their property. So we are aware of individuals in our mind.

3. Moreover, one cannot be aware of a composition except by being aware of the terms of the composition. But the composition 'Socrates is a human being' is formed by the mind: it cannot be formed by some sense-power, as sense-power cannot grasp the universal 'human being'. So the mind is aware of individuals.

4. Moreover, one cannot command any action without being aware of the object of that action. But the mind or reason commands the actions of sense-desire and temper, as is made clear in the first book of the *Ethics* [1103a1]. So since their objects are individuals, the mind is aware of individuals.

5. Moreover, Boethius tells us that whatever a lower power can do, a higher power can do. But the sense-powers, which are lower than the mind, are aware of individuals. So still more can the mind be aware of individuals.

6. Moreover, the higher a mind is, the more universal its

awareness is, as Dionysius makes clear in Chapter Twelve of the *Hierarchy of heaven*. But the mind of an angel is higher than the human mind: nevertheless, angels are aware of individuals. So still more the human mind.

But against this: Boethius says 'It is universal when thought of, individual when sensed'.

My answer is that it is clear from the last article that we must say that the human mind and the mind of an angel are aware of material things in different ways.

The awareness of the human mind bears on natural things princi- pally in virtue of the form: secondarily, it bears on matter in so far as it is related to the form. Every form, in its own self, is universal: so this relation to the form causes awareness of matter with a universal awareness only. Considered in this way matter is not the principle of individuation: matter is the principle of individuation in so far as it is considered as individual, i.e. as matter marked out according to determinate dimensions. This is what individuates the form. That is why the Philosopher says in the seventh book of the *Metaphysics*, 'The parts of the human being are matter and form considered universally: the parts of Socrates are this form and this matter' [1035a27 ff].

Hence it is clear that our mind cannot be directly aware of the individual. We are aware of the individual directly through our sense-powers, which receive forms from things in a bodily organ. Hence they receive them subject to determinate dimensions, and, as such, as leading to an awareness of the individual matter. Just as the universal form leads to an awareness of universal matter, so the individual form leads to an awareness of matter which is marked out, which is the principle of individuation. But the mind does get itself involved with individuals coincidentally, in that it follows on from the sense-powers, which deal with individuals.

This following on occurs in two ways.

In one way, it is in so far as the movement of the sensitive part has its terminus in the mind. This happens, for example, in the change brought about in the soul by things. In this way the mind is aware of the individual: in virtue of a kind of turning back. This occurs in so far as the mind, in being aware of its object — some universal nature — goes back to an awareness of its own activity, and beyond that to the [intellectual] likeness which is the origin of its activity; and beyond that to the sense-image from which this likeness has been abstracted. In this way it acquires some awareness of the individual.

In the other way, it is in so far as the change initiated in things by the soul begins from the mind and goes into the sensitive part, i.e. in the way in which the mind governs the lower powers. It gets involved with individuals in this way through the 'individual reason': this is a particular power, also called the cogitative faculty, which has a definite organ in the body, a chamber in the middle of the head. The universal judgement which the mind has of things we can do cannot be applied to an individual action except by means of some inter- mediate power which grasps the individual. In this way we make a syllogism, whose major premiss is universal, i.e. the judgement of the mind; its minor premiss is particular, and is the application of the 'individual reason'; and the conclusion is the choice of an individual action, as is clear from what is said in the third book of the *De anima* [433a12 ff].

But the mind of an angel, which is aware of material things in virtue of forms which have immediate reference both to matter and to form, is aware by a direct glance not merely of matter considered universally, but also individually. And the mind of God is the same.

The answer to the first objection is that the awareness by which one is aware of matter according to its analogy with form does not amount to awareness of the individual thing, as is clear from the body of the article.

The answer to the second objection is that the arrangements that wise people make with regard to individual things come about in virtue of their mind only through the mediation of the cogitative faculty, whose task — as is clear from the body of the article — is to be aware of individual notions.

The answer to the third objection is that the intellect can compose a proposition about both individuals and universals in virtue of its awareness of the individual by a sort of turning back, as we have said.

The answer to the fourth is that the intellect or reason is aware in a universal way of the end to which, by its command, it directs the acting of the sense-desire and the temper. This universal awareness is applied to individuals by means of the cogitative faculty, as has been said.

The answer to the fifth objection is that what a lower power can do can be done by a higher power; but not always in the same way. Sometimes it is done in another higher way. In this way the intellect can be aware of the things that the senses are aware of, but in a higher way than the senses are. The senses are aware of them in virtue of their material characteristics and external accidents, but the intellect gets through to the inmost nature of that kind of thing, which is to be found in the individuals themselves.

The answer to the sixth objection is that the awareness of the angel's mind is more universal than the awareness of the human mind in that it reaches more things with fewer intermediaries. It is also more efficient in being aware of individuals, as is clear from what has been said.

Article 6

The sixth question is, does the human mind get its awareness from things which are sensed?

Apparently not.

1. Things which do not agree in matter cannot be related by acting and being acted on, as is clear from Boethius's book *On the two natures* and from the Philosopher in his book *De generatione et corruptione*.

But there is no common matter between our mind and things which are sensed. So things that are sensed cannot act on our mind in such a way that an awareness is imprinted in our mind as a result of them.

2.   Moreover, the object of the intellect is that which exists, as it says in the third book of the *De anima* [?429b15, 430b26]. But the essence of things is not perceived by the senses at all. So the awareness of the mind does not come from the senses.

3.   Moreover, Augustine says in the tenth book of the *Confessions*, speaking of the way in which we acquire an awareness of things that are thought of, 'They were there, I say, before I learned them' (he is speaking of things that are thought of in our mind), 'but they were not in the memory.' So it seems that the thought-likenesses are not drawn from the senses.

4.   Moreover, Augustine proves in the tenth book of the *De Trinitate* that the soul can only love what it is aware of. But people may love knowledge before they learn it, as is clear from the fact that many pursue it with a lot of effort. So before they learned that knowledge, it was within their intellectual grasp: so the mind does not draw knowledge from things that are sensed.

5.   Moreover, Augustine says in the twelfth book of *Super Genesim ad litteram*, 'The image of a body is brought about in the spirit, not by the body, but by the spirit, in itself, with a wonderful swiftness, inexpressibly distant from the slowness of the body.' So it seems that the mind does not draw the thought-likenesses from the senses, but itself forms them in itself.

6.   Moreover, Augustine says in the twelfth book of the *De Trinitate* that our mind judges of bodily things according to bodiless, everlasting descriptions. But the descriptions that we draw from the senses are not like this: so, the same as before.

7.   Moreover, if the mind draws its awareness from things that are sensed, this can only be in so far as the likeness which is drawn from the things that are sensed acts on the passive intellect. But such a likeness cannot act on the passive intellect. It does not act on it while it is still in the imaging faculty, because while it is there it is not yet actually thought of: it is only potentially thought of [something that can be thought of]. Nor does it act on the passive intellect when it is in the active intellect, since the active intellect does not receive likenesses: if it did, it would not be any different from the passive intellect. Nor does it act on the passive intellect when it is in the passive intellect itself, since a form which is already in a subject does not act on that subject, but is in some way at rest in it. Nor does it act on the passive intellect when it exists on its own, since thought likenesses are not substances, but belong to the category of the accidents, as Avicenna says in his *Metaphysics*. [Hence it does not exist on its own at all.] So it is completely impossible for our mind to draw knowledge from things that are sensed.

8.   Moreover, that which acts is of a nobler sort than that which is acted on, as Augustine makes clear in the twelfth book of his *Super Genesim ad litteram*, and as the Philosopher does in the third book of the *De anima* [?429a12]. But that which receives is related to that

which it receives as that which is acted on to that which acts. So since the mind is of a much nobler sort than things that are sensed, and than the senses themselves, it could not receive any awareness from them.

9. Moreover, the Philosopher says in the seventh book of the *Physics* that the soul comes to know when it is at rest [247b11]. But the soul cannot receive any awareness from things that are sensed unless it is acted on by them. Ergo, etc.

But against this: as the Philosopher says, and as experience shows, when a sense is lacking a kind of knowledge is lacking. For example, blind people have no knowledge of colours. This would not happen if the soul acquired its awareness from something other than the senses. Therefore it acquires awareness through the senses from things that are sensed.

2. Moreover, all our awareness arises originally from our knowledge of the first unprovable principles. But an awareness of these arises in us from the senses, as is made clear at the end of the *Posterior analytics* [?96b35 ff]. So our knowledge has its origin in the senses.

3. Moreover, nature does nothing without a point, nor does nature fall short in what is necessary. But our senses would have been given to us pointlessly if we did not gain awareness of things through them.

My answer is that we must say that there was a great diversity of opinion on this point among the ancients.

Some claimed that our knowledge takes its origin wholly from something outside us, something separated from matter. This group was divided into two factions.

One group, the Platonists, claimed that the forms of things that are sensed were separated from matter, and could thus be actually thought of. Individuals in nature came to be by sensed matter participating in these forms, and human minds had knowledge by participating in them. So they claimed that these forms were the origin of coming into existence, and of knowledge. The Philosopher tells us about this in the first book of the *Metaphysics* [987a29 – 988a16].

This claim is adequately refuted by the Philosopher. He shows that one should not posit that the forms of sensed things exist anywhere but in sensed matter, since the universal forms cannot be thought of without sensed matter taken universally, e.g. no snub without nose.

So there were others who did not claim that there were separated forms of sensed things, but they claimed that there were only intelligences — what we would call angels — and these separated forms are the whole origin of our knowledge. This is why Avicenna wanted to have it that just as sensed forms are only received in sensed matter through the influence of the active intellect, in the same way forms that are thought of are only imprinted on human minds by the active intellect. This active intellect would not be a part of the soul, but a separate substance, according to him. Nevertheless, the soul needs the senses to stir it up and make it ready for knowledge, so to speak: just as agencies here below prepare the matter to receive the form from the active intellect.

But this view does not appear reasonable. According to this view, there would be no relation of necessary dependence between the awareness of the human mind and the sense powers. The opposite is clearly true: on the one hand, when a sense is lacking, there is a lack of knowledge about what is sensed by it, and on the other, our mind cannot actually consider even what it knows (in the sense of *knows as a habit*), without forming some sense-image. As a result, when the organ of the imaging-faculty [in the brain] is damaged this consideration is obstructed. Moreover, this view denies the proximate origins of things, if everything here below receives its forms, both sensed and thought of, immediately from this separated substance.

Another view was taken by those who claimed that our knowledge has its origin entirely from some interior cause. These too fall into two schools.

One school claimed that human souls have in themselves a consciousness of everything, but that by the union of the soul to the body this consciousness gets shadowy. So they said that there was no need to reject study or the senses as if they were obstacles to knowledge. They said that learning was just remembering: it is clear that we are reminded of things that we knew before by seeing and hearing.

But this view does not seem reasonable. If the union of soul with body is natural, it cannot be that natural knowledge is entirely obstructed by it: so, if this opinion were true, we would not be completely ignorant of the things which we cannot sense.

This view fits the claim that souls were created before bodies, and then joined to them. In that case the composition of soul and body would not be natural, but would be something that happens accidentally to the soul. Both the faith and the views of the philosophers judge that this opinion should be rejected.

The other school said that the soul is the cause of its own knowledge. It does not acquire knowledge from sensed things, as if the likenesses of things reached the soul in some way from the action of sensed things. Rather it is the soul itself which forms likenesses of sensed things, when sensed things are present.

This view does not seem wholly reasonable. No agent acts except in so far as it is in a state of actuality; so if the soul forms the likenesses of everything in itself, then it should have those likenesses of things in it in a state of actuality. This brings us back to the last view, which said that knowledge of everything is set in the soul by nature.

So the judgement of the Philosopher seems more reasonable than any of the above views. He said that the knowledge in our mind comes partly from inside, partly from outside. It does not come only from things which are separated from matter, but also from sensed things themselves. When we relate our mind to sensed things outside the soul, we find that it has a double relation to them.

One relation is that of actuality to potentiality. This is in so far as things outside the mind can potentially be thought of. The mind itself is actually thought of: so in virtue of this relation we posit that there is in the mind an active intellect, which makes things actually thought of.

The other relation is that of potentiality to actuality. This is in so far as the forms of determinate things are in our mind only potentially, while they are actually in things outside the soul. In virtue of this relation we posit that there is a passive intellect in our soul, whose role it is to receive the forms which are abstracted from sensed things, and made such that they can be actually thought of by the light of the active intellect. Now, this light of the active intellect originally comes into the soul from separated substances, especially God.

So, according to what we have said, it is true that our mind gets knowledge from sensed things. Nevertheless, it is also true that the soul itself forms likenesses of things in itself, in so far as the forms which are abstracted from sensed things become actually thought of — so that they can be taken into the passive intellect — in virtue of the light of the active intellect. So too, then, all knowledge is in a certain sense originally planted in us, in the light of the active intellect, through the mediation of universal conceptions. We are at once aware of these by the light of the active intellect, and we judge about other things by their means, as if they were universal principles, and we are aware in advance of other things in them.

So according to what we have said there is some truth in the claim that we were already conscious of the things that we learn.

The answer to the first objection, then, is that sensed forms, or forms abstracted from sensed things, cannot act on our mind except in so far as they become immaterial in virtue of the light of the active intellect. In this way they are made, as it were, homogeneous with the passive intellect and act on it.

The answer to the second objection is that a higher and a lower power do not act on the same object in the same way: the higher acts in a superior way. So the senses are not made so effectively aware of a thing by the form they get from it as the intellect is. The senses are led by this form to an awareness of the external accidents, while the intellect gets through to the pure essence of the thing, separating it from all material characteristics. So 'The awareness of the mind has its origin in the senses' does not mean that the senses grasp everything that the mind is aware of, but rather that the mind is led from what is grasped by the senses to something beyond. This is like the way in which the thought of sensed things leads one to think of divine things.

The answer to the third objection is that what Augustine says refers to the pre-awareness of individuals in the awareness of the universal principles. So in this sense it is true that we already had in our soul the things that we learn.

The answer to the fourth objection is that people can love knowledge before they acquire it, in so far as they are aware of it with some kind of universal awareness, i.e. by being aware of the usefulness of that knowledge, either by seeing it, or in some other way.

The answer to the fifth objection is that 'the soul brings about

forms in itself' means that the thought-of forms which are made by the
action of the active intellect bring about forms in the passive intellect,
as we have said. As a result of this the imaginative power can form the
forms of various different sensed things. This is particularly clear
when we imagine things that we have never perceived with the senses.

The answer to the sixth objection is that the first principles, of
which we have an inborn awareness, are sort of likenesses of the
uncreated truth. So when we make judgements on other things by
their means, we are said to judge of things by immutable descriptions, or by the uncreated truth. But what Augustine says here refers
to the higher reason, which remains in the contemplation of eternal
things. But though it is of a higher dignity, its operation comes later,
since 'For the invisible things of him from the creation of the world
are clearly seen, being understood by the things that are made'
[Rom. 1:20].

The answer to the seventh objection is that when the passive
intellect receives the likenesses of things from sense-images, the
sense-images are related to it as secondary and instrumental active
causes. The primary and principal active cause is the active intellect.
So the effect of the action which remains in the passive intellect
follows the nature of both, not just of one of them: the passive
intellect receives the forms as actually thought of, as a result of the
power of the active intellect, but as the likenesses of determinate
things as a result of the awareness of the sense-images. That is why
forms which are actually thought of do not exist on their own either
in the imaging faculty or in the active intellect, but only in the
passive intellect.

The answer to the eighth objection is that although strictly speaking the passive intellect is of a nobler sort than the sense-image, there
is nothing to stop the sense-image being relatively of a nobler sort:
i.e. in so far as the sense-image actually is a likeness of such and such
a thing, and there is no likeness of it in the passive intellect except
potentially. So in some way the sense-image can act on the passive
intellect by the power of the light of the active intellect, just as colour
can act on the sight by the power of physical light.

The answer to the ninth objection is that the rest in which knowledge comes to its completion means that there is no movement of the
natural passions. It does not mean that there is no movement or
being acted on in the general sense, in which any receiving is called
'being acted on' and 'being moved': the sense in which the
Philosopher himself says in the third book of the *De anima* that
thinking is a kind of being acted on [?431a7].

Passage 10: The immortality of the soul

The *Quaestio disputata de anima* seems to date from after the composition of the first part of the *Summa theologiae*, around 1269. There is a
parallel in the *Summa* to the passage collected here at I q.75 a.6.

Quaestio disputata de anima, article 14

The fourth question is whether the human soul is immortal. Apparently it is mortal.

1.   Ecclesiastes says in Chapter Three [verse 19]: 'The death of man and of beasts is one, and the condition of them both is equal.' But when beasts die, their soul dies too. So when human beings die their soul perishes.

2.   Moreover, that which ceases to exist and that which does not cease to exist are of different categories, as it says in the tenth book of the *Metaphysics* [1058b26]. But the souls of beasts and the souls of human beings are not of different categories, since human beings and beasts are not. So the souls of human beings and the souls of beasts are no different with regard to ceasing to exist and not ceasing to exist. But the souls of beasts perish: so the human soul perishes too.

3.   Moreover, Damascene says that the angels receive immortality by [grace or] favour, not by nature. But the angels are not of a lower nature than the human soul: so the human soul is not naturally immortal.

4.   Moreover, the Philosopher proves in the eighth book of the *Physics* [266a12] that the first initiator of change has infinite power, since it initiates change during an infinite time. So if the soul has the power of lasting an infinite time, then it follows that its power is infinite. But there is no infinite power in a finite essence. So if the soul does not perish, it follows that its essence is infinite. But this is impossible, since only God's essence is infinite. So the human soul is not imperishable.

5.   But, it was objected [by the bachelor?], the soul is imperishable not by its own essence, but by the power of God. Against this there is the following: what does not belong to a thing by that thing's own essence is not essential to it. But perishable and imperishable are predicated in an essential manner of whatever they are predicated of, as the Philosopher says in the tenth book of the *Metaphysics* [1059a1]. So if the soul is imperishable, it must be imperishable by its own essence.

6.   Moreover, everything that exists is either perishable or imperishable. So if the human soul is not imperishable in virtue of its own essence, then it is perishable in virtue of its own essence.

7.   Moreover, everything imperishable has the power to exist always. So if the human soul is imperishable, it follows that it has the power to exist always. So it cannot have existed after having not existed: which goes against the faith.

8.   Moreover, Augustine says that just as God is the life of the soul, so the soul is the life of the body. But death is to lose one's life: so by dying one loses one's soul, and it is taken away.

9.   Moreover, form only exists in that in which it exists. So if the soul is the form of the body, it cannot exist except in the body: so when the body perishes it does.

10.   But it was objected that this is true of the soul in so far as it

is a form, but not in its own essence. But against this, the soul is not the form of the body in a coincidental way: if it were, since the soul makes a human being to exist in virtue of being the form of the body, it would follow that the human being is only a coincidental existent. Now, what belongs to something in a non-coincidental way fits it in virtue of its nature. So the soul is a form in virtue of its nature. So if in virtue of being a form it is perishable, then it will be perishable in virtue of its own nature.

11.   Moreover, when things come together in one existence, they are so related that when one of them ceases to exist the other one does so too. But the soul and the body come together to bring about one existence, i.e. the existence of a human being. So when the body perishes the soul does too.

12.   Moreover, the sensing soul and the reasoning soul are one in substance in the human being. But the sensing soul is perishable; so the reasoning one is too.

13.   Moreover, the form should be in proportion to the matter. But the human soul is in the body as form in matter. So since the body is perishable, so is the soul.

14.   Moreover, if the soul is separable from the body, then it must have some non-bodily performance, since no substance is idle. But there cannot be any non-bodily performance of the soul: not even thinking, which is the most plausible, since there is no thought without sense-images, as the Philosopher says [431a16], and there are no sense-images without a body. So the soul cannot be separated from the body, but it perishes when the body perishes.

15.   Moreover, if the human soul is imperishable, this can only be because it is something that thinks. But thinking does not belong to it, since the highest part of a lower nature imitates in some way the action of a higher nature, but does not attain to it. (For example, monkeys in some way imitate human performances, but do not quite attain them.) It seems, in the same way, that the human being is the highest thing in the order of material things, and so imitates in some way the action of intellectual separated substances, namely thinking: but does not attain to it. So there seems to be no need to claim that the human soul is immortal.

16.   Moreover, all or at least most of the individuals of a species attain the performances that belong specially to that species. But very few people attain to thought. So thinking is not a performance that belongs especially to the human soul: so the human soul does not have to be imperishable just because it is capable of thought.

17.   Moreover, the Philosopher says in the first book of the *Physics* [187b26] that everything finite gets eaten up if you are for ever taking a bit away from it. But the natural good of the soul is a finite good. So since the natural good of the human soul is forever being diminished by some sin or other, it appears that in the end it will all be taken away: so the human soul at some time perishes.

18.   Moreover, when the body is weak the soul is weak too, as is clear from its performances. So when the body perishes the soul perishes.

19.   Moreover, everything that comes from nothing can go back to nothing. But the human soul is created from nothing, so it can go back to nothing. So it follows that the soul is perishable.

20.   Moreover, so long as a cause is there, its effects are there too. But the soul is the cause of the life of the soul. So if the soul is there for ever, then the body is alive for ever, which is obviously false.

21.   Moreover, everything that exists in its own right is a 'this something' that belongs to a category and a kind within a category. But the human soul is apparently not a 'this something', and cannot be put in a category or a kind within a category, since it is a form. To be in a category or a kind within a category belongs to something made up [of form and matter], not to either matter or form, except in [some reductive sense,] some sense in which the application of being in a category can be brought back to them. So the human soul does not exist in its own right; so when the body perishes it cannot remain.

But against this, we have what the Book of Wisdom says in chapter two [verse 23]: 'God created man incorruptible, and to the image of his own likeness he made him.' So we can gather from this that human beings are indestructible — i.e. imperishable — in so far as they are in God's likeness. But human beings are in the likeness of God in virtue of their soul, as Augustine says in his book *On the Trinity*. So the human soul is imperishable.

Moreover, that which perishes has a contrary, or is made up of contraries. But there is no contrariness about the human soul: things which are contrary in themselves are not contrary in the human soul. After all, the descriptions of contrary things in the soul are not contrary. So the human soul is imperishable.

Moreover, the heavenly bodies are said to be imperishable, because they do not have matter as things which come to be and perish do. But the human soul is wholly non-material, as is obvious from the fact that it accepts the likenesses of things in a non-material way. So the soul is imperishable.

Moreover, the Philosopher says that the intellect is as separated from what perishes as is the everlasting [413b25 f]. But the intellect is a part of the soul, as he says. So the human soul is imperishable.

My answer is that the human soul must be completely imperishable. To make this clear we must realise that what follows on something else in its own right cannot be separated from it. You cannot separate being an animal from a human being, and you cannot separate being odd or even from a number. Now it is clear that existence follows on in its own right from the form: everything exists in virtue of its own form. So existence cannot be separated from the form. So things that are made up of matter and form perish because they lose the form which brings existence with it. But the form itself cannot perish in its own right: only coincidentally. When the thing made up [of matter and form] perishes, the form perishes coincidentally, in that the existence of the thing made up, which is in virtue of the form, fails — that is, if the form is such that it is not something that itself has existence, but is only that in virtue of which the made-up thing exists.

If, then, there is some form which is something that has its own existence, then that form must necessarily be imperishable. This is because something that has its own existence does not lose existence unless it loses its form: so if the thing that has its own existence is itself a form it is impossible for it to lose its existence.

Now it is clear that the originating principle in virtue of which a human being thinks is a form that possesses an act of existence in its own right, and is not merely that by which something exists. This is because thinking, as the Philosopher explains in the third book of the *De anima* [429a27], is not an activity carried out by any bodily organ. One cannot find any bodily organ that can receive all the natures that can be sensed, above all because what receives must be devoid of the nature of the thing received, as the pupil of the eye is devoid of colour. But all the bodily organs have some nature that can be sensed. The intellect, however, with which we think, can be aware of all the natures of things that can be sensed: so it is impossible that its performance, thinking, should be carried out by any bodily organ. So it is clear that the intellect has its own performance in its own right, and the body has no share in it. Now everything performs according to its manner of existence: what possesses an act of existence in its own right performs in its own right, while the things that do not possess an act of existence in their own right do not have performances in their own right. It is not heat that heats things up in its own right, but a hot thing. So it is clear, then, that the originating principle of thought, in virtue of which a human being thinks, possesses an act of existence that is on a level higher than that of the body, and that does not depend on the body.

It is clear, too, that this kind of originating principle of thought is not something made up out of form and matter, since likenesses are received in it in a completely non-material way. This is obvious from the fact that thought is of universals, which are considered in abstraction from matter and from the characteristics of matter. We are left, then, with the conclusion that the originating principle of thought, by which human beings think, is a form that possesses its own act of existence: hence it has to be imperishable. This is what the Philosopher says, too: that the intellect is something divine and everlasting.

But we showed in the earlier questions that the originating principle of thought by which a human being thinks is not some separate substance, but is something that exists in a human being in the way that a form does, i.e. the soul or part of the soul. So we are left with the conclusion from the above that the human soul is imperishable.

All those who claimed that the human soul perishes missed out one of the parts of the foregoing argument. Some claimed that the soul is a body, and claimed thus that it is not a form but something made up of form and matter. Others thought that the intellect is no different from the senses, and so claimed that it has no performance without a bodily organ, and hence that it does not possess an act of existence on a higher level than that of the body; and hence, that it is not a form that possesses its own act of existence. Others claimed that the intellect by which a human being thinks is a separate substance. We have shown above [in previous articles of this question] that all these views are false. So we are left with the conclusion that the human soul is imperishable.

We can find evidence for this from two sources. Firstly, from the side of the intellect: even those things which are in themselves perishable are imperishable in so far as they are grasped by the intellect. This is because the intellect grasps things in a universal way, and in this way they do not come to perish. Secondly, from the natural tendency, which can never be frustrated in anything. We see that human beings have a natural tendency towards going on for-ever. And this is quite reasonable: existence is in itself something desirable, and so a thinking being that grasps existence as such, not here and now, has a desire for existence without qualification, at all times. So it seems that this tendency is not vain, but that human beings are, so far as their thinking soul is concerned, imperishable.

The answer to the first objection is that in the Book of Wisdom Solomon is trying to provoke, and speaks sometimes in the character of a wise man, and sometimes in the character of a fool. The saying adduced here is said in the character of the fool. Or you could say that the passing away of human beings and beasts is said to be the same, with reference to the perishing of the thing made up of form and matter: in either case this occurs by the separation of the soul from the body, though the human soul continues after the separa-tion, while the soul of the beasts does not.

The answer to the second objection is that if the human soul and the soul of the beasts were to be put in categories, it would follow that they were of different categories, if we were looking at it with reference to the nature of the categories. In this way the perishable and the imperishable must differ in category, though they can agree in some common description — so if we look at it from a logical point of view they can be put in one category. Now the soul does not belong to a category as if it were a species within the category, but rather as a part of a species. Both kinds of thing made up [of form and matter] are perishable: both that which has as a part the human soul, and that which has as a part the soul of a beast. So there is nothing in this to stop them being in one and the same category.

The answer to the third objection is that, as Augustine says, true immortality is true unchangeability. But unchangeability by choice, i.e. the choice that can change from good to bad, is possessed by both the soul and the angels by favour.

The answer to the fourth objection is that existence is related to the form as something that follows on from it in its own right, not as an effect is related to the power of an agent, or as change is to the power of that which initiates the change. So indeed, if something could initiate change during an infinite time, then this would reveal infinite power in the initiator of change. But something's existing for an infinite time does not reveal that it has an infinite form in virtue of which it exists. Similarly, the fact that two-ness is always even does not show that it is infinite. Rather, the existence of something for an infinite time reveals infinite power in the *cause* of its existence.

The answer to the fifth objection is that 'perishable' and 'imperishable' are essential predicates because they follow on from the essence as a formal or material originating principle, not as an active originating principle. The active originating principle of the everlastingness of some things is external to them.

This also makes clear the answer to the sixth objection.

The answer to the seventh objection is that the soul has the power to exist always, but did not always have this power. So it does not have to have existed always, it only needs never to cease in the future.

The answer to the eighth objection is that the soul is said to be the life of the body in so far as it is the cause of life, as the form is the originating principle of existence. This is because for living beings to exist is to be alive, as the Philosopher says in the second book of the *De anima* [415b13].

The answer to the ninth objection is that the soul is a form in such a way that it possesses its own existence that does not depend on the existence of that of which it is the form. This is shown by its performance, as we have shown.

The answer to the tenth objection is that though the soul is essentially a form, nevertheless something can correspond to it as being a form of such-and-such a kind, i.e. a self-existing form, that does not correspond to it as being a form. This is just as thinking does not correspond to a human as being an animal, though a human being is essentially an animal.

The answer to the eleventh objection is that though the soul and the body come together in one human existence, nevertheless this existence comes to the body [as a gift] from the form. So the soul passes on to the body its own existence, by which it self-exists, as has been shown in the foregoing questions. So even when the body is removed the soul continues.

The answer to the twelfth objection is that the sensing soul in brute animals is perishable; but in the human being, since it is of the same substance as the reasoning soul, it is imperishable.

The answer to the thirteenth objection is that the human body is matter which is in proportion to the human soul, as far as its performances are concerned. But perishing and other failings happen by material necessity, as has been shown above. Or one can say that perishing occurs as a result of sin, not as a result of the way in which human nature was first set up.

The answer to the fourteenth objection is that what the Philosopher says here — no thought without sense-images — is to be understood with reference to our state in the present life, in which human beings think in virtue of their souls: the way in which a separated soul thinks will be different.

The answer to the fifteenth objection is that though the human soul does not attain the manner of thinking according to which higher substances think, it nevertheless attains to some kind of thinking, which is enough to show its imperishability.

The answer to the sixteenth objection is that though very few people attain to the level of complete thought, nevertheless everyone attains to the level of some kind of thought. It is very clear that the first principles of demonstration are general conceptions of the soul, which are grasped by means of the intellect.

The answer to the seventeenth objection is that though sin takes away grace altogether, it does not take anything away from the nature of a thing. It does, though, take away a certain tendency to or aptness for grace: and in so far as sin brings in something to do with the contrary tendency, it is said to take away something from the natural good [of the soul], i.e. aptness for grace. But it never takes away the whole of the natural good: under the contrary tendencies the potentiality still continues, though farther and farther away from being actualised.

The answer to the eighteenth objection is that the soul does not get weak when the body does — not even the sensing soul gets weak. This is clear from what the Philosopher says in the first book of the *De anima* [408b21], that if an old man were to receive the eye of a young one, he would see as well as the young one. From this it is obvious that the weakness of an action does not occur because the soul is weak, but because the organ is.

The answer to the nineteenth objection is that what comes from nothing can go back to nothing, if the hand of Providence does not keep it [in existence]. But we do not call things perishable just because of that: we call them perishable because they have some originating principle of perishing. This is why perishable and imperishable are essential predicates.

The answer to the twentieth objection is that though the soul, which is the cause of life, is imperishable, nevertheless the body, which receives life from the soul, is subject to change. In this way it drifts away from the condition which makes it fit to receive life: and so it happens that a human being perishes.

The answer to the twenty-first objection is that though the soul can exist in its own right, it does not have a species [to itself] in its own right, since it is a part of a species.

6

Aquinas on Ethics

An introduction to Aquinas on ethics

Free will

Since for St Thomas thought has a universal, non-material character, it follows that there is little difficulty for him with the problem of free will. Aquinas assimilates his talk of volition to what he has said about natural tendencies. In 'An introduction to Aquinas on metaphysics' we saw that natural tendencies 'are according to a form': they stem from a naturally inherent form. Rational desire or appetite, the will, is nothing other than a tendency stemming in a similar way from a form that is intentional or thought of. A similar account applies to non-rational desire, whether in a human being or a brute animal: non-rational desire is nothing other than a tendency that stems from a sensible form as represented in the sense image (passage 11).

Since the form that is thought of is necessarily universal, as we have seen, the tendency that arises from it cannot be determined to one individual manner of realisation: so the will is free. The notion of descriptions, *rationes*, is also to be found playing an important role here: even the non-determined tendency which a certain thought-of form tends to give rise to need not in fact arise, as one need not be considering that thing under the description whose form would give rise to that tendency. Even non-human animals have a degree of 'freedom' or at least indetermination, which results from the fact that the manner of receiving a form in the imaging faculty, though material, is not exactly the same as that uniform way in which the same form is received in its natural subject. It exists in the animal as an object of the senses and the imaging faculty.

Despite the fact that St Thomas's answer to the problem of free will is quite simple, he nevertheless conscientiously discusses all the difficulties. A number of these are, unavoidably, of a purely theological nature: Aquinas dismisses many of them quite briefly, holding that the fact that the will acts only in virtue of God's action on it no more determines the will than the fact that the weather exists in virtue of God's action determines the weather. There are other objections, though, that, if suitably updated, form standard objections today. We do not normally nowadays think of the stars as exercising a determining influence on the will (passage 11, objection 21): but one's genetic make-up is a similar kind of objection which can be met by a similar answer. In the same way, what is alleged of the determining force of custom, in the words of St Augustine (objection 23), could be just as well rephrased in terms of conditioning.

Aquinas does not deny that there is a great deal that is determined in human actions and will: just as he does not deny that there is a great deal of indeterminism in animal 'actions'. (He would clearly not subscribe to the problem known as 'Buridan's ass': that problem was probably known to Aquinas, as it is found much before his time — and not at all, incidentally, in the works of Buridan. Dante quotes a version of it, which seems to imply that within a few years of St Thomas's death it was already a commonplace in intellectual circles.) One cannot not want to live well, in some sense: and one cannot, therefore, fail to want what one is actually considering as a necessary means to that end. But it is worth noticing on this point that Aquinas thinks that not only can one have various erroneous ideas of what well-being consists in, one can also be aware, correctly, of many different ways which genuinely do produce it. He is also commendably down-to-earth in his view that there is naturally more determination in those with strong characters or tempers, or with specific customs.

The human being and human good

The will is called a faculty of the soul, as is the intellect: and we are aware that Aquinas thought that the soul survived death. But we must not allow our discussions of will, intellect or soul to blind us to the fact that for Aquinas the soul is not the person: 'The soul is not I' is something that he explicitly says. The human being is a kind of animal, and an animal is a kind of body: so a human being is not a kind of soul but a kind of body. This clearly anti-Platonic claim makes a definite difference to his ethics. A good human being is one that has all the excellences which enable that kind of animal to live well by carrying out its specific performance (passage 12, *lectio* 10, section 11).

This view of ethics is of course very Aristotelian. It is based on the notion of human flourishing or well-being, and that of the virtues or excellences that make this possible. This ethics is emphatically not one that is based on merit: Aquinas would regard our modern system, which has the categories that are appropriate to a merit system, without having a God by whom this merit would be judged, as incoherent. An illustration may make this clear. If we consider two people facing equal dangers in the fulfilment of some duty or worthwhile end, then, other things being equal, we are inclined to think of the one that fears more rather than less, but overcomes that fear, as being the more courageous. This is because we admire such a person more: we think, surely rightly, that such a person would have more merit in the sight of God — if only we believed in God. For Aquinas, as for Aristotle, the more courageous person is precisely the one that fears less rather than more. The question foremost in their minds is not 'Which is more meritorious?' but 'Which would I rather be, given the choice? Which would it be better to be? Which more resembles the way I would bring up my children to be?'

This is the experiential basis of Aquinas's concept of human well-being. His theoretical explanation, collected here, is of great interest, but it is less convincing. Following Aristotle, Aquinas looks for evidence of the end of human life in the performances that are specific to human beings (passage 12, *lectio* 10, section 2). 'Specific' does not mean merely 'possessed by human beings alone'. Human beings differ from most other animal species in many ways: for example, there are very few other animals that do not have a part of their body that they cannot scratch. This does not make a life of scratching a plausible candidate for the end of the human being.

Aquinas seems to want to illustrate the concept of 'end' by appealing to the ends of different parts of the body, and to the different functions of people with different skills in society. Each of these ends is a performance. The first of these does not look very hopeful: a part of animal has an end in relation to the life of the whole animal, but to what whole does an individual animal stand as a part? It is true that there is the life of the species, and that one very specific performance of the rabbit, say, is to produce other rabbits: but one should not want to claim that the end of the life of the individual human being is the life of the species, though this may be a part of that end.

It seems as if Aquinas wants to short-circuit the discussion. When a thing has a specific performance, then its end or excellence is to do that specific performance well. The fact that among animals only human beings are capable of thought is undoubtedly a phenomenon of great importance: it certainly appears that the exercise of thought in life is a specific performance of the human being. If we admit this, have we not been given the end, the excellence, and the specific performance all at once? Aquinas seems to think so: and while it is easy to pick holes in this or that point of the theory, it is not easy to rid oneself of the feeling that to reject this view is to reject one's own nature.

Natural law

The stress given here to these Aristotelian aspects of Aquinas's ethical thought should not be taken to imply that he ignores merit. Rather he gives it a firm footing in the providence of God, who sees all — even the heart and bowels — and governs all. Our natural appreciation of human good and evil is a natural consequence of our rationality: but even what comes by nature is a free gift from God, as our very existence is. Aquinas holds that our natural awareness of good and evil is in fact, under one description, a promulgation to us of the will of the supreme governor of the universe: a natural law. Since there is nothing that can come to us except from God's hand, it is thus absurd to suppose that we can get some good or avoid some evil — in virtue of God's will — precisely by flouting that will as naturally promulgated to us in our rational understanding of good and evil. A deep attachment to excellence and the good life is not only the only good and reasonable option, it is, given the providence of God, the only one which makes any practical sense. Honesty is not only the best policy, it is the only policy: as we can be sure that God's will will never be frustrated in the long run.

Passage 11: Free will

Though this question is normally collected as a part of the *De malo*, it was in fact disputed on its own in 1270. A parallel in the *Summa theologiae* is I q.83, especially article 1.

De malo, question 6

The only question here is, do human beings have a free choice of their actions, or do they make their choice of necessity?

Apparently they make their choice not freely, but of necessity.

1. Jeremiah says at 10:23, 'The way of a man is not his: neither is it in a man to walk and to direct his going.' But that in respect of which human beings are free is their own: it is something put within their dominion. So it seems that human beings do not have free choice of their ways and actions.

2. But it should be objected [by the bachelor?] that this refers to the carrying out of people's choices, which sometimes is not in their power. Against this counter-objection we have what the Apostle says in Romans 9:16: 'It is not of him that willeth (i.e. willing is not) nor of him that runneth (i.e. running is not), but of God that sheweth mercy.' Running belongs to the outward carrying out of actions, but willing belongs to the inward choice. So inward choices are not in people's power: God gives them to us.

3. But it should be objected that the change by which people make a choice is initiated by some inward influence, i.e. by God, in a fixed way. But this does not go against freedom. Against this counter-objection is the fact that all animals initiate change in themselves by appetite. But non-human animals do not have free choice because change is initiated in their appetite by something external, i.e. by the influence of the heavenly bodies, or by the action of some other body. If, then, change is initiated in the human will in a fixed way by God, it follows that human beings do not have free choice of their actions.

4. Moreover, an action is forced when its originating principle is outside the subject, and the victim of force does not contribute anything to it. So if the originating principle of a choice which is made voluntarily is outside the subject — in God — then it seems that the will is changed by force and of necessity. So we do not have free choice of our actions.

5. Moreover, it is impossible that a human will should not be in accordance with God's will: as Augustine says in the *Enchiridion*, either a man does what God wills or God fulfils his will in him. But God's will is changeless; so the human will is too. So all human choices spring from a fixed choice.

6. Moreover, there can be no actuality of a potentiality that is not directed to its own object. For example, the actuality of sight can only occur in the presence of what is seen. But the object of the will is

the good; so the will cannot desire anything but the good. Therefore it necessarily desires the good, and does not have free choice of good or bad.

7. Moreover, every potentiality that is related to its object as that which is changed is related to that which changes it is a passive potentiality. Its activity, then, is not strictly acting, but being acted on. That which is sensed changes the senses in this way, so sense is a passive potentiality, and so to sense is in some way to be acted on. But the will is related to its object in the same way as that which is changed is related to that which initiates change in it: the Philosopher tells us in the third book of the *De anima* [435b15] and the twelfth book of the *Metaphysics* [1072a26] that the desired is something that initiates change in something else, not something that is changed, while desire is something that initiates change in something else, and that is itself changed. So the will is a passive potentiality, and to desire is to be acted on. But that which acts on any passive potentiality of necessity changes it, if its action is sufficient. So apparently the will is changed of necessity by that which is desired. So human beings are not free to desire or not.

8. But it should be objected that the will is related by necessity to the last end, since everybody necessarily wants to live well, but is not so related to that which is for this end. Against this counter-objection, the end is an object of the will, but so is what is for the end: they both fall under the description 'good'. So if the will is changed towards its end of necessity, then apparently it is also changed of necessity towards that which is for the end.

9. Moreover, where there is one and the same initiator of change, and one and the same thing that is changed, there is one and the same kind of change. But when someone desires both the end and what is for the end, then we have one and the same thing being changed — the will — and one and the same thing that initiates change — since no one desires what is for an end except in so far as they desire the end. So the kind of change is one and the same: so if we desire the end of necessity, then we desire what is for the end of necessity too.

10. Moreover, the intellect is a potentiality which is separate from matter: so is the will. But the intellect is changed of necessity by its object: one is compelled by the force of reason to assent to a truth. So by the same token the will is changed of necessity by its object.

11. Moreover, the character of the first initiator of change remains in all subsequent initiators of change, because all subsequent initiators of change change other things in so far as they are changed by the first initiator. But the first initiator of change in the order of voluntary changes is the desired thing which we grasp. Now, if we can prove that something is good, the grasp of the desired thing is subject to some kind of necessity: so this necessity apparently is passed on to all the subsequent changes. So change is initiated in the will not freely but of necessity.

12. Moreover, that which initiates change in something else is something real in the world, rather than something of the mind. But

the Philosopher tells us in the sixth book of the *Metaphysics* [1027b25] that good is in things, while true is in the mind. So the good is something real in the world, while the true is something in the mind. So the good, rather than the true, meets the description of being something that changes something else. But the true initiates change in the intellect of necessity, as we have said. So the good initiates change in the will of necessity.

13. Moreover, love, which belongs to the will, is a more vehement change than is awareness, which belongs to the intellect. As Dionysius says in the fourth chapter of *On the divine names*, awareness produces a likeness, while love produces a transformation. So the will is something that is more subject to change than is the intellect. So if change is initiated in the intellect by necessity, it seems that still more it is so in the will.

14. But it should be objected that the action of the intellect follows a change that starts in the world and proceeds into the soul, while the act of the will follows a change that starts in the soul and proceeds into the world. So the intellect falls rather under the description of 'passive', while the will falls under that of 'active'. So it is not acted on of necessity by its object. But against this counter-objection, assent belongs to the intellect, and consent to the will. 'Assent' signifies a change in favour of the reality which is being assented to, just as 'consent' signifies a change in favour of the reality consented to. So the change of the will no more starts from the soul and proceeds into the world than does that of the intellect.

15. Moreover, if the will is not changed by necessity with regard to some things that are desired, then we must say that the will is equally related to opposites. This is because 'not necessarily' is equivalent to 'possibly not'. But everything that is in potentiality to opposites is not brought to be one or other of them in actuality except by some actual existent, which makes that which existed potentially to exist actually. Something which makes something actually exist is called its cause. So it will be necessary, if the will desires something in a determinate way, for there to be some cause that makes it desire that thing. But once we have the cause, the effect must follow, as Avicenna proves. This is because if once we have the cause, the effect need not follow, then we will need something else to bring the potentiality into actuality: so the cause will not be a sufficient cause. So the change in the will by which it desires something is of necessity.

16. Moreover, no power that is equally related to opposites is an active power, since every active power can do that act with reference to which it is active. But the impossible does not follow from the possible: it would follow that two opposites are true at the same time, which is impossible. But the will is an active power. So it is not equally related to opposites, but necessarily ends in one or other of them.

17. Moreover, the will sometimes begins to make a choice when it was not previously making a choice. So either it has changed from the characteristics it previously had, or not. If not, then it follows that it is not choosing now any more than it was before, so it would be

choosing without choosing, which is impossible. But if its character has changed, then it must have been changed by something, since everything that is changed is changed by another. But that which initiates change imposes necessity on the changed, or it would not suffice to change it. So the will is changed of necessity.

18.   But it should be objected that these arguments are conclusive only for material potentiality, which exists in matter; not for the immaterial potentiality which the will is. But against this counter-objection, the originating principles of all human knowledge are the senses. We cannot know anything except in so far as it falls under the senses — either itself or its effects. But a power which is equally related to opposites does not fall under the senses: and in its effects which do fall under the senses, we do not find two contrary acts existing at the same time. Instead, we always see that one of two determinately becomes actual. So we cannot judge that there is an active potentiality in human beings which is related equally to opposites.

19.   Moreover, since potentiality is attributed relative to an actuality, as one actuality is related to another, so are the potentialities of those actualities related. But two opposed actualities cannot exist at the same time; so there cannot be one potentiality which is related equally to two opposites.

20.   Moreover, according to Augustine in the first book of *On the Trinity*, nothing is the cause of its own existence. So by the same token nothing is the cause of its own change. So the will does not change itself, it needs to be changed by another. This is because it begins to act after having earlier been not acting, and everything that is like this is changed in some way. That is why we say that it is not the case that God began to desire after not having desired, because God is unchanging. So the will must be changed by something else. But that which is changed by another undergoes some necessity from that which changes it. So the will desires necessarily and not freely.

21.   Moreover, everything that has many forms can be brought back to something that has one form. Changes in humans are diverse and of many forms. So they can be brought back to the changes of the heavens, which are uniform, as their cause. But that which is caused by the changes of the heavens happens of necessity: since a natural cause necessarily produces its effect unless there is some obstacle. But there is nothing that can be an obstacle to the changes of a heavenly body, and so impede its effect, since the activity of that impeding agent must also be brought back to some originating principle in the heavens as its cause. So changes in the human apparently occur of necessity, not by free choice.

22.   Moreover, if one does what one does not want to do, one does not have free choice. But people do what they do not want: compare Romans 7:15, 'The evil that I hate, that I do'. So human beings do not have free choice of their actions.

23.   Moreover, Augustine says in the *Enchiridion* that by making bad use of free will people lose it and lose themselves. But to choose freely belongs only to those that are [still] in possession of free will.

So human beings do not have free choice.

24. Moreover, Augustine says in the eighth book of the *Confessions* that when custom is not opposed, necessity arises. So it seems that at least in people who are accustomed to doing something, change in the will is brought about of necessity.

But against this we have what Ecclesiasticus says [15:14]: God made man from the beginning, and left him in the hands of his own counsel. But this would not be the case if we did not have free choice, which is the desire for what has previously been deliberated on, as it says in the third book of the *Ethics* [1112a15]. So human beings have free choice of their actions.

Moreover, rational potentialities are equally related to opposites, according to the Philosopher. But the will is a rational potentiality, since it is in the reason, as the third book of the *De anima* [432b6] says. So will is equally related to opposites, and is not changed necessarily in favour of one of them.

Moreover, people have dominion over their own acts, as the Philosopher says in the third book of the *Ethics* [1113b7]: they have it in them to act and not to act. But this would not be so if we did not have free choice of our actions.

My answer is that some claimed that the human will is changed of necessity to desire something; but they did not claim that the will is forced. Not everything that is necessary is forced or violent, only that whose originating principle is outside. So there are some natural changes which are necessary, but not violent. The violent excludes the natural as much as it does the voluntary, since the originating principle of both these is within, while the originating principle of the violent is outside.

But this view is heretical: it takes away the reason for merit and demerit in human actions. It does not seem either meritorious or demeritorious, after all, for someone to do of necessity, in this way, something he cannot avoid. Also this view is to be classed among the 'aberrant' philosophical views: it does not only go against the faith, but overturns all the principles of moral philosophy. For if there is nothing free in us, but the change by which we desire comes about of necessity, then we lose deliberation, exhortation, command and punishment, and praise and blame, which are what moral philosophy is based on.

This kind of view that destroys the principles of some part of philosophy is called an 'aberrant' position. An example is the view that there is no change, which destroys the principles of natural science. People are led to put forward such views partly through perverseness, and partly through sophistical arguments, which they cannot resolve, as the fourth book of the *Metaphysics* [1009a17] says.

To make clear the truth about this question we must first realise that in human beings, just as in other things, there is an originating principle of their own actions. This active or change-initiating originating principle in human beings is strictly speaking the intellect and the will, as it says in the third book of the *De anima* [433a9]. Now, this originating principle partly corresponds to the active originating

161

principle in the things of nature, and is partly different from it. It corresponds in the following way: in natural things we find the form, which is the originating principle of action, and the tendency which follows on from the form, which is called 'natural appetite'; and it is from these that action follows. In the same way, in human beings we find the thought-of form, and the tendency of the will which follows on from the form that is grasped; and the external action follows on from these. The difference is that the form of a natural thing is a form made individual by matter. So the tendency which follows on from it is determined one way [to one thing]. The thought-of form is universal, and many things can be included under it; so since actions are individual things, and no individual thing can match the potentiality of the universal, the tendency of will is indeterminately related to many things. For example, a craftsman conceives the universal form of a house, under which the different kinds of houses are included; his will can tend to his making a square house or a round one, or of any shape. The active originating principle in brute animals is half-way between the two. The form which is grasped by the senses is individual, as is the form of a natural thing: so from it there arises a tendency towards one action, as there does in natural things. But the same form is not always received [uniformly] in the senses as it is in natural things (e.g. fire is always hot); rather it is received now one way, now another — now as a pleasing form, now as a distressing one. Hence the animal at one time flees, and at another pursues. This is what it has in common with the active originating principle in human beings.

Secondly we have to realise that there are two ways for a potentiality to be changed. In one way, on the side of the subject; on the other on the side of the object. 'On the side of the subject' is as when the sight is changed by a modification of the characteristics of its organ to see more or less clearly: 'on the side of the object' is as when the sight sees now white, now black. The first kind of change belongs to the exercise of the activity, i.e. it is exercised or not, better or worse. The second kind of change belongs to the specification of the activity, since the activity is specified by its object.

But we should realise that in natural things the specification of an activity is by its form: the exercise comes from the agent, i.e. what causes the change. That which changes another acts for an end: so we conclude that the first originating principle of change, with relation to the exercise of an activity, comes from the end. But if we think of the objects of will and intellect, we will find that the object of the intellect is the first originating principle in the category of formal cause, since this object is the existent and the true. The object of the will, on the other hand, is the first originating principle in the category of final cause, since the object of the will is the good, under which all ends are included, just as all forms that are grasped are included under the true. So the good, in so far as it is a form that is grasped, is included under the true as being something true: while the true, in so far as it is the end of the activity of the intellect, is included under the good, as being some individual good.

So if we think of the change in the powers of the soul from the side of the object that specifies the act, the first originating principle of the change comes from the intellect, since this is the way in which the good which is thought of changes the will itself. But if we think of the change in the powers of the soul from the side of the exercise of the activity, then the originating principle of the change comes from the will. This is because the power to which the chief end belongs changes to actuality the power that has control over that which is for the end. For example, it is the military art which changes the harness-maker's art towards acting. In this way the will changes itself and all the other powers. I think because I want to: and in the same way, I use all my powers and habitual dispositions because I want to. That is why the Commentator defines 'habitual disposition' in the third book of the *De anima* as 'that which people can make use of when they want'.

So to prove that change is not brought about in the will of necessity, we have to think of the change in the will from both sides: with regard to the exercise of the activity, and with regard to the determination of the activity, which comes from the object. With regard to the exercise of the activity, then, it is clear, first of all, that the will initiates change in itself. It changes itself just as it changes the other powers. It does not follow from this that the will is in potentiality and actuality at the same time in the same respect. In the case of the intellect, people who are finding something out initiate a change in themselves towards knowledge, by proceeding from one thing they knew to something they do not know, except potentially. In the same way, one can be actually wanting something, and so change oneself towards actually wanting something else. For example, you want to be healthy, and so change yourself towards wanting to take the medicine. You want to be healthy, so you begin to deliberate about what makes you healthy: and when the deliberation is concluded you want to take the medicine. So in this way the deliberation was prior to the desire to taking the medicine, and the deliberation came from your will as you wanted to deliberate.

So the will changes itself by means of deliberation: but deliberation is an inquiry which is not demonstrative. It can come out either way; so the will does not change itself of necessity. But the will does not always want to deliberate, so there must be something that changes it towards wanting to deliberate. But if it is changed by itself, then, again, the change in the will must be prior to deliberation. We cannot go on to infinity in this line, so we must claim that a will that is not always actually wanting is changed, with regard to this first change in the will, by something external, by whose influence the will begins to want.

Some claimed that this influence comes from the heavenly bodies. But this cannot be the case. The will is in the reason, as the Philosopher says in the third book of the *De anima* [432b6]. Now the intellectual reason is not a bodily power, so it is impossible for the power of a heavenly body to initiate change in the will directly. To claim that the human will is changed by the influence of the heavenly bodies, just as the appetites of brute animals are changed, is a result of the view of those who held the position that the intellect is no different from the senses. The Philosopher applies to them in the *De anima* the words of some poet that 'Such is the will that is put in men by the father of gods and men', i.e. the heaven or the sun [427a25].

We are left, then, with Aristotle's conclusion in the chapter on good luck [*Eudemian ethics*, 1248a25 ff], that that which first initiates change in the will and the intellect is something which is superior to them, i.e. God. God initiates change in everything according to the description under which they can be changed. For example, he changes light things to move upwards, and heavy things downwards; and in the same way he changes the will in accordance with its character. He does not change it of necessity, but in such a way that it is undeterminedly related to many different things. It is clear, then, that if we think of the change in the will from the side of the exercise of the activity, change in the will is not brought about of necessity.

But if we think of the change in the will from the side of the object that determines the act of will to want this or that, we must realise that the object that initiates change in the will is a fitting good which is grasped. So if some good is proposed that is grasped under the description 'good', but not under the description 'fitting', it will not change the will. Deliberation and choice have to do with individuals, since the action is an individual. So what is grasped as good and fitting must be grasped as good and fitting in the individual case, not only in a universal way.

If, then a thing were to be grasped as good and fitting with regard to all the individual elements that can be thought of, then it would change the will of necessity. That is why people of necessity desire well-being, which was defined by Boethius as 'the state which is complete in the gathering together of all goods'. I say 'of necessity' with regard to the determining of the activity, since the opposite of well-being cannot be desired. 'Of necessity' does not apply with regard to the exercise of the activity, since it is possible that a person at such-and-such a time does not want to think about well-being. This is because the activities of the mind and of the will are also individuals. But if a good is such that it is not found to be good with regard to all the individual elements that can be thought of, it will not change the will of necessity, even with regard to the determining of the activity. Someone could want its opposite, after all, even when thinking of it, since its opposite may be good and fitting with regard to some other individual element which has been thought of. For example, that which is good for the health may not be good to the taste, and so on.

The will may be more drawn to what is presented under one particular characteristic than to what is presented under another, in three ways. In one way, the first may have more weight, and so change the will in accordance with reason: e.g. when someone chooses what is helpful for the health, rather than what is helpful to some whim. In another way, one may think about one individual circumstance and not of another. This happens especially when there is some good opportunity presented for it either from within or without, so it crops up in such a thought. The third way comes from a person's characteristics: as the Philosopher says, 'As a man is, so will his end seem to him' [1113a32]. So the will of a quick-tempered person and the will of a calm person will be changed with regard to a thing in different ways, since different things are fitting for them. In the same way, a sick person and a healthy person react to the same food in different ways.

If, then, the character in virtue of which a person sees something as good and fitting is inborn and not subject to the will, then we choose what we choose of natural necessity, just as we all naturally desire to exist, to live, and to think. But if the character is not inborn, but is subject to the will, e.g. when one is disposed by a habitual disposition or an emotion to see something good or bad in this individual thing, then the will is not changed of necessity. One can get rid of these characteristics, so as not to see things in that way. For example, one can calm one's anger, so as not to judge someone in anger. But it is easier to get rid of an emotion than of a habitual disposition.

So the will is changed of necessity towards some things, from the side of the object: but not to everything. But on the side of the exercise of the activity, it is not changed of necessity.

The answer to the first objection is that the actuality spoken of there can be understood in two ways. In one way, we can understand the Prophet to be speaking of the execution of a choice: it is not in one's power to bring entirely to effect what one has deliberated in one's mind. It can be understood in another way: even the inner will is changed by some higher originating principle, i.e. God. That is why the Apostle says 'It is not of him that willeth (i.e. willing is not) nor of him that runneth (i.e. running is not)' — it does not belong to them as if they were the first originating principle — 'but of God that sheweth mercy'.

And this also makes clear the answer to the second objection.

The answer to the third objection is that brute animals are changed by the influence of a higher agent towards something determinate, in accordance with the way the individual form is; it is the conception of the individual form which the sense appetite springs from. God does indeed change the will, however, in an unchanging manner, because of the manner of acting of God's change-initiating power, which cannot fail. But because of the nature of the will which is changed — which is such that it is related indifferently to different things — this does not lead to necessity, but leaves freedom untouched. In the same way divine providence works unfailingly in everything, but nevertheless effects come from contingent causes in a contingent manner, since God changes everything in a relative way, relative to the manner of existence of each thing.

The answer to the fourth is that the will does contribute something when change is initiated in it by God: it is the will itself that acts, though the change is initiated by God. So though its change does come from outside as far as the first originating principle is concerned, it is nevertheless not a forced change.

The answer to the fifth objection is that there is a way in which the human will is not in accordance with the divine will, i.e. in so far as it wants something that God does not want it to want, e.g. when it wants to sin. But it may not be the case that God wants the will not to want it. If God did want the will not to want it, then it would not want it, as the Lord does everything that he wills. Though in this way the human will is not in accordance with God's will with regard to the change in the will, it must always be in accordance with regard to the outcome or result: the human will always brings about the result that God is bringing about by means of the human will. As regards the manner of wanting, however, the human will does not have to match the will of God: God wants each and everything eternally and infinitely, but people don't. As Isaiah says at 15:9, 'As the heavens are exalted above the earth, so are my ways exalted above your ways.'

The answer to the sixth objection is that since the good is the object of the will, one can maintain that the will never wants anything except under the description 'good'. But since many different things fall under that description, one cannot maintain that because of this the will is changed of necessity towards this or that.

The answer to the seventh objection is that something active does not change something else of necessity except when it is more power-ful than that which is passive. Now, the will is in potentiality with regard to the universal good, so no good is more powerful than the power of the will so as to change it of necessity, except something that is good according to all ways of thinking about it. Only the complete good, i.e. well-being, is of this kind: the will cannot fail to want it, at least not in the sense of wanting its opposite. It can, however, not be actually wanting it, as it can turn away the thought of well-being, since it changes the intellect towards its activity. Hence in this way not even well-being is necessarily wanted; just as people would not necessarily be heated [when standing in front of a fire], if they could keep heat away from them when they wanted.

The answer to the eighth objection is that the end is the reason for wanting what is for that end. So the will is not related to the two things in the same way.

The answer to the ninth objection is that when one can attain an end in only one way, then there will be the same reason for wanting the end and wanting what is for the end. But that is not how it is in the case suggested, since once can attain well-being in many different ways. So even though people want well-being of necessity, they need not want any of the things that lead to it.

The answer to the tenth objection is that there is a certain simi-larity between intellect and will, and a certain dissimilarity. The dis-similarity is with regard to the exercise of activity. The intellect is changed towards acting by the will, while the will is not changed by any other power, but by itself. But as regards the object both sides are similar: just as the will is changed by necessity by what is in every way good, but not by an object which can be taken as bad under some description, so the intellect is changed of necessity by a neces-sary truth which cannot be taken as false, but not by a contingent truth, which can be taken as false.

The answer to the eleventh objection is that the character of the first initiator of change continues in the changed in so far as the latter is changed by the initiator of change. In this way the changed acquires a likeness of the initiator of change, but it does not have to become a total likeness of it. Hence the first change-initiating originating principle is not itself in process of change, but this is not the case with other initiators of change.

The answer to the twelfth objection is that the fact that the true is a sort of something existing in the mind makes it more formal than is the good, and more of a change-initiating force under the description of being an object. But the good is more of a change-initiating force under the description of being an end, as we have said.

The answer to the thirteenth objection is that love is said to transform the lover into the beloved, in so far as by love the lover is changed towards that which is loved. Awareness produces a likeness in so far as a likeness of that of which one is aware comes into existence in the one who is aware. The first of these two belongs to an imitation whose origin is the agent that seeks an end: the second, to an imitation that is according to a form.

The answer to the fourteenth objection is that 'to assent' does not pick out a change of the intellect towards the world, but rather one that is towards the conception of the world which is in the mind. The intellect assents to this when it judges it to be true.

The answer to the fifteenth objection is that it is not every cause that brings on its effect of necessity; not even every sufficient cause, either. This is because a cause can be obstructed, so that sometimes its effect does not follow. This is the way it is with natural causes, that do not necessarily produce their effects, but only in most cases, since in a minority of cases they are obstructed. So the cause that makes the will want something does not have to do this of necessity: an obstruction can be presented by the will itself, either by putting aside the thought that leads to wanting it, or thinking of the opposite, i.e. that what is being put forward as good is not good in some respect.

The answer to the sixteenth objection is that what the Philosopher proves by this thesis is not that a power that is related equally to contraries is not active, but rather that an active power that is related equally to contraries does not produce its effect of necessity. If you did claim this it would clearly follow that contradictories would both be true. But if we grant that there is some active power that is equally related to opposites, it does not follow that opposites can be the case at the same time. Even if both the opposites to which the power is equally related are possible, one is not co-possible with the other.

The answer to the seventeenth objection is that when the will begins to make a choice from a fresh start, it undergoes a change from its previous state or characteristic, in so far as before it was potentially choosing, and now it is actually choosing. This change is brought about by some initiator of change, to the extent that the will changes itself towards acting, and also to the extent to which it is changed by some external agent, i.e. God. But it is not changed of necessity, as we have said.

The answer to the eighteenth objection is that the originating principle of human awareness is in the senses. But not everything that a person is aware of has to be subject to the senses, or something whose sensed effect we are immediately aware of. After all, the intellect thinks of itself in virtue of its own activity, which is not subject to the senses; and in the same way it thinks of the internal activity of the will, in so far as change is initiated in the will in some way by the activity of the intellect. In another way the activities of the intellect are caused by the will, as we have said. This is in the way in which an effect is known from its cause, and a cause from its effect. But even if we grant that the power of the will which is equally related to opposites cannot come to our awareness except through a sensed effect, even so the argument does not follow. The universal, which exists always and everywhere, comes to our awareness through the individuals that are here and now; and first matter, which is in potentiality with regard to various forms, comes to our awareness through the succession of forms, which are not, however, in the matter at the same time. In the same way we are aware of the power of the will that is equally related to opposites, not because opposite activities exist at the same time, but because they succeed one after the other from the same originating principle.

The answer to the nineteenth objection is that the thesis 'As one actuality is related to another, so are the potentialities of those actualities related' is in one way true and one way false. If we take 'actuality' indifferently as corresponding to potentiality as the latter's universal object, then the thesis is true: for hearing is related to sight as sound is to colour. But if we take it as what is included under the universal object as an individual activity, then the thesis is not true: there is only one power of sight, though white and black are not the same. So though at one time there exists a power of will which is equally related to opposites, nevertheless those opposites to which the will is equally related do not exist at the same time.

The answer to the twentieth objection is that one and the same thing does not initiate change in itself in one and the same respect, but it can initiate change in itself in different respects. In this way the intellect, in so far as it is actually thinking of the premisses, brings itself from potentiality to actuality with respect to the conclusions. In the same way the will, in so far as it actually wants an end, brings itself into actuality with respect to what is for the end.

The answer to the twenty-first objection is that the changes in the will, since they have many forms, can be brought back to some originating principle that has one form. This is not the heavenly bodies, but God, as we have said — if we accept the premiss that God directly changes the will. But if we are speaking of the change in the will in so far as it is changed by something outside it which happens to be sensed, then the change in the will can indeed be brought back to the heavenly bodies. But nevertheless the will is not changed of necessity: for it is not necessary that on being presented with pleasant food the will should desire it. Nor is it true that what is caused by the heavenly bodies springs from them of necessity: as the Philosopher says in the sixth book of the *Metaphysics* [?1027b7], if every effect comes from some cause, and every cause produces its effect of necessity, it would follow that everything that happens is necessary. But both of these are false: some causes, even if they are sufficient causes, do not produce their effects of necessity, since they can be obstructed. This is clearly the case in all natural causes. Nor, again, is it true that everything that happens has some natural cause. Things which occur coincidentally do not occur through any active natural cause. This is because what is coincidental is neither an existent nor one and the same thing. So the occurrence of an obstruction, which is something coincidental, cannot be brought back to the heavenly bodies as to its cause, since the heavenly bodies act in the way that a natural cause does.

The answer to the twenty-second objection is that people who do what they do not want to do may not have freedom of action, but they have freedom of choice.

The answer to the twenty-third objection is that by sinning people lose free will in so far as they lose freedom from guilt and wretchedness, not in so far as they lose freedom from being forced.

The answer to the twenty-fourth objection is that custom does not bring about necessity without qualification, but rather especially in sudden actions. By deliberating a while the person who is accustomed to doing something can act against custom.

Passage 12: Human well-being

This passage appears to date from 1271. It is thus contemporary with the ethical treatise in the *Summa theologiae*, the *Secunda secundae*. A parallel to this piece, however, is to be found earlier, at I–II q.1.

Commentary on the Ethics, Book I, *lectiones* 9 – 10 (Aristotle's text: 1097a16 – 98a22; commentary: Marietti, sections 103 – 30)

Lectio 9

1. After discussing the opinions of other people on human well-being, the Philosopher here discusses his own view of it. First he shows what human well-being is: secondly, he speaks of a certain inseparable property of well-being [in *lectio* 18]. The first part has two parts: in the first of these he shows what well-being is; in the second he rules out a certain difficulty [in *lectio* 15]. On the first of these he does two things: first he shows what well-being is, then he shows that the views he has given on it agree with everything that people say

about well-being [in *lectio* 12]. On the first of these he does two things: first he puts forward some general descriptions and characteristics of well-being, which are more or less obvious to everyone. Then he looks into the essence of well-being, [in *lectio* 10]. On the first of these he does two things. First he claims that well-being is the last end; then he lays down the characteristics which a last end must have, [at section 5 below].

2.   First, then, he says that after having dealt with those matters which have to do with the views of others, he should come back again to the good that we are investigating, i.e. human well-being, and investigate what it is. On this we should first consider that there seem to be different goods aimed at in the different activities and skills. The good aimed at in medicine is health, the good aimed at in the military arts is victory, and in every other art some other good.

3.   If we were to ask what is the good aimed at in each art or in each business, we should know that it is that for the sake of which everything else is done: in medicine everything is done for the sake of health, in warfare everything is done for the sake of winning. In architecture everything is done for the sake of building the house. It is the same in any other business: there is some good aimed at, for the sake of which everything else is done. But the good that is aimed at in any activity or choice is called the end. 'End', then is just that for the sake of which things are done.

4.   If, then, some end at once turns up to which everything that is done by human skills and activity is ordered, that end will be the good that is brought about without qualification, i.e. that which is sought in all human deeds. But if several goods should turn up to which the ends of different skills are directed, our rational inquiry should go beyond that fact of there being several, to reach some one thing. For there must be one last end of the human being as a human being, because there is only one human nature. In the same way there is one end for a doctor, as a doctor, because there is one craft of medicine. This last end of the human being is called human good, or well-being.

5.   Then he lays down two characteristics of the last end. First, it should be complete; second, it should be self-sufficing. This is because the last end is the farthest limit of natural change in desire; and for something to be the farthest limit of natural change, two things are required. First, it should be a state which embodies a determinate form: it should not be a state which is merely on the way to having a determinate form. Kindling a fire does not reach its limit when things are prepared for the reception of the form [of fire], but in the actual form [of fire] itself. That which has a determinate form is complete; that which is disposed for the reception of a form is incomplete. Hence the good which is the last end should be some complete good. Secondly, the limit of natural change should be

complete; nature is not defective in things which are necessary. In this way the limit of begetting a human being is not a human being that lacks some limb, but a complete human being. The last end, likewise, being the limit of desire, must necessarily be self-sufficient, i.e. some complete good.

6.   But we should consider, on this topic of the completion of the final good, that just as the agent initiates a change towards an end, so the end initiates change in the desire of the agent. Hence the degrees of the ends should correspond to the degrees of the agents. There are three kinds of agent. One is very incomplete: it does not act by virtue of its own form, but only in so far as it is in process of change which is initiated by something else. This is the way in which a hammer shapes a knife. For this reason the effect — the form which has been imposed — bears no similarity to this agent, but rather to that which initiates the change in it. A second kind of agent is complete: it acts according to its own form, as fire heats; but it needs to have change initiated in it by some principal agent first. To this extent it is in some way incomplete, by sharing in the incompleteness of the instrumental agent. The third kind of agent is most complete: an agent that acts according to its own form, and does not have change initiated in it by anything else.

7.   It is similar with ends. There are things that are desired not because of any formal goodness which is existent in them, but only in so far as they are useful as a means to something else; e.g. a bitter medicine. Then there are things which are desirable on account of something they have in them, but also for the sake of something else, like a warm and pleasant-tasting medicine. This is a more complete kind of good. But the most complete kind of good is that which is so desired for its own sake, that it is never desired for the sake of anything else. The Philosopher here distinguishes these three degrees of goods. He says that what has been said about the last end needs to be further developed by looking into the characteristics which are required for being the last end.

8.   There seem to be several degrees of ends. Some ends we choose only for the sake of something else; e.g. riches — which we do not desire except in so far as they are useful for a human life — or flutes for making music, and in general all instruments, which we do not try to get unless we need to use them. It is clear, then, that all these ends are incomplete. But the best and last end should be complete. Hence, if there is only one thing that is complete, it should be the last end which we are seeking. But if there are many complete ends, then the most complete of them should be the best and last. It is clear that just as that which is desirable in its own right is more complete than that which is desirable for the sake of something else, so that which is never desired for the sake of something else is more complete than those things which, besides being desired for their own sake, are also desired for the sake of something else.

9. Thus what is absolutely complete is that which can always be chosen for its own sake and never for the sake of anything else. Now, human well-being seems to be of this kind: we never choose it for the sake of something else, but only for its own sake. Honour, and pleasures, and thought, and virtue, we certainly choose for their own sake: for we would choose them or desire them even if we got nothing else out of them. But we do also choose them for the sake of well-being, in that we think that through them we will lead a life of well-being. But no one chooses well-being for this reason, nor for the sake of anything else. Hence we are left with well-being as the most complete of goods, and hence as the last and best of ends.

10. Then he deals with the way in which well-being is self-sufficient. First he discusses what belongs to the definition of sufficiency; then he discusses the 'self-' part [section 13].

First, then, he says that the same conclusion seems to follow from the consideration of self-sufficiency as from that of completion: i.e. that well-being is the best and last end. This is because the two points follow one from the other. The complete good, in fact, seems to be self-sufficient, since if it were to some extent not sufficient for something, then it would not seem to set desire completely at rest. Thus it would not be a complete good. But when he says *self*-sufficient good, he does not mean that it would suffice for just one man living a solitary life: he means it suffices for his parents and children and wife and friends and fellow-citizens. It should, in fact suffice to provide for them by offering them all the help that they need in temporal things, and by counselling and teaching in spiritual things. This is because the human being is naturally a social animal. Hence it will not suffice a person's desire, that he should be able to provide for himself; he will have to be able to provide for others too. But, we must understand, this is so up to a point.

11. For if someone were to want to extend this not only to his own relatives and friends, but to his friends' friends too, this would go on for ever. If this were so, if well-being demanded this infinite sufficiency, no one could arrive at sufficiency, and so no one could lead a life of well-being. The Philosopher is speaking in this book of well-being as it can be possessed in this life, since the well-being of the next life is beyond all rational inquiry. What the limit should be, up to what point well-being should be sufficient, is to be examined again elsewhere, in the *Economics* or the *Politics*.

12. He has made it clear, then, for whom the complete good, or well-being, should be sufficient: not just for one man, but for himself and for everyone whom he is responsible for. So here he sets out what it is that is called self-sufficient. He says that what we call self-sufficient is that which would make life worthy of choice even if that was all one had, without any need for anything coming from outside. This fits well-being very well. The movement of the will would not have reached its limit, if there remained something left outside which

a man needed. This is because everyone who needs something desires to have what he needs. Hence it is clear that well-being is a self-sufficient good.

13. Then he explains the definition of self-sufficiency, as far as the 'self-' part is concerned. A thing is called self-sufficient if it is taken as sufficient in isolation from everything else. This can happen in two ways. It happens in one way because the complete good which is called self-sufficient is not capable of receiving an increase of goodness from any additional good. This is the way it is with the one who is wholly good, i.e. God. Just as a whole plus its part is not something greater than the whole, since the part is itself included in the whole, so no partial good increases God's goodness, since that good is only good in virtue of sharing in the divine goodness. But in the other way something is said to be sufficient on its own, without anything else added, if it has within it everything that a human being necessarily has need of.

14. In this way the well-being that we are now speaking of is self-sufficient: it contains within itself everything that is necessary of itself — not, though, everything which a person could get. Hence it could be better by having something added to it. But the human will does not for that reason remain in a state of disquiet: desire which is ruled by will, as the man of well-being should have, is not in a state of disquiet about things which are not necessary, even if they could be got. This characteristic, then, is said to fit well-being most of all: it would be worthy of choice even if it had nothing added to it.

But if it has anything added to it, even the least of goods, then it will clearly be more worthy of choice. The reason is that by adding on we get a superabundance or increase of good. And just in so far as something is a greater good, to that extent it is more worthy of choice.

15. At the end he sums up what he has said: well-being, being the last end of everyone who acts, is a complete good, and self-sufficient.

Lectio 10

1. After stating the conditions of human well-being, the Philosopher here investigates its definition. He does three things here. First he shows that this inquiry is necessary: then he hunts for a definition of well-being [section 27]. Then he shows that the definition he gives will not do, and that more needs to be said [in *lectio* 11].

He says first, then, that everyone admits that well-being is some best thing, whose nature is such that it is the last end and a complete self-sufficient good. But very clearly something must be said about well-being, so that we can know what it is more specifically.

2. Then he investigates the definition of well-being. First he asks

after its genus; then he asks after its species [section 10]. First he shows that well-being is a performance of a human being. Then he shows that it is some performance specific to a human being [section 3]. Then he shows what is the performance that is specific to a human being [section 4].

He says first, then, that what well-being is can be made clear if we take into account the performance of the human being. The good of everything that has a specific performance is that performance, and that thing's being well consists in its doing that. For example, the good of a flute-player consists in his performance; and the same with someone who makes statues, and with any kind of craftsman. The reason for this is that the final good of a thing is its last completion. Now form is the first completion, but performance is the second completion. If some external thing is said to be an end, this can only be so through some performance, through which human beings get that thing, either by making it, as the builder makes a house, or because they use it or enjoy it. Hence we conclude that we must look for the final good of a thing in its operation. If, then, human beings have a specific performance, then necessarily their final good will consist in their specific performance. Well-being is the human being's final good: so well-being is the specific performance of the human being.

3.   If well-being is said to consist in anything else, it will be either because by it a person becomes fit for this kind of performance, or because it is something that one can achieve by performance, as when we say that God is the human being's blessedness.

4.   Then he proves that there is a performance specific to the human being. He does this in two ways; first, by means of what is coincidental to the human being. It is coincidental to a human being to be a weaver, or a cobbler, or a teacher of grammar, or a musician or anything else of that kind. But all of these things have their specific performance. If not, these things would be idle and vain for a human being. But if it is unsatisfactory that that which is directed by human reason should be idle and vain, it is much more unsatisfactory that that which is by nature, which is directed by the reason of God, should be so. Since, then, human beings are things that exist by nature, it is impossible that they should be idle by nature, which they would be if they had no specific performance. There is, then a performance which is specific to the human being, as there is a performance which is specific to what the human being is coincidentally. The reason for this is that everything, be it natural or artificial, exists in virtue of some form, which is the originating principle of some performance. Hence, just as each thing has its own specific existence in virtue of its form, so it has also its own specific performance.

5.   Secondly, he shows the same conclusion from the parts of the human being. We should attribute the same performance to a whole and to its parts. As the soul is the actuality of the whole body, in the same way parts of the soul are the actualities of parts of the body. In

this way sight is the actuality of the eye. But every part of the human being has its own specific performance: e.g. the performance of the eye is seeing, that of the hand is feeling, that of the foot walking, and so on for each part. It is clear, then that the whole human being has some specific performance of its own.

6. Then he inquires into the specific performance of the human being. It is clear that the specific performance of each thing is that which corresponds to it in virtue of its form. The form of the human being is the soul; it is by the actuality of the soul that the human being is said to be alive. This is not in the sense in which being alive is existing, for living beings: rather in the sense in which being alive means some performance during a life, such as thinking or feeling. It is clear, then, that human well-being consists in some performance during a life.

7. You could not say that any kind of living brings with it human well-being: living is common to us and to plants. The well-being we were looking for is some good which is specific to the human being: it is called 'human good'. For the same reason we should distinguish between well-being and the kind of life which is called nutritive or vegetative; for this too is common to us and the plants. From this we can conclude, too, that well-being does not consist in the health, beauty, strength, or swiftness of the body, since all these are acquired through the operations of that kind of life.

8. After the nutritive or vegetative life we come to the sensitive life. This, too, is not specific to the human being, but belongs also to the horse and the ox and to any kind of animal. Hence well-being does not consist in this kind of life either. From this we can conclude that well-being does not consist in any kind of sensible experience or pleasure.

9. After the nutritive life and the sensitive life there is nothing left except the life which consists in performance according to reason. This kind of life is specific to the human being: the human species is distinguished by this, its rational part. But there are two kinds of rational part. One is rational by participation, that is, by its being persuaded and governed by reason; the other is rational by its essence. It has in itself the capability of reasoning and thinking. This part is what is more principally called rational, as that which is x in its own right is always more principally x than that which is x in virtue of something else. Now since well-being is the most principal good of the human being, it follows that it should be found more in that which is rational by its essence than in that which is rational by participation. Hence we can conclude that well-being consists in the life of contemplation more principally than in the active life: that it consists more in the exercise of the reason or intellect, than in the exercise of the appetite under the direction of reason.

10. Then he goes into the specific differences of well-being. There

are two of these, so there are two parts here. [The second part starts at section 12.]

First, he concludes from what has gone before that the specific performance of the human being is a performance of the soul, a performance which is in accordance with reason, or is at least not devoid of reason. He says this because of the performance of the appetite under the direction of reason. It is a universal truth that when a thing has a performance which is specific to its kind, that is the same performance as the performance of a good thing of that kind — that is, unless we should add to the mention of performance something about excellence. The performance of a harpist is to play the harp, and the performance of a good harpist is to play the harp well. It is the same in all other cases.

11. If, then the performance of human beings consists in some kind of life, that is, that life in which they perform according to reason, then it follows that the good of human beings will be their performing well according to reason. The best human beings, those who have a life of well-being, will do this best of all. It is a part of the description of excellence that anything that has an excellence performs well in performing according to it: as, for example, the excellence of a horse is that according to which it runs well. If, then, the performance of the best of human beings, those that lead a life of well-being, is to perform well, or perform best, according to reason, it follows that human good, or well-being, is a performance according to excellence. So if there is only one excellence of human beings, the performance which is according to that excellence will be well-being. But if there are more excellences, then well-being will be the performance which is according to the best of them. Well-being, after all, is not just the good for human beings, but the best.

12. Then he investigates the other specific difference of well-being. For well-being, we need also as much continuity and perpetuity as possible. The appetite of a being with intellect naturally desires this; the intellect does not perceive our existence only under the aspect of 'now', as the senses do, but our existence, without qualification. Existence is desirable in its own right. The animal, perceiving by its sense its own existence under the aspect of 'now', desires to exist now: but human beings, similarly, grasping their own existence without qualification, desire to exist without qualification: always, not just now. Hence it belongs to the definition of complete well-being that it should be continuous and perpetual. This is not possible in our present life: hence in our present life complete well-being is impossible. But the well-being which is possible in this life should at least be in a complete life, i.e. in the whole of a human life. Just as the arrival of one swallow does not mean the arrival of summer, and neither does one fine day, so it is not by one performance that a human being reaches a state of well-being. It is only reached when a human being continues good performance throughout a whole life.

13. It is clear, then, that well-being is a performance which is specific to the human being, according to excellence, in a complete life.

Latin – English Glossary

absolute: without any relation to anything else.
actio: acting.
actus: actuality.
adaequatio: match, matching.
aequalitas: equating.
appetitus: desire, appetite.
assimilatio: likening.
cogitativa: 'cogitative' faculty; animal intelligence.
cognitio: [generally] awareness.
cognoscere: to be aware.
comparatio: being related.
componere: (1) [in logical sense] to compose; (2) [in metaphysical sense] to put together.
compositio: (1) [in logical sense] composing; (2) [in metaphysical sense] putting together.
conditio: characteristic.
consignificare: to consignify.
convenire: (1) to fit; (2) to correspond to; (3) to come together; (4) to be akin to.
conversio ad phantasmata: to turn back to sense images.
converti: to be a convertible term.
convertibile: convertible term.
contingens: contingent.
contingere: to be [contingently] possible.
correspondere: to correspond.
corruptibilis: perishable.
definitio: definition. See **ratio**.
determinatum: (1) determinate; (2) determined; (3) definite.
dictio: locution.
differentia: specific difference.
dispositio: qualification.
divisio: dividing.
ens: the [actually] existent.
ens per accidens: the coincidentally existent.
ens per se: the existent in its own right.
enunciatio: indicative sentence.
esse: (1) actual existence; (2) to [actually] exist; (3) to be the case; (4) to be (especially in passage 1).
esse ut verum: existence in the sense of the true.
existere: to exist [perhaps more accurately] to be present.
felicitas: [human] well-being.
finalis: final, in the sense of 'as an end'.
forma intelligibilis: thought-of form.
genus: (1) category; (2) kind.

habitudo: relation.
habitus: habitual disposition.
importare: to convey.
inconveniens: unsatisfactory.
inesse: to exist in.
inhaerere: to inhere; to be in.
intellectus: (1) intellect; (2) thought.
intelligere: to think.
intelligibilis: thought-of.
motus: change.
movere: to initiate change.
moveri: to change; be changed; have one's change initiated.
mutatio: change.
nomen: (1) noun; (2) name.
notitia: consciousness; notion.
operatio: performance.
oratio: expression.
passio: being acted on.
per accidens: coincidentally.
per prius et posterius: said in a principal sense and secondary related senses.
per se: in itself; in its own right.
per se sufficiens: self-sufficient.
perfectio: completion.
perfectus: complete.
phantasia: imaging faculty.
phantasma: sense-image.
potentia: potentiality.
praedicamentum: category.
principium: (1) originating principle; (2) principle; (3) premiss.
proprium: inseparable property.
quidditas: essence.
ratio: (1) description; (2) reason; (3) argument.
reflexio super phantasmata: turning back to sense images.
scientia: knowledge.
scire: to know.
secundum quid: relatively; in a relative sense.
significare: to signify.
significatio: significance; signification.
similitudo: (1) likening; (2) likeness.
simpliciter: without qualification.
species: (1) species; kind; type; (2) likeness.
species intelligibilis: thought-of likeness.
sub diversas rationes: under different descriptions.
subsistere: to self-exist.
substantia: substance, in three different senses: a substantial individual; the kind to which such an individual belongs; and what such an individual is.
sufficiens per se: self-sufficient.
unum per accidens: one and the same thing coincidentally.

unum per se: one and the same thing in its own right.
verbum: verb.
volitio: desire.
vox: utterance.

English – Latin Glossary

acted on, being: *passio*, the correlative of *actio*, acting. One of the accidental categories.

acting: *actio*. One of the accidental categories.

actual existence: *esse*. See under **existence**.

actuality: *actus*. This notion has its origin in the analysis of change, and a distinction between what a thing can be (is in potentiality) and actually is (is in actuality). Aquinas also uses the word to distinguish between having an active potentiality to do something — first actuality; and to be actually doing it — second actuality. See the analysis of change in Chapter 3, 'Introduction to Aquinas on metaphysics'.

actually existent: see under **existent**.

akin to: one of the translations of *convenire*, also translated as 'come together with', 'correspond to', and 'fit'.

appetite: used to translate *appetitus*: but also 'desire' and 'tendency' have been used.

argument: one of the words used, in appropriate contexts, to translate *ratio*. Other translations are 'description' and 'reason'.

aware, be aware of: *cognoscere*. See under **awareness**.

awareness: the usual translation of *cognitio*. This should not be understood in the sense of consciousness: it rather means 'being aware of an individual, thinking accurately about it'. This rather forced translation has been used to avoid having to talk of 'knowing' an individual. Thus 'know' has been left for *scire*.

be, being: occasionally used — especially in passage 1 — to translate *esse* and *ens*. See under **existence** and **be the case**.

being acted on: *passio*, the correlative of *actio*, acting. One of the accidental categories.

be the case: used to translate *esse* in its veritative sense, in logical and epistemological contexts: especially in passages 2 and 8.

case, be the: see under **be the case**.

category: used to translate *praedicamentum* and also *genus*. This latter word is also often translated as 'genus' and 'kind'.

change: as a noun, this translates *motus* (also 'process of change'), and occasionally *mutatio*. As a verb 'change' is seldom used, except in contexts where it is clear whether it is being used in a transitive sense or an intransitive sense: generally in the latter. For the transitive sense of 'change' (translating *movere*) the usual expression has been 'initiate change [in something else]': and for the intransitive sense, (*moveri*) 'be in process of change' or 'have one's change initiated by another'.

character: used to translate *conditio*.

characteristic: used to translate *conditio*, especially in the context of *conditiones materiales*, material characteristics, in passage 9.

cogitative faculty: *potentia cogitativa*. Also called 'particular reason'. That faculty which accounts for animal intelligence, and also for the way in which human beings are able to relate their abstract and universal knowledge to their individual and concrete actions. See passage 9.

coincidental, coincidentally: used to translate *per accidens*, as opposed to *per se*, translated as 'in its own right'. Something can exist in its own right or coincidentally, be one and the same thing in its own right or coincidentally, be true or good in its own right or coincidentally, or be a cause or an effect in its own right or coincidentally. All these notions are linked. See Chapter 3, 'Introduction to Aquinas on metaphysics' and Chapter 5, 'Introduction to Aquinas on truth, knowledge and the mind', and passages 3 and 8.

come together: one of the translations — the most literal — of *convenire*, also translated as 'be akin to' 'fit', 'correspond to'.

complete, completion: translate *perfectus* and *perfectio*. In a few contexts — e.g. in passage 12 — the more obvious translation 'perfect' might be more appropriate, but in general the notion is more that of complete existence than of complete goodness. But for Aquinas these notions are connected: see Chapter 5, 'Introduction to Aquinas on truth, knowledge and the mind'.

composing: *compositio*. This translation is used only in logical contexts: the composing or putting together of subject and predicate which makes up an affirmative indicative sentence. It is opposed to dividing, *divisio*, which is the separation of subject and predicate which makes up a negative indicative sentence. The word *compositio* in metaphysical contexts is translated as 'making up' or some analogous phrase.

consciousness: used to translate the rather rarely-used word *notitia* in a couple of contexts. 'Awareness' would perhaps be more accurate, but that word is being used for *cognitio*. It should be understood as being conscious *of* a thing. Also translated as 'notion'.

consignify: *consignificare*. Used of the manner in which a word brings with it some meaning beyond that of its straightforward signification, e.g. in the way in which verbs, besides signifying a certain acting, also consignify a time in virtue of their tensing.

contingent: *contingens*. That which can be the case or not.

convertible term: *convertibile*. Used of the expressions of 'transcendental' notions such as existent, true, etc. See Chapter 5, 'Introduction to Aquinas on truth, knowledge and the mind', and passage 8.

convey: *importare*. Used only in the context of a non-semantic contribution to a sentence by some part of it, e.g. the copula conveys the composing.

correspond to: one of the translations of *convenire*, also translated as 'be akin to', 'come together with', and 'fit'. The same word is also used in epistemological contexts, especially passage 8, to translate *correspondere*.

definite: used occasionally to translate *determinatum*, usually translated 'determinate' or 'determined'.

definition: *definitio*. A definition, for Aquinas, is always a definition of a thing, not a word. It is the most accurate of *rationes* or descriptions: see under **description**.

description: one of the words used to translate *ratio*, especially in logical contexts. A description, in this context, is an aspect of a thing which is picked out by a way of thinking of it or describing it, or by a particular expression which is applied to it. It is thus quite similar to our concepts of 'sense' and of 'being considered, etc., under a description'. A word — like 'true' — can be applied loosely or analogously, but there will be only one sense in which 'the description is completely met'. The most complete and accurate of descriptions of a thing is the definition. Other words used to translate *ratio* are 'argument' and 'reason'.

determinate: the usual translation of *determinatum*. Used adverbially especially in the context of passage 2. The same word is also translated as 'determined' and 'definite'.

difference, specific: see under **specific difference**.

disposition, habitual: used to translate *habitus*.

dividing: see under **composing**.

essence: used to translate both *essentia* and *quidditas*. See Chapter 3, 'Introduction to Aquinas on metaphysics'.

exist: *esse*. See **existence**. Also *existere*, rarely: this word might often have been better translated as 'to be present'. 'To exist in' translates *inesse*, the manner of existence of an accident. The ugly expression 'to self-exist' translates and explains *subsistere*.

existence: used to translate *esse*, to be, especially in the contexts of actual existence and existence in the sense of the true — see Chapter 3, 'Introduction to Aquinas on metaphysics'. Actual existence is a generalisation of what 'being alive' is for animals and plants: it is something that belongs to an individual and as such can be expressed by a first-level predicate, which is true or false of individuals. Existence in the sense of the true is the notion of there being something of a certain kind. It applies, then, to anything that can be a subject of a sentence, or anything that is in a kind that has instances, including things that are non-actual, like numbers or the dead. But it is not something that belongs to an individual, and so cannot fittingly be expressed by a first-level predicate: only by a second-level predicate, a predicate that is true or false of what first-level predicates refer to. See especially passage 3.

existent: *ens*. See under **existence**.

expression: *oratio*. An *oratio* is a syntactically complex expression. It may or may not be an indicative sentence: both 'Pale Socrates' and 'Socrates is pale' count as expressions in this sense. See passage 1.

final: *finalis*, used in the sense of 'as an end or goal', not in the sense of 'ultimate, last'.

fit: one of the translations of *convenire*, also translated as 'be akin to', 'come together with', 'correspond to'.

habitual disposition: see under **disposition, habitual**.

human well-being: see under **well-being**.

imaging faculty: a deliberately ugly rendering of *phantasia*, which is meant to draw attention to itself. See Chapter 5, 'Introduction to Aquinas on truth, knowledge and the mind' and passage 9.

in its own right: *per se*. See under **coincidental**. This expression is also (rarely) translated as 'on its own', in appropriate contexts.

indicative sentence: see under **sentence, indicative**.

inhere: *inhaerere*, the relation which accidents stand in towards their substantial subject.

initiate change: see under **change**.

inseparable property: *proprium* as a noun. An accident which is inseparable from its subject, but not part of its essence, e.g. the colour of
Socrates's eyes.

intellect: *intellectus*. See also under **thought**.

kind: used as a loose translation of both *genus* and *species*, where these are
not being distinguished.

know: *scire*. See under **awareness**.

knowledge: *scientia*. See under **awareness**.

likeness: usually a rendering of *species*, in a context of the theory of knowledge. Also translated as 'thought-likeness', even when not explicitly
qualified by *intelligibilis*, when the context demands it. 'Likeness' is also
used in other contexts to translate *similitudo* — usually translated as
'likening'.

likening: usually a translation of *similitudo*, but (rarely) also of *assimilatio*.

locution: *dictio*. A word which Aquinas uses in the context of passage 1
instead of *verbum*, word, which he is there giving the technical sense of
'verb'.

make up (and analogous expressions): *componere* in the metaphysical
context. A corporeal substance is made up of form and matter —
though, more strictly, we should say 'made up by the form out of the
matter'. See especially passage 6, and relevant parts of Chapter 3,
'Introduction to Aquinas on metaphysics'.

match, matching: *adaequatio*. This notion is of crucial importance in St
Thomas's theory of truth and knowledge. It should not be understood
as a mere 'correspondence': rather it is identity of form. See the discussion in Chapter 5, 'Introduction to Aquinas on truth, knowledge and
the mind'.

name: the usual translation, outside passage 1, of *nomen*. It should be
noticed that Aquinas uses this word to apply to common nouns and
even adjectives, not just proper names.

notion: a translation used for the rather rare *notitia* in certain contexts.
Also translated as 'consciousness'.

noun: the translation given in passage 1 of *nomen*. It might often have
been more accurately translated as 'non-complex grammatical subject': even what are grammatically adjectives count as nouns for
Aquinas

on its own: a translation used for *per se* in a very few contexts.

originating principle: *principium*. See under **principle, originating**.

performance: the usual translation of *operatio*. This word is also (rarely)
translated as 'operation'.

perishable: *corruptibilis*. Used only of that which has a tendency to cease to
exist, not of that which can be annihilated by God's will but has no
natural tendency to cease existing.

potentiality: *potentia*. See under **actuality**, and also Chapter 3, 'Introduction to Aquinas on metaphysics'.

premiss: a (rare) rendering of *principium* in appropriate contexts.

principle: used for *principium* (usually 'originating principle') in the
context of discussing scientific knowledge, etc. The same word is sometimes translated as 'premiss' in other contexts.

principle, originating: usual translation of *principium*. It may be the point of origin or the cause.

process of change: *motus*. See under **change**.

property, inseparable: *proprium* as a noun. See under **inseparable property**.

qualification: *disposito*.

qualification, without: *simpliciter*. Opposed to *secundum quid*, relatively or in a relative sense.

reason: *ratio*, in the appropriate contexts. Other words used to translate *ratio* are 'argument' and 'description'.

relating: *comparatio*. See under **relation**.

relation: used to translate *relatio*, one of the accidental categories, but also *comparatio*. This word is usually found in a logical or epistemological context, where it is often translated as 'relating', as in 'the relating of subject to predicate'. The same word is used sometimes to translate *habitudo*. 'Without any relation to anything else' translates *absolute*.

relatively, in a relative sense: *secundum quid*. Opposed to *simpliciter* — without qualification.

right, in its own: *per se*. See under **coincidental**.

said in a principal sense and secondary related senses: translates *dicitur per prius et posterius*, Aquinas's usual way of characterising an analogical expression.

self-exist: *subsistere*. See under **exist**.

self-sufficient: *per se sufficiens* or *sufficiens per se* in passage 12.

sense-image: *phantasma*. See Chapter 5, 'Introduction to Aquinas on truth, knowledge and the mind' and passage 9.

sentence, indicative: *enunciatio*. A true or false proposition.

significance, signification: used indifferently for *significatio*.

signify: *significare*. This ugly rendering has been used to avoid the associations of the word 'mean'. The notion of signifying is closer to our notion of reference.

specific: the usual translation of *proprius* as an adjective. The rendering is slightly inaccurate, as often things are *propria* to an individual.

specific difference: *differentia*. The qualification which is used to divide up a genus into its species. For example 'rational' is the specific difference which distinguishes the human species from the rest of the animal genus.

think: used to translate *intelligere*. The normal translation of this word in translations from classical Latin, and in many translations of Aquinas, is 'understand'. But you can *intelligere* a thing, and *intelligere* is an activity, which indicates that the verb is just an etymologically appropriate standard translation of the Greek verb *noein*, to think of. Hence *intelligibilis* in *species intelligibilis* and *forma intelligibilis* is translated as 'thought-of'.

thought: often used to translate *intellectus* or parts of the cognate verb. See under **think**.

thought of: see under **think**.

turning back to sense images: *conversio ad phantasmata* or *reflexio super phantasmata*.

type: occasionally used as a translation of *species*, when contrasted with 'kind' as a translation of *genus*.

unsatisfactory: translates *inconveniens* uniformly. In context a stronger word might occasionally have been used, e.g. 'absurd'.

utterance: *vox* in passage 1. Aquinas himself gives a definition of it as 'sound from the mouth of an animal accompanied by some imaging'.

verb: in passage 1, the translation used for *verbum*, translated as 'word' in other contexts.

well-being: *felicitas*. See passage 12.

Notes on Reading

Aquinas

The work of Aquinas which the student is likely to find most accessible, in libraries if not for purchase, is the *Summa theologiae*. The best translation available in English is that published in sixty volumes by Eyre and Spottiswoode (London) between 1963 and 1975. It contains the Latin text as well as the translation, and also notes, introduction, appendices and glossary for each volume. The different volumes are by different translators, and are therefore irregular in manner.

Also fairly accessible should be the translation of the *Summa contra gentiles*, translated by A. C. Pegis, J. F. Anderson, V. J. Bourke and C. J. O'Neil, published as *On the truth of the catholic faith* (New York: Doubleday, 1955).

A large number of other works of Aquinas were translated in the 1950s and 60s in the United States, but are not easily available. There is thus little alternative for the moderately serious student but to learn Latin.

The texts used for this collection were of the series published by Marietti of Turin in the 1940s, 50s and 60s. They are the texts most likely to be in university libraries, and they contain useful features such as the numbering of sections within chapters or *lectiones*, and subject indexes.

Books on Aquinas

Perhaps the most interesting introduction to Aquinas's philosophical thought on a number of key topics is the essay entitled 'Aquinas' by Geach in *Three philosophers* (G. E. M. Anscombe and P. T. Geach, Oxford: Blackwell, 1961, pp. 67 – 125). The essay entitled 'Aristotle' by Anscombe (pp. 1 – 63) also contains much material that is useful for an understanding of Aquinas's basic philosophical notions.

Other general introductions are one by Frederick Copleston — published under the title *Aquinas* by Penguin (Harmondsworth, 1955), and under the title *Thomas Aquinas* by Search Press (London, 1976) — and Anthony Kenny's *Aquinas* (Oxford: Oxford University Press, 1980).

For information on the life of Aquinas, and the contexts in which his work was done, the best book is James A. Weisheipl O.P., *Friar Thomas d'Aquino* (New York: Doubleday, 1974).

On individual themes dealt with in this collection P. T. Geach's *God and the soul* (London: Routledge and Kegan Paul, 1969) is very valuable, particularly the papers entitled 'What do we think with?' (pp. 30–41), 'Form and existence' (pp. 42–64) and 'What actually exists?' (pp. 65–74), which deal with the notions of form, actual existence, and thought and the mind.

On the existence of God, perhaps the best place to start is with the chapter on cosmological arguments in Brian Davies, *An introduction to the philosophy of religion* (Oxford: Oxford University Press, 1982, pp. 38–49).

On the problem of future contingents, there is a discussion by A. N. Prior in the paper 'The formalities of omniscience', collected in his *Papers on time and tense* (Oxford: Clarendon Press, 1968, pp. 26–44).

Index

20–28 *passim*, 47–8, 53,
116, 133–4

fate 16, 40, 42–3
form, 3, 10–12, 30, 56–7, 103,
170
  accidental 19, 57, 64, 78
  action and 171, 174–5
  artificial 19, 67–8, 91, 96
  essence and 69–70, 74, 83
  individualised 69, 165
  of expression 24
  of noun 20
  sensed 93, 96, 97
  soul as 146–51
  substantial 57, 65–9, 78,
    81–3, 89–97 *passim*
  tendency and 153, 162
  thought-of 68, 119–22,
    135–45, 153, 162
free-will 3, 16, 19, 42–6 *passim*,
153–4, 157–69 *passim*
Frege 5, 9, 14, 49–50, 55–7
future contingents 3, 8, 15–17,
30, 189

Geach, P. T. 3, 51–2, 56–7,
114, 188–9
geometrical objects 58, 82, 89,
136
Gilson, E. 52
God
  as creator 54, 104
  ethics and 155–6
  existence of 3, 49–50, 74,
    99–103, 104–13
  foreknowledge of 16, 44–5
  language about 14
  nature of 103
  the will and 154, 157, 164–8
    passim
good
  appetite and 132
  existent and 115, 117, 126–7
  final 174
  God and 14, 43, 125, 130
  human 45–6, 97, 147,
    154–6, 170–6
  will and 39, 45–6, 150,
    157–9, 162–7

heavens
  Aristotle's views on 99, 101,
    103, 111–12
  necessity and 40, 42, 75,
    88–9, 148, 157, 160,
    163–4, 168–9
Hilary (of Poitiers St) 128
Hume, David 4, 59, 71, 74

identity 14, 58, 114–17 *passim*,
125
  of form 69, 185
  related to true and existent
    125–6
imaging faculty (*phantasia*)
  118–19, 122, 141, 143,
  145, 153–4
imagination 18, 121, 137, 145
indicative sentences (*enunciationes*)
  12, 18, 129
  affirmative — *see* affirmation
  distinctions of 31–2
  future 15, 32–3, 36–8, *see*
    also future contingents
  indefinite 39
  negative — *see* negation
  opposed pairs of 31, 33, 35,
    48
  subjects of 25
  see also propositions
individual 9, 11–12, 22, 62
  accidental 19, 52, 62, 64
  as subject 90
  coincidental 62
  contingency and 33
  essence 70
  existent 52, 61–2, 65, 68, 83
  form and 56–7, 69, 120, 139,
    162, 165
  good 45, 97, 162–4
  identity of 58
  knowledge of 43, 87, 121–2,
    138–44 *passim*, 162, 167
  matter and 68–9, 138
  predicates true of 49–51, 90
  substances 78, 81–4, 91
individuation 69
inflections (grammatical) 21–3,
27, 31
inherence 24–5, 30, 62, 64, 86

DATE DUE	
DEC 1 4 2007	
DEC 1 8 2010	

GAYLORD   PRINTED IN U.S.A.